KT-434-029

Cyprus

Travellers' Guide

Cyprus

by Hazel Thurston

with 16 photographs by
Guy Gravett

Jonathan Cape London 1971

First published 1967
Reprinted 1970
Revised edition 1971
Reprinted 1972
Text and maps © Copyright Helga Greene 1967, 1971
Photographs © Copyright Guy Gravett 1967
Maps by Janet Landau
General Editor: Judith Greene

ISBN o 224 00500 6

Made and Printed in Great Britain
by Richard Clay (The Chaucer Press) Ltd, Bungay, Suffolk,
for Jonathan Cape Ltd, 30 Bedford Square, London WC1

CONTENTS

CONTENTS

CONTENTS

Acknowledgments

I should like to thank the Cyprus authorities and all the individuals in London and Nicosia who placed their resources at my disposal when I was writing this book. The Cyprus Tourist Organization was particularly active on my behalf.

So many people went out of their way to assist me during my visits to Cyprus that it would take a whole chapter to name them all. However, special thanks are due to Mr Savvas Patsalides, Mr Nicos Kofou and Mr Plato Christodoulides of the Tourist Department for making my time pleasant as well as productive. I am also greatly indebted to Professor Karageorghis, Director of the Department of Antiquities, and Professor G. S. Eliades, Hon. Curator of Paphos District Museum, for their co-operation and to the Department of Antiquities, whose official site plans have been of the greatest value. Among the many individuals who welcomed me, I must add my special thanks to Anastasis and Jean Kariliou of the Hesperides Hotel, Kyrenia, who provided a comfortable and friendly home base during my successive travels about the island.

I hope that the many others whom I have been unable to name will accept my overall thanks for their generous help, without which no comprehensive guide could have been written.

Vouni Palace

Melons

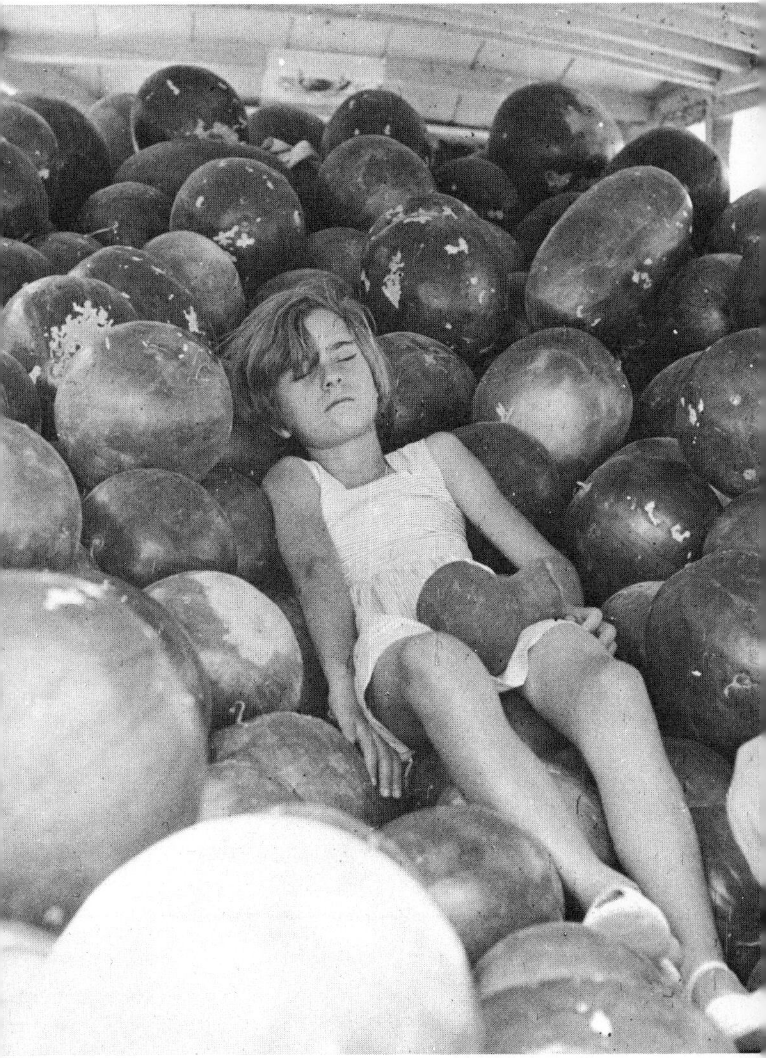

Wine harvest

Church of St Barnabas and St Hilarion, Peristerona

Deserted monastery, Larnaca-tis-Lapithou

Stavrovouni Monastery

Transporting young trees

Ayios Panteleimon, Myrtou

Temple of Apollo, Curium

	Half day
rona 50 m.) m.)	St Chry Castle (pp. 131 Bellapa St Hilar Asinou
ou . 148) 206–7) amondhi	Bellapa St Hilari
d	
a	Kiti Chu Tekké o
a via –53 –7	Kolossi (Curium (11 m.)
	Palea Pa tou Ron 9 Ay. Neo pp. 270

INTRODUCTION

Because Cyprus has no railway system, and the more regular bus services run directly between the six main towns, each of which is the capital of a district, the most practical method of arranging a guidebook is to take these towns as centres for sightseeing trips. Direct and indirect routes noting places of interest between the towns have also been included (see pp. 278–9 and Diagram of Routes on p. 31).

The policy of recommending tours has been dispensed with in the case of the towns themselves. This is because, with the exception of Paphos, where the sites are scattered over a large and featureless area, the distances are not great, and walking from place to place is the best way of getting around, perhaps with the aid of an occasional taxi. Reference to town maps in conjunction with the chart opposite will suggest the order in which various places of special interest may be visited according to individual preferences and schedules.

As there is a great deal to see in and around each of the six towns, a car is not an absolute necessity. Yet without some form of independent transport in country districts the visitor might find himself being whisked past some of the most charming features, and some of the more remote (and major) sites might never be visited at all. This guide therefore covers the six centres on the assumption that the reader will be able to hire, beg or share a car, this being the only really comprehensive way of getting around. Yet by being selective, and by making use of local transport (and advice), visitors to Cyprus will find that it is possible to follow, in principle if not with complete faithfulness, most of the routes outlined in this book. And there will be side benefits. For travellers without the constraints of a schedule or too great a dependence upon physical comfort, local bus travel is indeed the best method, not so much for lengthy visits to historical and archaeological sites, as for getting acquainted with the people and customs of the country.

Of course, selectivity is in any case essential in the planning of a holiday. It is unlikely that many people will contemplate exploring the whole of Cyprus in one visit. A choice will probably have to be made between staying in perhaps one or two of the major sea-side resorts such as Famagusta or Kyrenia, spending a few days in

B

Nicosia, the capital; investigating the industrial liveliness of Limassol; exploring the remote, almost archaic Paphos district or retreating to the invigorating hill resorts. I should hate to think that at my instigation anyone felt compelled to see everything I have written about, devoured it too indigestibly and came away with a flagging appetite.

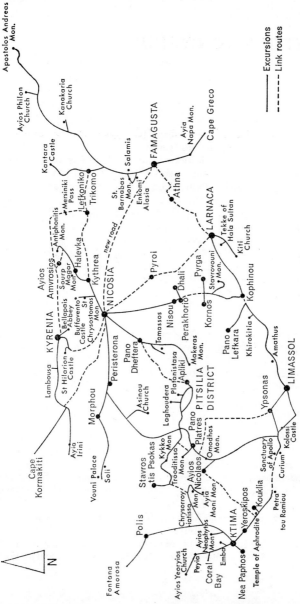

Diagram of Routes

Excursions ——————
Link routes — — — —

GETTING TO CYPRUS

AIR

More than twelve major airlines fly into Nicosia International Airport. Direct flights from London are operated by B.E.A. and Cyprus Airways, also via Athens (Olympic Airways), providing regular daily services to and from England.

Other daily communications include Athens (Cyprus Airways), Beirut (Middle East Airlines) and Tel Aviv (El Al Israel Airlines). B.O.A.C.'s scheduled flights from East Africa to London touch down at Nicosia twice weekly.

European main cities are served by Interflug (Berlin), Cyprus Airways (Frankfurt), Malev (Budapest), Turkish Airlines (Istanbul), Aeroflot (Moscow), Czechoslovak Airlines (Prague), Alitalia (Rome) and Balkan (Sofia) and Rhodes by Olympic Airways.

Regular services to the Middle East are operated by Alia Royal Jordanian (Amman and Benghazi); Turkish Airlines (Adana and Ankara); and United Arab Airlines (Cairo).

The above services are liable to be augmented in the future, and new communications put into operation.

Nicosia International Airport has a modern terminal building, equipped with duty-free shops. A £1 million improvement scheme has included extended runways for the use of Boeing 747s, and stringent safety precautions have been installed on the recommendation of the British Airline Pilots' Association.

SEA

Though cruise ships put in at Famagusta, Larnaca and Limassol, there are no scheduled passenger sailings from the United Kingdom. However, limited accommodation is available on cargo boats (Westcott and Laurence Lines) between London and Famagusta/Limassol, a voyage of approximately twelve days. Regular passenger services are operated from French, Italian, Yugoslavian, Israeli and Greek ports by the Adriatica Line, the Hellenic Mediterranean Lines, Typaldos Lines, Epirotiki Line, Jadrolinija and the Compagnie Française de Navigation Maritime and Zim Navigation, while the Black Seas Steamship Line steamers call at intermediate ports between Odessa, Famagusta and Alexandria. The Piraeus is the principal port of embarkation from Greece.

Tourist offices, travel agents and steamship companies will furnish current fares and scheduled sailings by these and other services.

RAIL

The fastest rail service to Athens (56 hours) for the Piraeus as the point of embarkation for Cyprus is from Liverpool Street to connect with the Akropolis Express at Ljubljana, Yugoslavia. This international train may also be boarded at Munich. Other connections may be made with the Hellas Express at Cologne, the Tauern-Orient Express at Munich, the Istanbul Express at Stuttgart and the Orient Express direct from Paris.

ROAD

Cars may be brought into Cyprus without formality for any period up to six months, provided that the importer is a bona fide visitor entering for non-immigrant purposes, such as touring, recreation or study. Other persons will require a Carnet des Passages en Douane, or must make a deposit as required by the customs authorities.

Recommended routes to Limassol are by Zim Navigation from Marseilles or Genoa, or by Efthymiadis Lines for Marseilles, Naples or the Piraeus.

Third-party insurance with a Cyprus insurance company is compulsory.

An international driving permit is required, or a current driving licence issued in a European country may be used in conjunction with a temporary driving licence obtainable from police stations, and costing 500 mils or 50p (approx. $1.22).

INCLUSIVE TOURS

So-called package holidays, which quote an inclusive price for air travel, accommodation at selected hotels, tips and transport to and from Nicosia airport, are excellent value. It is perhaps not generally realized that this arrangement involves no regimentation in respect of such things as sightseeing, and participants are left alone except in so far as they themselves request assistance in planning their day-to-day existence. Another thing to remember is that the saving is so great when compared with the ordinary air fare plus individual hotel terms that it is possible to treat oneself to the pleasures of occasionally eating out locally, or of staying in other parts of the island overnight, without unduly taxing the budget.

Inclusive tour operators will quote either for travel by charter flights or by scheduled services. There are over forty travel organizations providing this type of holiday, of whom one may quote as specialists Exchange Travel, Horizon and Cook's Silver Wing, as well as American Express.

PASSPORTS AND CUSTOMS

A currently valid passport is required. No visa is necessary for nationals of Austria, Belgium, the British Commonwealth, Denmark, Finland, France, West Germany, Greece, Iceland, Southern Ireland, Italy, Liechtenstein, Luxembourg, the Netherlands, Norway, San Marino, Spain, Sweden, Switzerland, the U.S.A. or Yugoslavia who intend staying three months or less. Permits for longer visits may be issued by the Chief Immigration Officer, Nicosia. Entry visas are required for holders of foreign passports not mentioned above, but visa fees are waived in the case of Czechoslovak, Israeli, Spanish, U.A.R. and U.S.S.R. passports. Visas are not required for visitors in transit for a stay of up to five days who can produce a through ticket and an entry visa for the country of their ultimate destination.

An international vaccination certificate is required only by visitors from countries infected by smallpox.

Bona fide personal possessions are exempt from duty if brought in within six months before or six months after the arrival in Cyprus of their owners. Wireless equipment should be declared. Sporting guns must have a temporary permit from the Minister of the Interior, but the importation of other classes of fire-arms is absolutely prohibited. The entry of dogs is also prohibited except in accordance with quarantine regulations.

TRAVEL IN CYPRUS

BUS AND TAXI SERVICES

As Cyprus has no railway system, the towns and the country districts are linked by bus and taxi services. However, although inter-town buses usually run until dusk, the country bus services are timed to bring villagers and their produce to market early in the morning, returning about midday when business is done. They are therefore of little use to tourists who are based on the towns and resorts, and whose requirements probably lie in the opposite direction. The average bus fare for a distance of 25 miles is 100 mils (10p or $0.24).

Inexpensive taxi services augment the buses. Seats may be booked in advance in taxis operating regularly and frequently between the majority of main towns, also between Nicosia and Limassol and the hill resorts. However, the volume of traffic between Nicosia and Kyrenia does not justify a regular service. These taxi services run on time, pick you up at your hotel or private address, and deposit you wherever you please when your destination is reached. The cost is approximately 200 mils (20p or $0.48) for 25 miles. For instance, the statutory fare between Nicosia and Famagusta is 350 mils per seat.

Bus and taxi services are run by private operators, and there are no comprehensive timetables. However, cyclostyled sheets giving schedules, prices, and addresses and telephone numbers of operators and agents are available from Tourist Information Bureaux.

COACHES

Details of coach tours may be obtained from Tourist Information Bureaux, or from the larger hotels. Such tours, which are seasonal, are also advertised in the *Cyprus Mail*, the English language newspaper, published daily except Mondays.

TAXIS

Taxis are numerous in the towns, and operate from the offices of their owners rather than from taxi ranks. They are best contacted by telephone if no taxi office is in your vicinity. Taxis are distinguishable from private cars either by an illuminated sign or by a broad yellow horizontal band around their bodies. (Self-drive cars usually have a distinguishing white band.) At the time this book goes to press a specimen rate is 50 mils (5p or $0.12) per mile. A private taxi from Nicosia to Famagusta costs £3 ($7.50).

For longer distances payment is by time, and it varies from 600 to 750 mils per hour. But when engaging a taxi for excursions into the country a private arrangement should be made with the taxi operator, and advice will be forthcoming from the local Tourist Information Bureau or your hotelier. As a rough guide, a chauffeur-driven car – which is what the taxis are – should cost from £3·50 ($8.50) inclusive per day.

CAR HIRE AND DRIVING

However well organized regular transport may be, and however productive of local colour and interesting acquaintanceships, a visitor bound for the archaeological sites, churches and beauty spots outside the main towns must devise some form of independent transport if he wishes to come and go at will. Numerous firms specialize in self-drive car hire. Charges average from £2·50 ($6) daily, £16·80 ($40) weekly and £60 ($150) monthly, varying according to the size and make of car. Drivers not in possession of an international driving permit must obtain a temporary licence (see p. 33).

The Survey of Cyprus Motor Map, 8 miles to the inch, and obtainable in a single sheet from booksellers, is adequate for general purposes. Asphalted roads are marked in red. This map is periodically revised in an attempt to keep up to date with road developments. It is relevant to remark here that continuing road improvement schemes lead to the elimination of bends, etc., as well as the by-passing of towns and villages, so that our figures may err on the side of overestimation. A scale of 4 miles to the inch would be preferable for the use of adventurous motorists. However, at the time of going to press this is not available in up-to-date form.

As a piece of extraneous information, it is worth noting that the first trigonometrical survey of the island was published in 1885 as a result of the work of Captain (later Lord) Kitchener, who was Director of Surveys in Cyprus, 1880–3. His map was on a scale of 1 m. to the inch.

The main roads are excellent, well cambered and with good surfaces, though care must be taken when using their shoulders for passing other traffic. The occasional pothole must be watched for. Plenty of time should be allowed when covering distances on minor roads, especially in the mountain districts, since inevitable hairpin bends and steep gradients add to fatigue and put high speeds out of the question.

International road signs have been erected throughout the island. Place names are given in the English form, as well as in Greek capitals – thus constituting a first step towards familiarity with the alphabet. 'LEFKOSIA', the ancient name for Nicosia, occurs infrequently.

The rule of the road is to the left.

ACCOMMODATION

HOTELS

An up-to-date list of hotels is published annually in a brochure obtainable free from Tourist Information Bureaux and travel agents. It is compiled as the result of registration, classification and inspection by the Hotels department of The Cyprus Tourist Organization.

However, due to a continuing boom, even the official guide has difficulty in keeping pace with an energetic state-subsidized programme of new hotels and improvements to those already existing. Though at the time of going to press the lists of hotels given in our own guide in their appropriate sections are correct, they are unlikely to remain comprehensive, and should therefore be read in conjunction with the official hotels guide, and in consultation with information centres, travel agents, etc., who are provided with current data.

Due to the demand for trained staff within the industry, a Hotels and Catering Institute and two Hotel Schools are in full operation. There is also a scheme whereby suitable trainees are sent abroad. The result is an excellent standard of service.

CATEGORIES AND PRICES

The present grading of hotels begins at *de luxe* and is scaled down from the 1st to the 4th category, with the 1st and 2nd categories subdivided into A, B and C. Classification by stars is soon to be introduced, bringing the hotel ratings into line with an internationally recognized system. Categories will remain based upon the number of bedrooms with private baths and/or showers, the standard of sanitary arrangements, the proportion of bathrooms per head and the general standard of public rooms, catering, service, etc. Almost all the hotels in villages, apart from the hill resorts, are 4th class. A badge denoting the class of each hotel is displayed at its entrance.

There are differences in price within a single category, as well as variations according to season, but the following prices (in mils) may be taken as minimal charges for one person, based on two sharing a room.

Category	Bed and Breakfast	Full board
De luxe	2,500	3,850
1st (A)	1,850	2,800
1st (B)	1,450	2,500
1st (C)	1,400	2,400
2nd (A)	1,250	2,100
2nd (B)	1,100	2,000
2nd (C)	1,000	1,800
3rd	900	1,600
4th	700	1,500

A ten per cent service charge is added.

The rates published against the name of each hotel in the official Hotels Guide may not be exceeded, but such extras as private baths or showers, better-situated rooms and air conditioning incur a reasonable additional payment. Many of the newer hotels, and recent additions to older ones, provide a bath or shower to each bedroom, but it is obvious that the lower categories cannot reach this standard.

Bed-and-breakfast rates are general practice, but full boarding rates are available for two full days or more if these are requested in advance. Alternatively, arrangements may usually be made for a price to include bed and breakfast and one main meal daily. The Cyprus Hilton and the Cypriana (Famagusta) quote for accommodation only.

Discounts from twenty-five to fifty per cent according to age are allowed for children occupying the same room as their parents. Members of the Armed Forces and their families on leave are allowed five per cent off the full boarding terms if the duration of their stay is three days or longer.

Municipal taxes in towns range from 10 to 35 mils, and hill resort taxes from 15 to 70 mils per person daily.

MONASTERIES

Visitors to the monasteries are made welcome. Though payment is not obligatory, it is customary to leave a small offering in the collection box which is usually to be found near the entrance to the church. There is no accommodation for women at Stavrovouni Monastery. The accommodation at the Monastery of Ayios Neophytos, Paphos district, is excellent. Facilities for overnight visits to St Chrysostomos and Sourp Magar monasteries have recently been discontinued.

REST HOUSE

A rest house is maintained at Stavros tis Psokas Forest Station for the use of visitors, who should apply by telephone to the Forestry Department of the Ministry of Agriculture in Nicosia (Tel. Nicosia 4000). A small charge is made to cover expenses. Though recently enlarged, accommodation is limited, so that visits are restricted to three nights.

YOUTH HOSTELS

Members of the International Youth Hostels Association may use hostels at Nicosia, Limassol, Troödos and Paphos. Application to be made to the President of the Cyprus Y.H.A., P.O.B. 1328, Nicosia, or to the hostels direct.

CAMPING

Organized camps at Troödos provide accommodation in tents and/or huts, with central buildings for meals, recreation, sanitation, etc.

Some sleeping accommodation may be available in the main buildings. Permission for independent camping must be obtained from appropriate District Officers.

VILLAS AND FLATS

Self-catering accommodation, which is so well suited to family life, is now available in most parts of the island, the demand having stimulated the growth of purpose-built flats, villas and bungalows to augment the previous private letting of small properties. Famagusta is particularly well provided with this type of accommodation. Lists of addresses may be obtained from Tourist Information centres abroad, as well as on the island itself. Olympic Airways offer inclusive terms for flight and accommodation, with or without a self-drive car. Travel agencies providing similar self-catering packages include Exchange Travel and Babet Holidays, a subsidiary of Babet Sales.

RESTAURANTS

Almost all hotels have restaurants and bars, with the standard of meals corresponding to their category. Also the majority of cafés in the cities, on the road and on the beaches supply local food and drink at inexpensive prices. These are usually indicated by the word *kentron* rather than *kapheneion*, which means coffee-house. The roadside 'stations', which often have more than one such eating and drinking place, as well as including petrol pumps and a telephone, and sometimes a police post, make good halting places at midday. These 'stations' have evolved from the staging posts which in the past were invaluable to horse-drawn traffic. National Tourist Pavilions at Curium, Salamis, Fontana Amorosa, St Hilarion Castle and Mount Olympus cater for visitors to sites remote from towns and villages. Some names and addresses of eating-places have been included in the appropriate sections of this guide, but our suggestions cannot be nearly as exhaustive as the cyclo-styled list of restaurants, cafés, etc., which is obtainable from all Tourist Information Bureaux on the island.

DEVELOPMENT SCHEMES

Large-scale projects already under way, or at the blue-print stage, will produce entirely new holiday complexes complete with hotels, restaurants, apartment blocks, sports facilities, shopping centres, etc. Among these are the Cyprus Government's 40-acre Golden Sands development at Famagusta, leased to a British firm, and another project planned for the hitherto 'off the map' Stazousa Point, 16m. east of Kyrenia. Some privately financed enterprises will also have properties for sale, either as an investment or to private buyers. Of these, the Coral Bay scheme (west of Paphos) and a £2 million development not far from Salamis are among the most ambitious. Further schemes under governmental consideration include developments in Kyrenia and Larnaca, as well as a scheme costing nearly £2 million for the Troödos hill resorts. This should be completed, in two phases, by 1977.

Wise decisions have been made in the imposition of height restrictions upon development schemes, which will prevent a recurrence of the Miami-like skyline of Famagusta – the one locale to which multi-storey buildings are appropriate.

PRACTICAL INFORMATION

CLIMATE AND CLOTHES

As the weather is largely predictable and of no unusual range, the inhabitants of Cyprus are fortunate people, concerned mainly with seasonal rainfall which will fill the cisterns and the river-beds and make the parched land of the plains burst into life and colour, producing a mass of exportable produce. Visitors to the island are luckier still as regards weather conditions, because they can practise a degree of pre-selection. For instance, snow fit for winter sports can be found on Troödos in January and February at a time when the plains have a mean daily temperature of 50° F. Conversely, when Nicosia's August maximum may be well into the hundreds, Troödos is likely to be twenty degrees lower, with a further substantial drop in night temperature. In this connection, it is only fair to add that the summer heat of Nicosia is mitigated not only by the dryness of the atmosphere but by an evening breeze which appears with the utmost punctuality. Also, the thermometer readings of the coastal towns, although not so very different from those of Nicosia, are deceptive in that sea breezes make for tolerance or even enjoyment of maximum summer heat, in the same way that fair weather and shelter can compensate for winter lows (daily mean 60° F.).

Two other major factors make up a climate: sunshine and rainfall. Records taken at Nicosia Airport show that, allowing for all possible hours of daylight, the sun shines 74 per cent of the time. Figures for the twelve months of the year are available, a random sample being March 62 per cent, July 90 per cent, October 80 per cent and January 57 per cent.

In view of the conformation of the island, with its two mountain ranges separated by a plain, rainfall is by no means uniform, varying considerably from district to district and from place to place. Nicosia is the driest town, as well as having the minimum humidity in hot weather, the average annual rainfall reading being 14·72 in. Kyrenia is the wettest (21·15 in.), hence the greenery and luscious fruit of the northern coastal strip.

The Troödos Mountains must be considered separately. Roughly, the greater the altitude, the higher the rainfall. Troödos Resort averages as much as 48·95 in., the preponderance of which occurs from late October to early May. During January to March this may be expected to precipitate in the form of snow. In the winter period, although the main roads are kept clear of snow and landslide, sightseeing off the beaten track is uninviting. Consequently many of the mountain hotels, except those connected with winter sports, are closed during the winter months and have their high season in the summer.

For the benefit of bathers, four seasonal sea temperatures may be quoted here: January 61·4° F. (16·4° C.), April 65·5° (18·6° C.), July 79·4° F. (26·3° C.), and October 77° F. (25·1° C.).

To sum up, the climate is good and healthy. Vanished are the days when Crusaders putting in at the ports on the south coast of Cyprus expected to have as many of their number taken by fever as by the swords of the Saracens. In fact, drainage and modern pest control have reached such a high standard of success that it is said that the incidence of the mosquito has to be made the subject of a report to the authorities. This is a slight overstatement.

Meteorological records show a favourable climate all the year round in comparison with other Mediterranean countries. However, spring (from early March) and autumn (until the end of November) are the most suitable seasons for average northern visitors – especially those who propose spending a good deal of their time in energetic sightseeing.

Tweeds and woollen clothing are suitable for the winter months, but as spring comes these will soon be discarded in favour of light-weight materials. In summer the most comfortable and gay sports clothes may be worn, with the provision of something warmer after sundown at the higher altitudes. Cypriot women are modest in their apparel, and 'way out' clothes may attract unwelcome attention in places far from the populated areas. Care must be taken by women to be 'decently' dressed when visiting churches. Outside one of these there is a notice reading: 'Ladies in shorts not allowed in the church. Please see the caretaker for a skirt.' The best hotels are smart, and their patrons like to dress up in the evenings, without necessarily being absolutely formal.

HEALTH AND DRINKING WATER

There are twenty-two general hospitals on the island, in addition to others owned by the mining companies and run for the benefit of their employees, and two sanatoria. The general hospitals incorporate dental centres. About one hundred nursing homes and clinics cater for private patients. The mineral springs of the Troödos range have been recommended for the treatment of skin and rheumatic diseases.

Because the social insurance scheme does not include free treatment for foreigners, intending visitors should be reminded that it is possible to take out temporary insurance against accidents and illness during visits abroad. Details may be obtained from insurance companies and travel agents all over the world.

The climate of the island is healthy, as is demonstrated by a low death-rate and low infant mortality and the absence of quarantinable disease such as cholera, plague, typhus and yellow fever.

Tap water may be drunk in all the main towns, though in Famagusta it is apt to be heavily chlorinated, and bottled mineral water from Moutoullas in the mountains may be preferred. However, an improvement is anticipated with the introduction of a new source of supply from the Larnaca/Limassol area.

TOURIST INFORMATION

In these days of competitive tourism, the majority of Governments maintain tourist offices in foreign capitals for the purpose of providing useful and attractive information from which the basic plan for a holiday may be drawn up. These offices are the best source for up-to-the-minute information, especially in respect of countries which, as in the case of Cyprus, are in the process of developing their tourist industry, and where amenities are increasing year by year.

On arrival at a destination visitors are well advised to make full use of the local tourist offices, which exist for the sole purpose of helping them to get the greatest possible benefit from sightseeing, transport facilities, local entertainment and the hundred and one details of existence which differ just a little from country to country. The main Cyprus Information Bureau is in Nicosia, and there are sub-offices in Limassol, Famagusta, Larnaca and Paphos. The staffs of these offices know the island thoroughly and are proficient in languages. A full range of travel brochures is available, one for each of the six districts of Cyprus. Good advice on local events, tours, travel, etc., will be given to callers. A school for training tourist guides is yielding good results.

Information on all aspects of travel, both to Cyprus and inside the island, may also be obtained from:

United Kingdom	Cyprus Trade and Tourist Centre, 211–13 Regent Street, London, w.i.
U.S.A.	Embassy of Cyprus, 2211 R. Street, Northwest, Washington 11, D.C. 20008.
Egypt	Embassy of Cyprus, 3 Nabil El Quakad Street, Dokki, Cairo, U.A.R.
France	Ambassade de Chypre, 23 rue de Galilée, Paris 16e.
Germany	Zyprische Zentrale für Fremden Verkehr, 73 Ubierstrasse, 532 Bad Godesberg, Bonn.

Greece   Embassy of Cyprus,
                         16 Herodotos Street,
                         Athens.

ANCIENT MONUMENTS AND MUSEUMS

Ancient monuments and museums come under the administration of the Department of Antiquities, which is based on the Cyprus Museum, Nicosia. All such places are normally closed for public holidays. Hours of admission, which change according to season, are subject to alteration without notice. Though the prevailing times are given in the sections of this guide which deal with the relevant towns and excursions therefrom, visitors are advised to check these by obtaining from the Cyprus Museum cyclostyled sheets which set out fees and visiting hours for all the museums and ancient monuments in the charge of the Department of Antiquities.

Entrance fees vary between 25 and 50 mils for residents of Cyprus, and 50 and 100 mils for visitors. Bona fide students and architects may apply at the Department of Antiquities for a pass which will give them free access to the sites and museums under that department's control.

At many of the sites detailed leaflets prepared by specialists in the various fields concerned may be purchased from the custodian at 50 mils each. The full set is also on sale at the entrance to the Cyprus Museum in Nicosia. However, excavations by archaeological teams uncover new sites every year, or add to the scope of existing ones, so that the leaflets cannot keep pace. More recent information on the 'active' sites is contained in the Annual Reports of the Director of the Department of Antiquities, obtainable for 300 mils at the Cyprus Museum and at all District Museums.

BANKS AND CURRENCY

There are three leading local banks: the Bank of Cyprus (with branches in main towns), the Popular Bank of Limassol and the Turkish Bank of Nicosia. Five overseas banks have branches in Cyprus: Barclays Bank D.C.O., the National and Grindlay's Bank, the Chartered Bank, the National Bank of Greece and the Turkiye Is Bankasi. Banking hours are from 9 a.m. to 12 noon, including Saturdays.

Hotels, large shops and garages will also usually accept travellers' cheques.

Visitors may bring in an unlimited amount of sterling, provided that it is in the form of travellers' cheques, letters of credit, etc. Sterling notes brought in should not exceed £15, and Turkish money should not exceed TL 150. Information on the importation of other currencies should be obtained from banks.

Cyprus is in the sterling area, and 1,000 mils is equivalent to one Cyprus pound, which is worth £1 sterling ($2.60 approx.). You should check exchange rates with your bank as they are subject to considerable fluctuation. Notes are in denominations of £5, £1, 500 mils and 250 mils, and there are coins of 100 mils (10p), 50 mils (5p), 25 mils (2½p), 5 mils and 1 mil. Decimal coinage was introduced in 1955. The coins are similar in size to the equivalent British pieces, 100 mils being the size of 10p, 50 mils that of 5p and 25 mils that of a sixpence.

SHOPPING, SOUVENIRS AND CIGARETTES

A great many shops are small, and their proprietors choose to serve their customers themselves, with the result that they provide individual attention unknown in larger stores. The requirements of foreigners are well understood because of the presence in Cyprus of members of the Armed Forces and their families.* Narrow Ledra Street in Nicosia has a great many shops specializing in the tourist trade. In addition, each town has a municipal market patronized by local people, where native products in general command prices lower than those of the souvenir shops. These markets, of course, specialize in food, and their displays of fruit and vegetables are spectacular. The municipal market in Famagusta is especially showy, with each stall built up as for a horticultural exhibition.

Souvenir shops should not be despised, because they retail the adaptations which fit into the pattern of continental, transatlantic and British living. The chief things to look out for are Lefkaritiki lace, pottery from the Kyrenia district, Turkish Delight from Yeroskipos, woven linen and pottery from Phiti in the Paphos district, embroidery from Atheniou in the Larnaca district, baskets from Dhavlos and Phlamoudhi, and silver and brassware.

* Also personnel of the U.N. peace-keeping force.

The Cyprus Handicrafts Centre in Evagoras Avenue, Nicosia, sells traditional products. It is possible to arrange for cases of fruit in season to be delivered abroad by arrangement with shippers.

Shopping hours, which are elastic when the shops are owner-run, are from 8 a.m. to 1 p.m. and 4 p.m. to 7 p.m., except on Saturday, which is a half-day. In winter the lunch-break is shorter.

Cigarettes are sold in bars and cafés, as well as at numerous newspaper kiosks. Some well-known English brand names include tobacco grown in the Karpas, and these in King Size retail from 175–200 mils per 20. Imported English and American brands are more expensive, but there is no dearth of cheaper brands.

TIPPING AND BARGAINING

It is customary to tip the staff of hotels in recognition of special services, despite the 10 per cent service charge. Taxi-drivers, also, should be tipped, the scale varying in relation to the fare. Fifty mils would be generous for a minimum fare. Personal service of other kinds, from messengers or guides, for instance, should be rewarded, but if these services have been extended by way of hospitality, it is sometimes better to suggest that the recompense be passed on to a child or a dependant. Thus honour is satisfied.

There are no rules for bargaining, which must be left to the individual purchaser's discretion. The distinction between what is an eastern Mediterranean game but can also be an occasional cause for offence is a fine-drawn one. The best policy, if the asking price seems unreasonable, is to mention a lower figure, and if this is firmly refused to abandon the purchase – or else submit.

ENTERTAINMENT AND SPORT

BROADCASTING

Sound and television programmes in Greek, Turkish and English, sometimes sub-titled. The Forces Broadcasting Service also transmits on the 211-metre waveband. Programmes are advertised in the *Cyprus Mail*.

CABARETS	There are 'night-spots' in all the towns. Dancing and floor shows take place out of doors during the summer months.
CINEMAS	European and American films are shown in the towns and larger hill resorts – out of doors during the summer months. Many foreign films have Greek sub-titles, while Greek films are frequently sub-titled in English.
COFFEE-SHOP GAMES	Much time is spent on 'tric trac', a form of backgammon, and various card games while drinking coffee or wine.
CONCERTS AND THEATRICAL PERFORMANCES	Greek and Shakespearian drama and concerts are performed in the ancient outdoor theatres at Salamis, Curium and Soli. See also Cultural Festivals (p. 54).
FOOTBALL	Association Football is popular with town and village sides, and there are international fixtures, as well as regular matches against the Forces.
GOLF	At Nicosia and Pendayia (available for visitors who produce a club membership card).
HORSE-RACING	Every Sunday afternoon during the spring and autumn at Nicosia Race Club.
RIDING	Available in Troödos Mountains and by arrangement from main towns and resorts.
SAILING	Boats are for hire at the seaside resorts. Sailing clubs hold regattas at Kyrenia, Larnaca and Famagusta.
SHOOTING	Partridge: October–January; Wood-pigeon: June–September; Clay-pigeon shooting in Nicosia.
SQUASH RACKETS	In Nicosia.

SWIMMING	Famagusta, Limassol and Kyrenia have the best facilities, although all the coastal towns and many other places have pleasant beaches near by. There are no municipal swimming baths. Hotels with pools are indicated in the official Hotels Guide.
TENNIS	Spring and autumn Pan-Cyprian Tournament in Nicosia. Troödos Pan-Cyprian and Middle East Tournament in August.
WALKING	The mountain ranges provide interesting walking country.
WATER SPORTS	Water ski-ing, underwater sports, etc., at the main sea-side resorts, where equipment may be hired. Regattas and games organized by Famagusta Nautical Club January–March, November–December, and swimming and speedboat competitions April–October. Similar events at Kyrenia and Larnaca, June–September week-ends.
WINTER SPORTS	At Troödos from January to March. Equipment may be hired through the Cyprus Ski Club, Nicosia, and from shops and hotels in Nicosia and Troödos.

HOLIDAYS AND FESTIVALS

PUBLIC HOLIDAYS COMMON TO BOTH COMMUNITIES

January 1st	New Year's Day
March 25th	Greek Independence Day
October 1st	Cyprus Independence Day*
October 29th	Turkish Independence Day

* Recently moved from a date in August, because that month is too hot for full-scale celebrations.

Public Holidays for the Greek Community

January 6th	Epiphany
40 days before Easter	Green Monday
January 19th	Name day of Archbishop Makarios III
April 1st	EOKA Day
Movable	Good Friday
Movable	Easter Saturday
Movable	Easter Monday
October 28th	OXI day – Greece's defiance of Mussolini
December 25th	Christmas Day
December 26th	Boxing Day

Public Holidays for the Turkish Community

April 23rd	Children's Bairam
May 19th	Sports and Youth Bairam
August 30th	Zafir Bairam
Movable	Birthday of the Prophet
Movable	Sheker Bairam (Ramadan), two days
Movable	Qurban Bairam (Feast of Sacrifices), three days

Holy Days

The holy days of the Orthodox Church are celebrated by special services, and by customs, some of which may be traced from pagan times and which have been assimilated into the Christian calendar. The chief holy days are:

January 1st	New Year's Day (St Vassilios)
January 6th	The Epiphany
January 30th	SS Chrysostomos, Vassilios and Gregory
February 10th	St Charalambos
March 25th	The Annunciation
Movable	Good Friday
Movable	Easter Day
April 23rd	St George
May 21st	SS Constantine and Helena
Movable	Ascension Day
Movable	Whit Sunday
June 11th	St Barnabas

June 29th	SS Peter and Paul
August 6th	The Transfiguration
August 15th	The Assumption
August 29th	Beheading of St John the Baptist
	Nativity of the Blessed Virgin
September 14th	Exaltation of the Holy Cross
October 18th	St Luke
November 30th	St Andreas
December 12th	St Spyridon
December 25th	Christmas Day

FEAST DAYS

The feast days of the patron saints of monasteries and village churches are made the occasion for the gathering of devout and at the same time uninhibited sections of the peasant population. These days of rejoicing, with their processions along herb-strewn streets, their market stalls, and with villagers dressed in their finery, provide insight into a pattern of life which is fast disappearing. The following feasts, many of which combine with local fairs, are among the most important:

Fixed:

January 1st	Ayios Vassilios at **Nicosia**
January 6th	Feast of the Immersion of the Holy Cross at **Famagusta**
January 24th	Ayios Neophytos at **Ayios Neophytos Monastery**
February 2nd	Panayia (The Purification of the Blessed Virgin Mary) at **Chrysorroyiatissa Monastery**
March 25th	Panayia (The Annunciation) at **Lysi** (near Famagusta) and **Klirou** (Nicosia District)
April 23rd	Ayios Yeorghios celebrated in 144 villages
1st Sunday in May	St Makarios the Hermit at **Sourp Magar Monastery**
May 21st	Ayios Constantinos and Ayia Helena at **Tokhni** (Larnaca District)
June 10th–11th	Ayios Barnabas at **St Barnabas Monastery**
June 28th	St Paul at **Kato Paphos**

August 15th	Panayia (The Assumption) at **Kykko Monastery, Makheras Monastery** and **Apostolos Andreas Monastery** (14th–15th)
August 16th	**Akhiropiitos Monastery**
September 2nd	Ayios Mamas at **Morphou**
September 6th	St Michael the Archangel at **Lapithos, Arkhangelos Monastery** and other places
September 14th	Exaltation of the Holy Cross at **Stavrovouni Monastery** and **Omodhos**
September 28th	Ayios Neophytos at **Ayios Neophytos Monastery**
October 4th	St John Lampadistes at **Kalopanayiotis**
October 17th–18th	St Luke at **Famagusta**
October 26th	St Demetrios at **Leonarisso** (Karpas)
Movable: March–April	Palm Sunday at **St Memnon,** Famagusta; Good Friday Procession of the Epitaph.

Popular Festivals

Limassol Carnival	**Limassol** is *en fête* for one week fifty days before Easter, with processions, folk-dancing, singing and general merrymaking.
Green Monday	On the last Monday before Lent, in a survival of an ancient Dionysian feast, Cyprus people celebrate in the fields with special food and wine.
Orange Festival (Famagusta)	In March the orange harvest is celebrated for four days by parades, displays of folk-dancing, shows and free distribution of oranges.
Orange Festival (Morphou)	In May. Folk-dancing and singing, parades and agricultural exhibition. Local food served at night. Free oranges.
May Day (Anthestiria)	During the first fortnight in May all the principal towns celebrate a Flower Festival which is the direct successor of the Feast of Aphrodite. As in pagan times, the celebrations are at their most colourful in **Paphos**.

Cataclysmos (Pentecost)	Fifty days after Easter, Sea games, dancing and contests, said to be a survival of the Feast of the Paphian Aphrodite Anadyomene – the rising of the goddess from the waves – and later associated both with thanksgiving for Noah's survival of the Deluge and the Feast of Pentecost. Observed in all seaside towns, and **Karavas**.
Flower Festival	In May the Famagusta Philoptokhos Association holds a flower show and parade of decorated 'chariots'.
Cyprus Night (Larnaca)	Mid-June, one night of folk-dancing and singing, theatrical performances and local delicacies.
Annual Popular Fair (Famagusta)	During the last week-ends of June, arts and crafts exhibitions, dancing, musical performances and local food in the Municipal Gardens.
Festival of Folk Dancing (Limassol)	Early July. Displays in the Municipal Gardens.
Kyrenia Festival	At week-ends, from July–September. Cypriot theatre, folk-dancing and singing.
Agricultural Exhibition (Perapedhi)	Mid-August. Displays of agricultural products, folk- and modern dancing competitions. Local food.
Peach Festival (Kato Mylos, Limassol district)	Usually last week-end in August. Exhibition of agricultural produce. Dancing, local food. Free peaches.
Platres Folk Festival	In late August or the beginning of September, the mountain resort of **Platres** becomes a rallying place for the hill villagers. They compete in traditional dancing and singing, and bring their handicrafts for sale. Modern dancing and the election of 'Miss Platres'.
Prodhromos Festival	Village two-day fair at end of August. Sale of local products.

Lemon Festival	**Lapithos** in the Kyrenia District is famous for gardens and for lemon trees, and celebrates the citrus harvest in late August with singing, dancing and good food.
Lace Festival (Pano Lefkara)	Early September. Exhibition of traditional lace and embroidery.
Fig Festival (Zakaki, Limassol district)	Late September. Dancing, singing, local food, exhibition of agricultural products and free figs.
Wine Festival	**Limassol** celebrates the conclusion of the wine harvest (usually at the end of September) with wine-tasting, folk-dancing, singing and competitions.

CULTURAL FESTIVALS*

Salamis Festival	From June to September Greek and Shakespearian dramas are produced in the ancient amphitheatre at **Salamis.** (Plays are also performed in Othello's Tower at **Famagusta.**† Not unnaturally, Shakespeare's *Othello* is a favourite.)
Curium	Between June and September ancient Greek plays are produced in the theatre at the site of **Curium** near Limassol. Concerts by moonlight.
Week of Ancient Drama	The National Theatre of Greece produces classical plays at **Salamis** and **Curium** during September.
Musical Season	During the winter months **Nicosia** puts on a programme of concert and chamber music.

TRADE FAIR

International Trade Fair	Held annually in September at a permanent site on George Grivas Dighenis St in **Nicosia.**

* The dates of cultural festivals are governed by availability of first-class and often international theatre companies and concert performers.

† Discontinued at time of going to press.

POSTAL AND TELEPHONE INFORMATION

Postage Rates

Ordinary Mail	Letters not exceeding 28 grams	Postcards
	mils	mils
Inland	15	5
British Commonwealth	20	15
Foreign countries	20	25

Airmail	per 14 grams	Postcards
Egypt	40	20
France	50	25
Germany	50	25
Greece	30	15
Holland	50	25
Israel	40	20
Italy	50	20
Lebanon	40	20
Turkey	40	20
United Kingdom	50	20
U.S.A.	90	40

Daily airmail services to all countries.

Post Office Hours

    Weekdays: 8 a.m.–1 p.m., 2.30 p.m.–5.30 p.m.
    Saturdays: 8 a.m.–1 p.m., 4 p.m.–5 p.m.

Parcels and registered letters should be called for at central offices upon notification of their arrival.

Telegraph Rates	7 word min. Day	Overnight Letter
Inland	20 mils	—
Great Britain	80	40 mils
France	85	43
Greece	63	33
U.S.A.	108	55

Urgent telegrams are double the ordinary rate. Radio telephone services link with the majority of foreign countries. Cable and Wireless Ltd provide world-wide communication by cable, as well as communication with ships at sea.

TELEPHONE CHARGES

C.I.T.A. (Cyprus Inland Telecommunications Authority) runs the local telegraph and telephone systems and connections with external services. The internal telephone system is adequate. Most operators speak fluent English and will ascertain local numbers should these be in doubt. The telephone directory is printed in English, Greek and Turkish.

Typical charges for telephone calls are as follows:

	Day	*8 p.m.–7 a.m.*
Nicosia to:	*mils*	*mils*
Famagusta	100	65
Kyrenia	60	40
Larnaca	60	40
Limassol	100	65
Ktima (Paphos)	150	100
Troödos	100	65

WEIGHTS AND MEASURES

MEASURES OF LENGTH

British units of length are used, with the addition of the 'pic' (*arshin* in Turkish), which equals two feet. The Cyprus mile, of approximately three statute miles or one league (or a stage travelled by a laden donkey!), is unofficial and used solely by the peasants.

LAND MEASURE

$$1 \text{ evlek.} = 400 \text{ sq. yds.}$$
$$1 \text{ donum (or scala)} = 1,600 \text{ sq. yds. or approx. } \tfrac{1}{3} \text{ acre.}$$

MEASURES OF WEIGHT

Though English weights are recognized, the Cyprus standards are in more general use, except for postage.

1 dram = 0·112 oz.
100 drams (¼ oke) = 1 onje or onka
400 drams = 1 oke (2·8264 lb.)
44 okes = 1 Cyprus kantar
180 okes = 1 Aleppo Kantar (for carobs)
200 okes = 1 kantar (for fuel and onions)

MEASURES OF CAPACITY

English pints, quarts and gallons are usual, though the *oke* or *okka* (1·125 quarts) may be encountered in country districts. The Cyprus litre, used for oil, is 2·8 quarts. The old *kouza* (jar) of 2·25 gallons and the *gomari* or donkey-load (36 gallons) are rarely used.

ELECTRICITY

240 volts A.C., 50 cycles, single phase for lighting and domestic requirements. The larger hotels provide points for electric shavers, giving alternative voltages of 230/115.

TIME

Two hours in advance of Greenwich Mean Time, or seven hours in advance of Eastern Standard Time (U.S.A.).

GEOGRAPHY AND GEOLOGY

In the Cretaceous period of the Mesozoic Age, about a hundred million years ago, what is now Europe was almost entirely covered by a vast and very deep sea. Countless evolving creatures lived in this ocean, and over lengthy periods of time deposited their shells and bones on its bed. This residue formed a fine ooze which was subjected to such great and continuing pressure that it was converted into chalk and limestone. Where in addition the limestone met with great heat resulting from internal upheaval, the end product was marble.

Throughout the geological history of the earth its crust has cracked and crumbled under the huge strain of the cooling process. In accordance with the laws of nature, titanic damage occurred at the weakest spots – the geological faults. The ocean which extended across what is now land was one huge area of weakness, loaded unbearably by the accumulated weight of deposits by marine animals, and crushed simultaneously by the great land masses to north and to south. The outcome was that the floor of the ocean crumpled into folds, some of which emerged above the level of the sea. These were the Alps, the Carpathians, the Himalayas and the Atlas Mountains.

During the ages when these dramatic changes were taking place the ocean bed of the eastern Mediterranean cracked under the strain, and masses of molten rock broke through, to become islands, of which Cyprus is one. The new land masses were composed of igneous material overlaid by strata of limestone, sandstone and clay which had previously formed the bed of the sea.

In the case of Cyprus, there were at first two land masses separated by a shallow sea which was to become the fertile plain of the Mesaoria. The chief range, now known as the Troödos Mountains, was especially vulnerable to the elements. The sedimentary cap of rock from the sea-bed disintegrated and was washed away, so that the igneous rock became exposed. One effect has been that the Troödos range contains most of the accessible mineral wealth of the island: copper, asbestos, pyrites, other ores and their byproducts, which have for thousands of years been of prime importance in the economy of Cyprus.

The formations of the Kyrenia or Northern range are distinct, as can be seen at a glance. The igneous rock was thrust upwards in the same way, but due to less exposure to wind, rain and frost, and to the lower altitude, the sedimentary limestone has remained as a protective covering. This forms the crags, the embattled peaks, which make these mountains more spectacular than the major, southern group.

The rivers are dry in summer and early autumn, except as the result of some freak storm. After rain, as much water as possible is stored in reservoirs, and prevented from reaching the natural outlets to the sea.

FLORA

Apart from plantations aimed at halting the encroachment of sand (as at Ayia Irini and Salamis, where mimosa is doing admirable work), the principal districts administered by the Forestry Department are in the two mountain ranges. These areas total over 500 sq. m., of which perhaps 100 produce industrial timber for use in the mines, and for fuel, fruit boxes, etc. The remaining 400 sq. m. are the subject of long-term planning, because land reclamation is expensive. Its desuetude is in most instances due to forest fire, long-standing erosion and the depredations of goats. The whole huge area, roughly 17 per cent of the island, is fit for no other purpose except forestry, and awaits development with the aid of modern resources and sufficient funds. (Visitors with a special interest in forestry should contact the Ministry of Agriculture and Natural Resources, and it may be possible for a conducted tour of some of the forest areas to be arranged.)

The cedars in the southern range (*c. brevifolia*) are protected trees, and may not be cut or damaged. They are to be found in great numbers in the valley which bears their name. The Aleppo pine predominates on the mountains, and grows as high as 4,500 ft above sea-level, where it is replaced by the Troödos pine (*p. nigra*) with its characteristic straight trunk and curious flattened top. The dwarf golden oak is another feature of the Troödos range. It grows in the form of a bush, with attractive distinctive foliage, dark green on one side and yellow on the reverse. The lower slopes of the mountains are usually scattered with arbutus and juniper scrub, and the valleys are made especially picturesque by individual poplar and cypress trees. Cypresses, too, are employed as wind-breaks for the fruit plantations of the plains, and are often accompanied by groves of bamboo, and eucalyptus, which as well as absorbing water from the swamps makes very good fuel. Designated village fuel areas provide local supplies of firewood, thus preventing interference with the ordered growth of the plantations.

Olive and carob trees dominate the lower hills and coastal lands, but the olive trees do not appear to have received their due share of attention, or perhaps they are less noticeable in their haphazard positions than they would be in the attractive terraces favoured by other countries. They yield no exportable surplus either of oil or of fruit.

What we know as spring flowers come after the first autumn rains: dwarf narcissus, grape hyacinths and scilla among the first, followed by autumn-flowering cyclamen on the mountain slopes, and crocuses. Then, as true spring advances, the masses of colour re-emerge: pink thyme and vetches as cover, ranunculus and lupins, freesia-like gladiolus (*G. triphyllus*), cyclamen (*C. persicum*), whose tubers are relished by pigs, and which are at their most prolific near Kantara in March and April, and a peony (*P. arietina var. orientalis*) which flowers in May in Troödos. And there are clusters of a delightful miniature blue iris, a crocus (*C. cypria*) endemic to the island and an orchis (*O. Kotschyi*), which is rarer but can be located in the Paphos Forest. On lower ground, to the west of the Kyrenia range, there are wild tulips, the wine-coloured *T. cypria*, to be found near Myrtou, and the lighter-coloured *T. oculis solis*. Poppies and bright yellow oxalis grow at the wayside, and crops of flax add pale blue to the geometric patterns of new growth in the unfenced expanses of the Mesaoria. No one who has visited the northern range during the spring will ever forget the huge yellow umbels of the giant wild fennel (*ferula communis*) which seems to pose at every vantage point ready to be in the foreground of a picture. And everywhere there is the archaic asphodel, which has greater primitive significance than any other spring flower, for it was the one which Persephone plucked before she was carried off to the Underworld. In Cyprus the dead (or Plutonic) period is not the winter, but the days of summer drought.

The cherry blossom of Pedhoulas deserves a special pilgrimage in the Japanese tradition. The fruit-growing districts are at their most attractive twice yearly, in the flowering time and at harvest; Morphou for citrus, Trikoukkia for apples, Phassouri for all kinds of mass cultivation including bananas, and the Kyrenia coastal strip for, among other fruit, luscious apricots. In fact, anywhere in Cyprus where there is water and an adequate depth of soil there are orchards and vineyards, scenting the air and promising gastronomic pleasure. In the late autumn, when the wine harvest is finished, the bright orange and red foliage of the vines spreads in a fascinating patchwork over the mountains and hills.

FAUNA

'Cyprus rears many wild asses and rams, stags and hinds; but it has no bears, lions or wolves, or other dangerous beasts.'*

'There are in the mountains of Cyprus wild sheep, with hair like that of goats and dogs, which are said to be found nowhere else. It is a very swift animal and its flesh is good and sweet. When I was out hunting I saw several caught by dogs, and especially by the tame leopards of Cyprus.' †

The hunting leopards have gone the same way as the wild asses and deer, but the rare species of wild sheep, the moufflon, has survived to become one of the prides of the island. Throughout the history of Cyprus, these animals, with their agility and preference for the most inaccessible mountain regions, have constituted a challenge to the hunter. The Lusignans, the Frankish Crusaders who ruled for nearly three hundred years, were as fanatical sportsmen as the British. It is a great credit to the recent policy of the authorities that the breed has been preserved, not only in zoos and the special enclosure at Stavros tis Psokas but also in its natural habitat in the western spurs of the Troödos Mountains, in the region known as the Paphos Forest. This favourable state of affairs is the result of strict protection enforced at a time when the surviving breeding couples could be counted on the fingers of one hand.

* Wilbrand von Oldenburg (d. 1234) in *Excerpta Cypria*, by C. D. Cobham (Cambridge University Press, 1908), p. 13.
† Wilhelm von Bodensele, who visited Cyprus in 1333. Ibid., p. 16.

C

The moufflon are now on the increase, and are thought to number over 200. The breed may be seen in realistic surroundings in the enclosures of Stavros tis Psokas Forest Station (pp. 143–4).

This is the most noteworthy form of wild life in Cyprus. In fact, to the ordinary European observer there is no other species of special importance. One form of wild life which captures attention by its depredations is the rat, which lives in carob trees. It is noticeable that these large evergreen trees frequently have branches of brown withered foliage, due to the colonies of rats which inhabit them and eat the bark. Foxes and hares live in the mountains, and all over the island many different kinds of lizard and some snakes are to be found, but these are of passing interest except to the naturalist. Few of the snakes are poisonous, but the exception is the *coupli*, two to three feet long, which has a greenish skin and dark spots, and may be occasionally encountered at Salamis.

Domestic animals fare better in Cyprus than in many Mediterranean countries. In fact, any cruelty seems to arise from kindness, especially as regards cats, which are allowed to survive as they will, leading to gross over-population. In some monasteries, notably at the Monastery of St Nicholas of the Cats, near Akrotiri, and at Ayia Barbara below Stavrovouni, the cats are kept as snake-exterminators. Village dogs are rarely fierce, as though they have been taught to welcome strangers in the same tradition of hospitality as is practised by their masters.

Though mechanized transport is increasing in an island which is employing its resources to keep abreast with the times, donkeys are much in use for carrying loads, camels plough some of the smaller holdings in the Mesaoria and some bullock carts are still in use.

The Cyprus Ornithological Society, which was formed in 1957, has recorded over three hundred species of birds as having been reliably observed on the island. The majority of these are migratory, and it is from this group that the casual observer will derive most pleasure. For instance, between December and April each of the salt lakes near Larnaca and Akrotiri has a large flock of flamingoes. The same two regions harbour egrets, ibises, herons and other waders. The mass migration of storks and cranes is particularly spectacular, made the more fascinating on account of its regular pattern, not only as regards formation in flight but because of the predictability of the birds' arrival, usually for one night in early

August, *en route* for Egypt. Golden orioles are usually seen and cuckoos heard during the spring migration. Swallows may be expected on February 19th. Other winter visitors include several species of wild duck, wagtails, blackcaps and chiff-chaffs. The warblers and the blackcaps face the greatest danger on arrival because they are greatly sought after for eating, and are netted and trapped in bushes spread with bird-lime. The eastern spurs of the Kyrenia mountains are the surest locality for spotting the hoopoe, whose brilliant colouring and crest distinguish him from all others. Nightingales nest south of the Troödos range and at Lapithos near Kyrenia.

There are indeed very few migratory birds which do not habitually or occasionally visit or pass across Cyprus. The few resident birds are apt to develop distinctive features, and these modifications have been classified separately by ornithologists. The one bird peculiar to Cyprus is Cetti's Warbler, sometimes known as the Cyprus Warbler. This attractive little bird favours the Kyrenia range but can also be found nesting in bushes on the lower slopes of the Troödos Mountains. Rock doves are common in both ranges. The Little Owl and Scops Owl have managed to survive a reputation for being harbingers of death.

Of the larger birds, the griffon vultures of the Kyrenia mountain peaks have a peculiar fascination. Bonelli's Eagle breeds in both mountain ranges, as do fewer pairs of the Imperial Eagle. Other eagles have been sighted, but usually on migration. Buzzards come in large flocks, and are best seen at Akrotiri in September. The cliffs of Akrotiri have recently sprung into ornithological fame as the nesting place of the rare Eleonora's falcon, which was made the subject of a fascinating television programme in 1969. Partridges are common, but francolin – similar in their gait and flight, but larger – are most likely to be seen in the Kantara neighbourhood.

Spring and autumn are the best seasons for bird-watching. Members of the Cyprus Ornithological Society undertake bird-ringing under the auspices of the Natural History Museum, South Kensington, London.

MINING AND AGRICULTURE

The economy of Cyprus in the past has depended principally upon mining and agriculture. However, though the export of agricultural products, including wine, is on the increase – due as much to modern methods of cultivation as to new packaging methods, refrigeration and air transport – there is danger that the island's copper will be exhausted in the foreseeable future unless new sources of supply are located. Not only is this a grave state of affairs but it will be regretted by students of the past, who will invariably associate mining with the country's history.

Archaeologists have identified bronze ingots and artefacts, taken from excavated tombs, as having been produced in the third millennium B.C. Correspondence from the Kings of Alasiya to the King of Egypt in the form of the fourteenth-century B.C. Tell-el-Amarna tablets refers to gifts of copper. Homer in the *Iliad* says that Kinyras, King of Paphos, presented Agamemnon with a Cyprian *cuirasse* prior to the Trojan Wars (1194–84 B.C.), and in the *Odyssey* refers to trading transactions in metals. The Phoenicians carried on a trade in minerals before they settled in the island *c.* 1000 B.C. Besides this, detailed excavations of old mine workings, and analysis of neighbouring slag heaps, have proved that these antedate the Roman period, during which in A.D. 12 the Emperor Augustus Caesar assigned King Herod half the output of the copper mines of Soli in exchange for a cash payment. Mining declined under the Byzantines, Lusignans, Venetians and Turks, but was revived during British rule.

The American-owned Cyprus Mines Corporation of Skouriotissa (which means Our Lady of the Slag Heaps) has the most important and modern mine on the island. The ore is now brought from the Mavrovouni mine, processed at Xeros, and shipped from there, as indeed it was in antiquity. It is amusing to compare this go-ahead company's technology and its welfare arrangements with the account accredited to Galen, physician to Marcus Aurelius, who visited the Soli mines (and in all likelihood the actual Skouriotissa mine) in A.D. 166. He describes finding pools of tepid greasy water, green from what is now known as copper sulphate, suffocating air, nude slave workers and workings liable to collapse.

The Hellenic Mining Co. Ltd is the second largest producer of pyrites in the island, and owns several mines – one being near the ancient works of the city of Tamassos – as well as a great wine manufacturing and exporting business. Copper is mined by other companies near Polis (Polis-tis-Khrysokhou, the full name of the town, means 'city of the goldsmith'), which is adjacent to the site of ancient Marion and Arsinoe, and at Troulli, north-west of Larnaca. Near this latter village there are quarries yielding umber, which is still much used as a pigment. But perhaps Troulli is most famous for having been the scene of an ephemeral gold rush in 1936.

Asbestos – which is derived from the Greek word meaning unconsumed, i.e. indestructible by fire – is mined high on Troödos at Pano Amiandos, and is mainly of the quality used in the mixing of asbestos cement. These great mine workings are strangely impressive at such a height, if disfiguring to the landscape. The asbestos is taken by lorry to Limassol, and shipped from there. Chrome ore produced by another company on the northern slopes of the mountain is brought down by aerial ropeway to Kakopetria (near the church of St Nicholaos-tis-Steyis) before being transported to Famagusta. Copper and sulphur are mined at Mavrovouni, near Lefka, and shipped from Xeros, while iron pyrites comes from Mitsero in the Troödos foothills north-west of Kalokhorio and is exported mainly to Italy. Quarrying of lime for cement now scars the slopes above Kythrea, but this must be accepted as necessary to the country's economy. One side effect is the improvement of the road leading to Halevka.

It has been estimated that one-fifth of the population is connected to some degree with the wine industry, and that out of an agricultural community of some 64,000 families, half is engaged in the cultivation of the grape. The majority of farmers are smallholders. Big commercial interests are represented by the mining companies, the plantations near Limassol and the wine companies. Co-operative farming has never caught on with peasants renowned for their independence. The Abbey of Kykko is a considerable landowner, as well as having a large share in the capital investment of the island.

Many of the agricultural exports of Cyprus carry glamour, or at least the illusion of a residue of sunshine with them: nuts, oranges, lemons, grapefruit, pomegranates, raisins, currants, sultanas, figs, wines and brandy, grapes and melons, herbs and spices. New potatoes and carrots are the principal vegetables grown for export. Asparagus and strawberries are recent introductions to the export field, brought about by excellent air-freight links with the United Kingdom and northern Europe.

Wheat and barley for home consumption are grown extensively in the Mesaoria.

The principal wine-producing areas are high on the slopes of the Troödos mountains in the Nicosia and Paphos districts. The lowlands of the latter district, an area hitherto neglected, are coming into fuller production due to improved road and transport systems. The citrus and banana plantations of Phassouri, the orange groves of Morphou and the lemons of Lapithos and Karavas contribute in great measure to the economy. A thick-skinned oval variety of orange and the Valencia type are the most suitable to the climate and the overseas market. The produce of deciduous fruit trees is localized, as far as commercial output is concerned, to cherries from Pedhoulas, apples also from Pedhoulas and peaches and apricots from the lower slopes above Limassol. Strawberries are grown extensively near Morphou, almonds in the Pitsilia district and at Stroumbi, while pistachio nuts have added to the recovery of the previously impoverished Karpas region.

Surplus fruit and vegetables are canned, as well as being processed into juices, marmalade, jam and pickles.

The carob bean is the one unromantic exportable material. But even this has its attractions, because it is such a typical tree in the Cyprus scene, dotted on the land, never in groves, and affording shade to humans and animals. In the Paphos district the pigs make good use of this shelter. Some people dislike the smell of carob beans, which is pervasive and is apt to hang over Limassol during the harvesting season in the autumn.

No one who has ever smelled them at close quarters, can mistake them – carobs – those almost comic vegetables if that is what they should be called, which grow on evergreen trees and look like scarlet runners when they are new and green in early summer, hanging down in clusters from the branches. Later on, they turn black and hard, and a sort of honey drips from them and they haunt the Mediterranean ports with their unforgettable smell.*

These 'almost comic vegetables' form an important ingredient of cattle foods, and are also used in cosmetics, ice-cream, paper and man-made textiles. The pods and beans (known elsewhere as locust beans) are exported whole, kibbled or coarsely ground, as meal or in the form of gum – to the annual value of approximately one million pounds sterling.

One vanished reputation: though 'Chypre', the French name for Cyprus, has been adopted in the nomenclature of perfumery, there is no great perfume manufacturing industry in modern times, unlike in 1483, as reported by Felix Faber, a Dominican monk who visited Cyprus on two occasions on his pilgrimages to the Holy Land:

> Here are merchants from every part of the world, Christians and infidels. There are stores, great and precious, for the aromatic herbs of the east are brought here raw, and are prepared for the perfumer's art. The island itself abounds in dyes and perfumes, so that the stores of Nicosia are a source from which such drugs flow over the world.†

The Karpas is also the main source of Cyprus tobacco, a percentage of which goes into cigarettes sold on the island under familiar brand names, but a large proportion of which is exported. Great advances have been made in livestock and dairy production, resulting in the island's fare being of better quality and fresher than is common in countries of comparable geographical situation. Fat-tailed sheep are hardy and almost self-supporting, whereas dairy cattle – mainly of the shorthorn breed – are generally stall-fed. The local breeds of pigs – always a feature of Paphos husbandry – have been greatly improved by the introduction of Large White and Large Black strains. Poultry production has turned over from backyard farming to battery systems and the hatching of day-old chicks on a large scale, making an important contribution to the higher standard of living now apparent throughout Cyprus.

* *Stranger's Vineyard*, by Mona Messer (Stanley Paul & Co., 1939).
† *Excerpta Cypria*, pp. 41-2.

HISTORY

NEOLITHIC AGE (*c.* 5800–2500 B.C.)

The lower slopes of the two mountain ranges of Cyprus were inhabited long before the discovery of metals and their uses, and
early settlements have been identified in situations which were
favourable for husbandry, usually within reach of a spring or
perennial stream. The intriguing exception is on the rocky island
of Petra tou Limniti, a few miles west of Vouni Palace. This appears to be an inauspicious site for all but the beleaguered (and
unproductive for visitors, as well as being difficult of access). Of all
the Stone Age sites in Cyprus, four have been thoroughly excavated: Khirokitia, Kalavassos, Erimi and Sotira. Khirokitia is the
one which is the most rewarding to visit, because not only has it
been comprehensively investigated but it is well maintained in a
condition which affords a fascinating glimpse of a very early period
in man's history, when he was already occupied in agriculture and
the domestication of animals, and had also developed domestic
architecture in the form of *tholoi*, or beehive huts, made of baked
mud, but with a stone or pebble foundation. The Stone Age *tholoi*
of Cyprus are similar in structure to contemporary buildings in
Mesopotamia and in Crete. Obsidian implements used in the shaping
of stoneware also suggest outside influence, because obsidian is not
a native product. It may therefore be assumed that at this period
Cyprus was not without contact with the outside world. When
pottery later replaced stone for domestic use this appears as a sudden
adoption of new techniques preceded by no transition period –
another indication of the assimilation of foreign ideas and trends.

CHALCOLITHIC* AGE (*c.* 2500–2300 B.C.)

The discovery of copper *c.* 2500 was the beginning of what
amounted to an industrial revolution in Cyprus. This transition
period of two hundred years saw the mining of metal and the
establishment of trade with Egypt and other Mediterranean countries. The two centuries are characterized by more sophisticated
red polished and red-and-black pottery, such as has been found at
Ambelikou not far from Soli.

* *chalcos* = copper *lithos* = stone

BRONZE AGE (*c.* 2300–1050 B.C.)

Now that the production and export of copper was a well-organized industry, Cyprus assumed a position of great commercial importance in the civilized Mediterranean world. The island also laid itself open to infiltration from abroad – the first step towards the successive occupation by foreign powers which persisted until A.D. 1960. Though infiltration at first was insidious, it may be recognized at this early stage. The influence of Anatolia was the first to be implanted, and has survived in the pottery of the period. But at this stage of history Cyprus was not conquered. She assimilated the foreign culture and adapted it to her own requirements. By *c.* 2000 B.C. *tholoi* had been superseded by dwellings on a rectangular plan, and there is evidence of trade relations with Syria, Crete and Palestine. Bronze was by now in more general use than copper.

The religious practices of the Bronze Age in Cyprus are represented by a fascinating terracotta model of a sacred enclosure, discovered during the excavation in 1931–2 of a tomb at Vounous. The group appears to demonstrate that the sacrifice of bulls (and probably infants) played an important part in honouring the dead. In the cult of a snake goddess there could also be a link with the Minoan culture of Crete. An interesting companion piece, also in terracotta, of two pairs of oxen ploughing gives an indication of the high standard of husbandry among the people of the time.

During the Late Bronze Age, which as far as Cyprus is concerned is taken to have begun *c.* 1600 B.C., the island began to assume the historical role which her geography made inevitable, and which has persisted from those early days right through the centuries (and particularly during the Crusades) until the present time, and will no doubt continue into the future. Cyprus became a meeting-point of Eastern and Western civilizations, and therefore an important piece in the chess game of international power politics. Though prosperity and peace frequently accrued from relations with outside powers, independence came to be forfeited.

When Thothmes III, perhaps the greatest of the great Pharaohs of Egypt, came to the throne *c.* 1500 B.C. he had to contend with widespread revolt from his tributaries in Phoenicia, Syria and Mesopotamia. As was characteristic of this ruler, his victorious campaign was followed by programmes of reconstruction and stabilization. Though encircled, Cyprus appears to have suffered little from the concentration and consolidation of Egyptian power beyond her shores. She agreed to pay tribute, mainly in the form of copper, but the situation carried with it a large measure of protection, and it is clear that the island benefited from cultural as well as commercial exchange. Tombs of the period have yielded important finds, including gold, jewels, ivories and Egyptian scarabs.

The dependence of Cyprus upon Egypt lasted into the fourteenth century B.C., as evidenced in the Tell-el-Amarna tablets, a group of which consists of letters from the King of Alasiya to the King of Egypt, referring to the dispatch of consignments of copper. Alasiya is also mentioned in contemporary Hittite texts, and has been identified with the settlement of Enkomi, near Salamis, which was at that time engaged in the manufacture of metal goods for export.

The Egyptians were rulers rather than settlers, and therefore they left behind little in the way of architecture or monuments. But the island was not without colonists. Many of these were drawn from the surplus population of Mycenae, and from the fourteenth to the twelfth centuries Greeks returning from wars abroad established themselves first in the eastern districts of Cyprus and later spread across the island. In this way Paphos was founded by Agapenor, Kourion (Curium) by the Argives and Lapithos by the Laconians. By the time of the break-up of the Mycenaean Empire these settlers had formed themselves into powerful city-kingdoms which remained in existence until the period of Ptolemaic rule. The principal Greek settlements were at Salamis, Soli, Marion (Polis), Paphos and Curium. It should be remembered that though these colonists set themselves to reproduce the conditions of their native country by introducing kingship and bringing with them their own Greek cultural standards, religion, democracy, language and script, they maintained no political connection with the Greek State.

IRON AGE (c. 1000 B.C.)

For a period following the adoption of iron for the manufacture of weapons and implements, and the decline in demand for copper, Cyprus lost some of her links with the outside world. The very lively Achaean domination of Greece had been succeeded by a cruder, Dorian culture. Cyprus was to a large extent thrown back on her own insular resources and developed slowly, the main advances in technology being the potter's wheel, and the decoration of the product with geometric designs.

But though the influx of the Achaeans and their ideas had abated, a new influence was soon to be brought to bear upon Cyprus, this time from the East. The great trading nation of the Phoenicians, whose routes spread to the farthest known points of the world, would not be likely to remain blind to the potentialities of the richly endowed island on their doorstep. What began as straightforward trade developed into colonization, or take-over, which first concentrated upon Kitium (Larnaca) and costal areas and then encroached to inland settlements, but always with commerce as the set purpose.

ASSYRIAN AND EGYPTIAN PERIODS (*c.* 800–550 B.C.)

At a time when Greeks and Phoenicians were colonizing separate areas of Cyprus, and no doubt regarding each other warily, new powers were building up in the East. The Assyrian Empire had come into existence, and Sargon II, the ruler responsible for leading the Children of Israel into captivity, received the homage of seven Cypriot kings. (The relevant inscription is on a stele in the custody of the Berlin Museum.) In 668 B.C. ten local kings of Cyprus joined Assur-bani-pal the Assyrian in an expedition against Egypt. But the pendulum swung back: Egypt recovered, and Nineveh was taken by the Medes in 612 B.C. In 588–69 the Egyptians defeated the Cypriots and Phoenicians at sea, but did not immediately pursue victory to the point of conquest of the island. Egypt had now become the dominant power in the Mediterranean. Though Amasis (Pharaoh, 570–25 B.C.) fostered good relations with Greece, his diplomacy did not extend to Cyprus. He seized the island and exacted tribute, partly in the form of timber for shipbuilding, in which Egypt was deficient. Evelthon, King of Salamis, reigned supreme over the minor kingdoms of the island, and was responsible to Egypt. This was a period of prosperity, mirrored in the art of the day. The best of the Ayia Irini discoveries date from *c.* 625 to 560 B.C.

PERSIAN PERIOD (550–322 B.C.)

In those days the balance of power was never stable for long. It was now upset by Cyrus the Persian, who welded many tribes into a single force and moved against the combined strength of Egypt, Babylon, Lydia and Sparta. He defeated Croesus of Lydia at Sardis in 546 B.C., and was thereafter joined by the kings of Cyprus in a campaign against Amasis of Egypt – the step which followed the destruction of the Babylonian Empire. In 525 B.C. Egypt surrendered to Cambyses, the son of Cyrus.

The Persian Empire was at the height of its power during the reign of Darius. Cyprus had by then become part of a Persian province which included Phoenicia, Palestine and Syria. Though tribute had to be paid to the Persian overlords, and all military forces remained at their disposal, the island was permitted to retain its kings. This was a period of split loyalties, the Phoenician settlers being naturally orientated towards the Eastern conquerors, while the descendants of Greek colonists remained dissentient. Yet it was some years before the Greeks organized themselves for rebellion. In 499 B.C. Onesilos of Salamis headed all the other cities save one (Amathus contracted out) in revolt against his pro-Persian brother Gorgos, and succeeded in ousting him from the throne of Salamis. Success was short-lived. The Persian forces of Darius defeated him in the field near Salamis, and the revolt was crushed.

Though the kingdoms of Cyprus were still permitted to continue, from that date the Persians saw to it that the thrones were occupied by sovereigns friendly to themselves. It was at this period that the Palace of Vouni was built with the purpose of overawing neighbouring Soli, which was the last city to continue resistance against the Persian overlords. Because of their alignment with Persia, in 480 B.C. the city-kingdoms were obliged to join Xerxes in his operations against Greece. A result of this unwilling alliance was that the actions of the Cypriot fleet at the Greek Battle of Salamis came under justifiable suspicion.

The Greeks were sensible of the plight of their compatriots in Cyprus, and in 478 Pausanias the Spartan succeeded in liberating part of the island before he was forced to withdraw. In 467, when Cimon the Athenian had routed the Persians in Pamphylia, Cyprus was too far distant to benefit. Cimon therefore was sent to besiege Kitium, the main Persian stronghold, and to engage the Phoenician

fleet upon which the garrison relied. But he died during the operation. Though the Greek fleet did in fact meet and defeat the
Phoenicians off Salamis, the following year (448 B.C.) saw the
signature of the Peace of Kallias by Persians and Athenians, and
Cyprus was left to her fate.

With the strength of Athens in decline, and the Greek nation
split between Ionians and Dorians in the Peloponnesian War, it fell
to a local patriot to continue the struggle against the Persians and
their Phoenician allies. Again it was Salamis which produced the
leader, King Evagoras I, a remarkable man. Though he was
descended from Teucer, the founder and ruler of Salamis, he was
not born to kingship, but had dramatically wrested power from the
Tyrian Abdemon, a pro-Persian ruler.

The kingdom of Salamis flourished under the new king's rule.
Though his aim was to restore the Greek culture which had been
overlaid during the long period of Persian rule, and in spite of his
success in uniting Cyprus, with the exception of Soli, Kitium and
Amathus, he managed to remain for a long time on diplomatic
terms with both Greeks and Persians. Then, with assistance from
an Athenian navy and the king of Egypt, he bravely took the
initiative by capturing Phoenician cities and instigating revolt
against the Persians in Cilicia. But a set-back came in 387, when
Athens once more accepted the peace terms of the Persians.
Evagoras was left to continue hostilities single-handed. In 380–79
he was forced to surrender Salamis to overwhelming numbers of
attackers, and though he was still powerful enough to be able to
conclude a peace guaranteeing retention of the throne of Salamis,
he was forced to agree to pay tribute to the Persians, and to renounce sovereignty over the rest of the island.

After Evagoras was assassinated in 374–3 his son Nicocles
maintained the ideals of Greek culture. The next revolt came in 351,
when nine Cypriot kings rose against Artaxerxes III. Salamis was
again besieged by sea and land. Resistance was crushed, and Cyprus
reverted to Persian rule.

The next king of Salamis, Pnytagoras, accepted terms which
placed the Cypriot fleet at the disposal of the Persians. But when
the Persians needed help against Alexander the Great, Pnytagoras
and the kings of Cyprus sent warships to assist Alexander at the
Siege of Tyre in 332 B.C. This was the turning-point in the power

of the Persians, and thenceforward Cyprus was to be free from their domination.

HELLENISTIC PERIOD (322–58 B.C.)

It was Alexander the Great who was responsible for the spread of Hellenism. His ambition was to follow military conquests with the culture expounded to him by Aristotle. He was so successful in his campaigns that when he died no oriental opponent remained. But although there was no enemy, and although Alexander's successors were inspired by their dead leader's ideals and imperial policy, he left no competent heir, and fighting broke out between the Macedonian generals who sought to succeed him. Of these, Ptolemy, Satrap of Egypt and founder of a dynasty, set himself the task during the forty years of war which followed of holding Egypt and gaining control of Cyrenaica, Palestine and Cyprus.

In 318 B.C. he established a protectorate over Cyprus, which covered all but the kingdoms of Amathus, Kitium, Lapithos and Kyrenia, which had opted for rule by Antigonus, another Macedonian general, who had claims on Asia Minor and Syria as well as Cyprus. Ptolemy's forces under his brother Menelaus, with a navy commanded by Seleucus, another of Alexander's Macedonians, joined Nicocreon, king of Salamis, in operations against the strongholds of the supporters of Antigonus. These were vanquished with the exception of Kitium, under its king, Pygmalion. A year later Ptolemy came to Cyprus in person, took Kitium and executed its king, destroyed Marion and transferred its population to Paphos, and dispatched all the other recalcitrant kings as prisoners to Egypt. Nicocreon, king of Salamis, was appointed ruler of the conquered cities, while Menelaus was made *strategos* or military governor of the island.

The position remained thus until 306 B.C., when Antigonus dispatched his son Demetrius with 15,000 men and 100 ships to Cyprus. They landed on the Karpas Peninsula, where there were good harbour facilities. Menelaus met him in battle, but lost half of a large army, and had to retreat in disorder to Salamis. Here he was besieged by Demetrius, who brought up great engines of war against the defences of the city. Though Ptolemy came to the assistance of his brother, his fleet was decisively beaten off Cape Greco, and Menelaus surrendered.

Demetrius ruled for ten years as king of Salamis, until in 295 B.C. Ptolemy recaptured the island. Though Salamis was the one city to resist him, it was easily subjugated. Almost without interruption for the next three hundred years Cyprus now remained under the Ptolemies, who divided the island into four administrative parts: Paphos, Amathus, Salamis and Lapithos – all of which were ruled over by a *strategos* chosen from the aristocracy of the royal court at Alexandria. Paphos became the capital of the island.

During this period Alexandria was at its height as a great centre of learning and of luxury, and Cyprus was a valued possession of the Egyptian crown. Ptolemy Philadelphus, who succeeded Ptolemy I, built the city of Arsinoe to replace Marion and named it after his sister. When he deified her, her cult came to be identified with that of Aphrodite.

But the dynasty grew degenerate, lacking legitimate heirs, and there was a suggestion that the last true Ptolemy had bequeathed Cyprus to Rome. Consequently, when a Roman patrician was insulted by the nominal king of Cyprus, the bastard known as Ptolemy the Cyprian, the affair was used as an excuse for the annexation of the island. Cyprus became a province of the Roman Empire in 58 B.C.

ROMAN PERIOD (58 B.C.–A.D. 395)

Pretexts for aggression are frequently frivolous, and contrive to obscure real causes. In this case the build-up of the Roman Empire, and her rather uncharacteristic acquisition of sea power for use in the Carthaginian Wars, had led to recognition of the strategic importance of Cyprus – a role which the island has never been able to relinquish. The situation is best described by Strabo:

Now the Cypriots were first ruled in their several cities by kings, but since the Ptolemaic kings became lords over Egypt, Cyprus too passed to them, the Romans also contributing often their help. But when the last Ptolemy who reigned, a brother of the father of Cleopatra, the queen of our time, seemed both unsatisfactory and unthankful to his benefactors, he was deposed therefore, and the Romans occupied the island, and it became a separate imperial province. The king's ruin was chiefly due to Publius Claudius Pulcher. He fell into the hands of pirates, the Cilicians being then very active, and requiring a ransom he applied to the king, begging him to send and ransom him. He sent a very small sum [believed to have been two talents, about £500] so that the very pirates were ashamed to take it. They sent it back and released Publius without a ransom. When he was safe he bore in mind against both their favours, and becoming tribune grew so powerful that Marcus Cato (grandson of Cato the Censor) was sent to take Cyprus from its ruler. Ptolemy indeed succeeded in killing himself, but Cato swooped down and seized Cyprus, and disposed of the royal property and carried off the money to the common treasury of the Romans. From that date the island became an imperial province, as it is today. For a short interval Antony gave it to Cleopatra and her sister Arsinoe, but when he fell all his arrangements fell with him.*

Ptolemy was in fact offered the high priesthood of Paphos, but preferred death. The royal treasure of Salamis, which amounted to something like £1,700,000, was taken to Rome by Cato in person, where it arrived at an opportune moment for the replenishment of the imperial coffers. Cato desired to retain only the statue of Zeno the Philosopher (p. 215) and refused all other reward. He remained in the island two years, during which time Cyprus was reorganized as a part of the province of Cilicia.

In 52 B.C. the orator Marcus Tullius Cicero (106–43 B.C.) was appointed governor of Cilicia, and when he discovered that Cyprus was being administered harshly and crippled by taxation he made liberal fiscal reforms.

During the reign of Augustus, in 27 B.C., Cyprus was separated from Cilicia and became an imperial province under a military governor. The country was adjudged so peaceful as to require no garrison. A list of the Roman proconsuls, who ruled from Paphos, has been compiled by Dr Hogarth in an appendix to his *Devia Cypria*. The imperial finances were reorganized under Augustus Caesar, and for the first time money was forthcoming for large-scale public works in the provinces. Cyprus benefited in the form of harbour works, roads, bridges and aqueducts. The island grew prosperous by exporting wine, oil, corn and metals.

---

* Strabo, Book XIV, Chapter VI, in *Excerpta Cypria*.

In A.D. 45 one Sergius Paulus was proconsul of Cyprus and resident at Paphos. The two missionaries, Paul and Barnabas, appeared before him and pitted the strength of their faith and logic against the sorceries of a magician of the name of Elymas, leading to the distinguished proconsul's conversion, and to the firm establishment of Christian belief in the island of Cyprus.

The return of St Barnabas to his native Cyprus in company with his cousin Mark is recounted not in the Acts of the Apostles but in an apocryphal book known as the Acts of Barnabas.* This tells how the missionaries landed in the north of the island, but did not enter the city of Lapithos because a festival of idols was taking place there. They travelled through the Troödos Mountains, where they ordained Heracleidus as Bishop of Cyprus. But at Old Paphos, Curium, Amathus and Kitium they were shocked to witness heathen practices, and took ship to Salamis. Here Barnabas was martyred by the Jews. His remains were hidden in a cave, to be dramatically and opportunely rediscovered in A.D. 477.

The Jews in Palestine had never taken kindly to Roman rule, nor could they because they were subjected consistently to religious persecution. This pressure had in the past encouraged them to settle in Cyprus, and in A.D. 67, after an unsuccessful revolt which ended three years later with the fall of Jerusalem and the destruction of the Temple, there occurred an enormous influx of refugees to Cyprus, Cyrene and Egypt. From these countries of asylum they continued armed insurrection against the Romans, which was at all times harshly suppressed. In the case of Salamis alone, the city was partly destroyed, and 250,000 Cypriots are reported to have been killed. In A.D. 117 it was decreed that all Jews should be expelled from the island, and this policy was enforced so strictly that even if a Jew were shipwrecked on the coasts of Cyprus he was immediately slaughtered.

The removal of the Jews from Cyprus was the beginning not only of the uninterrupted spread of Christianity in the island but also of a period of great prosperity – so much so that the inhabitants earned a reputation for luxury, immorality and sloth. By the third century A.D., however, the Roman Empire had become weakened by plague, war and famine in the provinces, and revenues were depleted and the taxpayers exhausted.

* Ante-Nicene Christian Library (1870), Vol. XVI.

In A.D. 327, during the reign of Constantine, his mother the Empress Helena landed in Cyprus on her return voyage from Jerusalem, bringing with her portions of the True Cross, and the Cross of the Penitent Thief. This was a year of great distress and hardship, due to the famine which had followed a period of extreme drought. Not only did the Empress Helena found the Monastery of Stavrovouni as a shrine for the holy relics but she also took steps to alleviate the distress of the people by negotiating exemption from taxation on their behalf. Churches and schools were founded, and the fortunes of the island began to recover.

Constantine, who ruled A.D. 324–37, had embraced Christianity, and looked to it to become the power which would hold the Empire together. But the Church was divided, and he therefore convened the Council of Nicaea (A.D. 325) in Asia Minor. The result was the formulation of the Nicaean Creed, which stabilized Christian beliefs. However, the Christian Church of Cyprus, though having no doctrinal differences, claimed independence.

In the following decade Cyprus was ravaged by earthquakes, Salamis being the worst affected of its cities. In 334 and 345 it was almost wholly destroyed, and partially submerged by the encroaching sea. In 350 the city was rebuilt in a contracted form, renamed Constantia in honour of Constantine II and established as the metropolitan city of the island.

But in spite of the ideals of unity held by Constantine the Great, the Roman Empire was finally divided into two parts in A.D. 364, and Cyprus was in due course assigned to the Eastern Byzantine Empire, which had Constantinople as its capital.

BYZANTINE RULE (A.D. 395–1191)

Within the eastern division of the Roman Empire, Cyprus became one province of a political diocese administered from Antioch. However, in A.D. 478 its Church won autonomy through the claims of Archbishop Anthemios, who cited his discovery of the remains of St Barnabas as proof of direct apostolic foundation. But a new power was rising, stronger strategically than Byzantium, and as inspiring to its followers as Christianity. Islam had emerged as an almost irresistible force in the Mediterranean.

Byzantium was not strong enough to protect her outlying provinces from Arab attack. Damascus, Antioch and Jerusalem fell. Syria, Palestine and Egypt were conquered. In A.D. 647 Cyprus was invaded and, when offered the choice between acceptance of the Muslim faith or war, chose war, with the result that the new city of Constantia was destroyed. It was during this invasion that the lady known as Umm Haram, a relative of the Prophet Mohammed, died from a fall from her mule (p. 222).

By the time Byzantium had gathered strength for the relief of the island, the Muslim invaders had retired to Alexandria with seventy ships laden with booty. But in 654 the Arabs invaded Cyprus a second time and held the island for some years.

The long siege of Constantinople was followed by a truce between the two great powers. Justinian II and Abd al Malik reached an agreement wherein half of the taxes of the island should be paid to Byzantium. But Justinian II remained concerned about the position of Greek Cypriots. At first he attempted to reduce the number of Muslims in Cyprus, then realizing that if he persevered in this he would have no means of protecting the remaining Christians from reprisal, he ordered the mass emigration of Greek Cypriots to a new Christian city: Justinianopolis on the shores of the Sea of Marmara. At least part of the population departed. As a result of this depletion another Arab invasion followed in 692, and many Greek Cypriots were transported to Syria as prisoners, until in 698 the agreement between Byzantium and the Arabs was renewed, and prisoners and exiled Christians were repatriated to Cyprus.

From that period onwards Byzantium had imperfect control of the sea and Cyprus was exposed to constant attack by the fleets of Syria and Egypt. The position deteriorated still further in 802, when the Byzantine Emperor Nikephorus ceased payment of tribute to Caliph Haroun al Raschid. As a direct consequence, three great waves of invasion struck the island. Churches and ecclesiastical property were destroyed and thousands of Christians killed and captured, often to be taken away as slaves. It was at this time that the populations of the coastal towns – Paphos, Carpasia, Lapithos and numerous minor villages – were forced to move inland for protection. Great castles, including St Hilarion, Buffavento, Kantara and Limassol, were built.

The balance of power did not begin to shift until 964, when Cyprus was at last safe from foreign attack. Though very little has survived of contemporary secular architecture, the churches and monasteries built at that time as replacement and in thanksgiving are the best illustration of the climate of opinion in the island. After the liberation from Islam, culture in the island ran parallel to that of Constantinople. There were, however, periods of political uneasiness, and the following century saw at least two abortive rebellions against governors sent from Asia Minor. But under the aegis of more civilized governors from the Byzantine court more settled conditions prevailed. These are reflected in fine frescoes of the late eleventh and early twelfth centuries. Of greater importance than these political moves was the great split between the Orthodox and Latin Churches which mirrored the cleavage between the Eastern and Western Roman Empires. Rome and Constantinople vied with each other as rulers of the Christian world. Dissension came to a head when Constantinople's patriarch warned his people against the errors of the Latins. Rome excommunicated him and the schism was complete. The significance of this great rift, as far as Cyprus was concerned, was to become clear in the future, after the island had fallen under Lusignan rule, when Frankish domination resulted in persecution of the Orthodox Church of Cyprus.

The first of the Crusades by-passed Cyprus. Then in 1097 the Emperor Alexius thought to use a gathering of European princes as tools in reconstituting his empire on the shores of the eastern Mediterranean. Yet when these princes took Jerusalem they created a new kingdom and bestowed on it a code of law based on the feudal system. Antioch, Edessa and Tripoli were added to the domain of the third king of Jerusalem, Baldwin II (1118–31). The Byzantine Empire was too enfeebled to retaliate.

It was even too weak to take much action when Isaac Comnenus, great-nephew of the Byzantine emperor, set himself up as the independent sovereign of Cyprus. He had married the sister of William II, the Norman king of Sicily, who honoured this bond by sending a Sicilian fleet to defeat the rather ineffectual imperial forces opposing Isaac. He reigned tyrannically for seven years.

RICHARD CŒUR DE LION (A.D. 1191)

The next fateful change in the history of Cyprus arose entirely by chance in 1191. Four years previously, when Guy de Lusignan was king of Jerusalem, he had been overwhelmingly defeated by the forces of Saladin, and Jerusalem was taken. Nothing of the kingdom was left except the city of Tyre and the principalities of Antioch and Tripoli. Though de Lusignan was an unpopular figure, being regarded as an adventurer who had succeeded to the throne of Jerusalem solely on account of his marriage to Sybilla, who was heiress to the kingdom, the great European powers, England, France and the Holy Roman Empire, were so shocked by losses in the Holy Land that they reconciled their rivalries and mounted the Third Crusade. Acre was to be the first objective, with the aim of forming it into a base for land operations. In 1189 it was besieged by Guy de Lusignan, who, though he had been captured by Saladin and later released on parole, had returned to the attack. The forces of the Holy Roman Emperor, Frederick I, moved overland to his aid, while King Philip II of France and King Richard I of England approached by sea.

Though the French were able to sail direct towards Acre, the English fleet was dispersed by a great storm. Most of the ships took shelter off Crete and Rhodes, but three were wrecked within sight of Limassol. The survivors were captured by Isaac Comnenus, and their salvaged property seized. Meanwhile a fourth ship had been driven by the gale towards Limassol, having on board the king of England's sister, Joanna, Queen Dowager of Sicily, and his affianced bride, Berengaria of Navarre. When, instead of befriending the illustrious ladies, Isaac the tyrant insulted them, Richard reassembled his fleet and hastened to Cyprus to demand satisfaction for both wrongs. He was received with threats and taunts, and immediately gave battle, motivated additionally by the fact that Cyprus would make an excellent base and source of supply for the impending operations in Palestine.

The forces of Isaac Comnenus proved no match for English archers and armoured knights equipped for the Crusade. Richard's landing near Amathus met with immediate success, both in the initial operations and during the following day's great battle five miles from Limassol. Isaac took to the mountains, where he could not be followed without further preparation. Then, after many of his nobles had transferred their allegiance to the English king and Guy de Lusignan had arrived on the island with reinforcements, the tyrant offered terms which included the provision of gold, men-at-arms and his own services for the Crusade, with the surrender of his castles and his daughter's person as hostages. Yet as soon as these terms were accepted, he repudiated them and escaped by stealth from Limassol, where he had gone to vow allegiance to the English king.

The repeatedly outraged Richard put Guy de Lusignan in charge of land operations, while he deployed the English fleet around the island with the purpose of taking or intimidating every castle and stronghold. But although for a short time Isaac Comnenus eluded de Lusignan, first in Famagusta and then in the almost impregnable castle of Kantara, Richard was untroubled enough to be able to celebrate his marriage with great pomp in Limassol Castle. Berengaria was crowned Queen of England. According to a chronicler, 'there was joy and love enow'. Soon afterwards Isaac was captured while attempting to take ship from the Abbey at Cape Andreas in the Karpas peninsula. As he petitioned that he should not be put in irons, he was taken in silver fetters to captivity in Syria, where he died in 1194.

Resistance came to an end when Isaac's daughter surrendered the Castle of Kyrenia to Guy de Lusignan. She was dispatched with suitable honours to King Richard, who at that time was lying sick in Nicosia, and she thereafter became lady-in-waiting to Queen Berengaria and a popular figure at court.

Garrisons were placed in Cyprus when Richard, loaded with Isaac Comnenus's fabulous treasure, resumed his interrupted voyage to Acre. But when news followed him of revolt in Cyprus he began to regard the island as a doubtful asset, and sold it to the Knights Templar for 100,000 bezants.*

But the Templars were harsh rulers. Within a few months information was laid that a great uprising was planned for Easter 1192. They took refuge in their castle at Nicosia, but when their offer to withdraw from the island was refused they determined to fight, despite their inferior numbers. By sallying forth from the castle at dawn they crushed the rebellion by promiscuous and savage butchery. Yet, though temporary victory was theirs, they recognized that they would be incapable of holding the island by force. Accordingly they applied to Richard for permission to withdraw from their bargain.

---

* A gold coin, from the old French *besan* and Latin *byzantius*, 100,000 being estimated by De Mas Latrie in 1878 as worth £304,000.

Richard agreed to this proposition, though he did not return the Knights' first down-payment of 40,000 bezants. (The remainder of the agreed purchase money was to have come from taxation.) The Knights retained certain of their possessions in Cyprus, notably at Limassol.

Meanwhile Guy de Lusignan, who after the death of his wife Sybilla was deprived of the Crown of Jerusalem, was offered compensation by Richard in the form of the sovereignty of Cyprus – whether as a free gift or on terms similar to the transaction with the Templars is not known, though history suggests that Guy de Lusignan was a man unlikely ever to have discharged such a debt.*

LUSIGNAN DYNASTY (A.D. 1192–1489)

Domestic politics now took the form of the establishment of a feudal system of government, and the island was settled by the expedient of granting land to Crusaders in exchange for their military services. A strong hold was maintained over the native population.

For reasons which have never been divulged, Guy de Lusignan was never crowned king. Instead he was known as Lord of Cyprus. Upon his death, two years after the transference of the island to him, he was succeeded by his brother Amaury, who was recognized by the Holy Roman Empire and in 1197 crowned king in Nicosia. During his reign the Pope sent a commission to the island with the purpose of converting the Cypriots to the Roman Communion. Thus began three hundred years of oppression for the Greek Orthodox Church of the island.

After the Crusaders had in 1203 diverted their attention to Constantinople and sacked it, the Eastern empire was allocated among the European powers. This meant that Cyprus retained no political connection with the East, but became entirely dependent upon the sea power of the West. But she was useful, both strategically and commercially, and so received full measure of support.

At least as far as the ruling classes were concerned, this was a period of prosperity for Cyprus. Great cathedrals were built in

*Two versions of Richard's conquest of the island, recorded by Benedict of Peterborough (d. 1193) and the monk Neophytos, can be read and compared in *Devia Cypria*.

Nicosia and Famagusta, as well as the Augustinian (later Premonstratensian) Abbey of Bellapais and the château at Kouklia.
Castles within reach of the coast were refortified, with a view to
resisting internal risings, and keeping sea lines of communication
open in that contingency. The nobles of the period were renowned for their riches and for their luxurious way of life, which
included tournaments and sports, and hunting of wild beasts in the
mountains. But the people suffered greatly.

Because the kings of Cyprus were warlike, and apt to absent
themselves abroad where they were frequently killed in battle, the
sovereignty all too often devolved upon a minor, with his mother
as regent. It was natural that the widows should take counsel from
their own families, and it was through Eschiva d'Ibelin, mother of
King Hugues I (1205–18), that the great Frankish d'Ibelin family
assumed a power that was to rival that of the Lusignan dynasty.
During the long minority of Henri I, son of Hugues I, Jean
d'Ibelin fortified St Hilarion as a residence for the young king and
his sisters. But the Queen Regent quarrelled with d'Ibelin (also
known as the Lord of Beyrouth), and enlisted the help of the Holy
Roman Emperor Frederick II, who was on his way to Palestine.
Aware that Cyprus might well provide revenues to help finance his
Crusade (after all, the emperor had made Amaury king), he
undertook to deal with d'Ibelin.

Though at first it seemed that the emperor had come out best by
marrying the young king to Alix de Montferrat, a princess of
Norman lineage, by seizing the estates of d'Ibelin and his supporters, and by putting the island in charge of three barons adept
at extorting taxation, yet Jean d'Ibelin made a come-back and,
after a siege of the Castle of St Hilarion which lasted a year, regained possession of the person of the young king. The fighting
between the two factions continued for two years. A last stand was
made by the imperialists in the Castle of Kyrenia. During the
siege Alix de Montferrat died, and a truce was arranged for her
ceremonial funeral procession from Kyrenia to Nicosia, where she
was buried in the royal tomb. A year later the Emperor was forced
to relinquish all claim to control over Cyprus.

After Jerusalem had again fallen to the infidels in 1244 another
distinguished visitor landed in Cyprus. On what is known as the
Seventh Crusade, King Louis of France wintered with King
Henri in 1248. They sailed together to Egypt. In 1246 Henri's right

to the Crown of Jerusalem had been recognized by the Pope. By a Papal Bull of 1260, the activities of the Orthodox Church were seriously curtailed; all tithes had to be paid to the Latins, and in fact the Orthodox Church became subject to the Church of Rome.

The most splendid period of Lusignan rule in Cyprus covered the reign of Hugues IV (1324–59). Acre had fallen in 1291 to the Egyptian Mamelukes, a body of Turkish slaves from whom the Egyptian army was drawn, who had seized power to an extent which was reminiscent of the conquests of Saladin. After the fall of Acre, Cyprus became the natural centre of trade in the eastern Mediterranean – greatly favoured by Christian merchants desirous of political stability. Famagusta profited and became a fabulous city, rivalling Antioch, and the base for colonies of foreign merchants. Thus Ludolf, a Westphalian priest, who visited the island between 1336 and 1341, writes:

You must know that in Cyprus all the princes, nobles, barons and knights are the noblest, best and richest in the world. They live there now with their children, but they used to live in the land of Syria, and the noble city of Acon [Acre], but when that land and city were lost they fled to Cyprus, and there have remained until the present day.

Moreover there are very rich merchants, a thing not to be wondered at, for Cyprus is the furthest of Christian lands, so that all ships and all wares, be they what they may, and come they from what part of the sea they will, must needs come first to Cyprus, and in no wise can they pass it by, and pilgrims from every country journeying to lands over the sea must touch at Cyprus.*

In 1372 the traditional rivalry between Genoese and Venetians flared. The occasion of the coronation of King Pierre II as king of Jerusalem at Famagusta provided the spark for the fuse. A quarrel as to precedence arose – the Venetians insisted that it was their privilege to hold the right rein of the boy king's horse, leaving the left or inferior rein to the Genoese – and the result was large-scale fighting, fed by troops sent from Genoa. The king was captured, and his mother, Eleanor of Aragon, took refuge in Kyrenia Castle. Throughout a long siege the castle justified its reputation of being

* *Excerpta Cypria*, p. 20.

impregnable. Peace was concluded in 1374, but with the harsh condition that Cyprus was to cede the great city of Famagusta to the Genoese.

Pierre II was succeeded by his uncle, Jacques I (1382–98), who engaged in constant conflict with the Genoese of Famagusta. The walls of Nicosia had been built by his predecessor – they were to be levelled by the Venetians in 1564 – and now the king fortified Kantara and Larnaca, which had replaced Famagusta as the commercial centre of the island.

The reign of the next king, Janus (1398–1432), was distinguished by his wars with the Egyptian Mamelukes. In 1425 an Egyptian fleet sacked Limassol and Larnaca. Next year a still greater force landed at Limassol and marched on Nicosia. King Janus, who met the invaders at Khirokitia, was captured and his forces dispersed. The Mamelukes sacked Nicosia, breaking up the city with the utmost thoroughness, and departed to Alexandria with an immense amount of booty and prisoners whose fate was to be sold as slaves. King Janus was released after ten months on payment of a considerable ransom and the undertaking that the state would make an annual payment to Egypt in recognition of the suzerainty of the Sultan. The power of the Lusignan dynasty never recovered.

Religion and politics are never for long dissociated in the history – and the internal strife – of Cyprus. The Lusignans had been fanatically devoted to the Latin Church. But when King Jean II (1432–58) took as his second wife Helena Palaeologos, daughter of the ruler of the Peloponnese, she determined that she would make her own Orthodox Church supreme in the island. She attempted this by seeking to appoint her own nominee as Archbishop of Cyprus, but the move was circumvented by papal diplomacy, and the king was persuaded to overrule his wife. Further, Jean II was encouraged to marry his only daughter and heiress, Charlotte, to a staunchly Catholic Portuguese nobleman, John, Duke of Coimbra, who was created Prince of Antioch. But when he began to take part in state affairs and revealed his support of the Catholics Queen Helena saw to it that he was removed from court. He died soon afterwards in circumstances which suggest foul play.

Still more trouble was to arise from appointments to the archbishopric of Nicosia. The king appointed his illegitimate son, Jacques, and, though the consent of the Pope was withheld, insisted that he should enjoy all the privileges and revenues of the see.

Though Jacques was directly implicated in two murders, with one short interruption he continued as archbishop, and after the death of Helena in 1458 it was thought that the king intended making him heir to the throne. But Jean II died in the same year as his wife, and his daughter Charlotte succeeded at the age of twenty-two.

As the mother of Jacques had been Greek, he commanded the sympathy of the underprivileged classes in Cyprus. When he realized after his father's death that his power was in rapid decline, Jacques went to Egypt. Here he claimed that he was the rightful male heir, and appealed to the sultan in his capacity as suzerain of Cyprus. The sultan provided a fleet and Jacques landed at Larnaca in 1460. The people rose to his support, and Queen Charlotte with her second husband, Count Louis of the hated house of Savoy, took refuge in Kyrenia Castle. Though the castle was beleaguered for three years, it was never taken. In the end it was surrendered by treachery. The queen escaped to Rome, where she died in 1487 after having assigned her sovereignty to the house of Savoy.

Jacques had not waited for secession. In 1460 he was crowned king of Jerusalem, Cyprus and Armenia, though his titles went unrecognized by the Pope in Rome. In 1464 he succeeded in wresting Famagusta from the Genoese. He now contracted a most fateful marriage – to Caterina Cornaro, daughter of a Venetian nobleman. The Venetian Republic, alive to the possibilities – they had always coveted Cyprus as a trading centre and source of natural wealth – declared her an adopted daughter of the state, gave her a splendid dowry, and escorted her to Famagusta after a marriage by proxy. But the king died the following year, in circumstances which implicated the queen's uncles. His posthumous heir, Jacques III, lived for one year before also dying in a way which was notoriously suspect.

The adopted daughter of the Venetian state now sat on the throne of Cyprus, and was unshaken by a movement to replace her by a protégé of the Cypriot nobles. But although the Venetians had by now managed to infiltrate into all branches of the kingdom, and had withdrawn all real power from the queen, they could not rest assured that she would continue indefinitely as their pawn. In 1489 Queen Caterina was persuaded to accept voluntary and honourable exile in Italy where, with copious funds provided by the grateful Republic, her court became a centre for the culture of the Renaissance.

Venice announced that the Republic had taken possession of Cyprus with the free consent of its adopted daughter. A friendly alliance was arranged with Egypt. Peaceably, the Lusignan era had ended and the Venetian occupation begun.

VENETIAN RULE (A.D. 1489–1571)

The Venetian Republic's command of the sea in the Middle Ages had brought her vast profits in connection with transport and supplies for the Crusaders. Genoa had been her rival, until decisively beaten at sea in 1380. But 1486 was a more fateful year for the Venetians, because when Diaz discovered and charted a trade route to India via the Cape, this automatically eliminated the overland route from the eastern Mediterranean and Venice lost her monopolies. Nevertheless, for strategic reasons she needed a base in the East, and Cyprus, so assiduously prepared for that role, became the outpost of the Venetian Republic.

The new régime set out to be moderate according to the standards of the day. The Lusignan code of government was retained. The Orthodox Church now went unmolested. Taxation was not to be increased. Yet because the occupation was primarily military, other considerations were treated with indifference. Trade declined, agriculture fell into neglect and the standard of living of the people deteriorated. Very soon a visitor to the island was writing:

> ... all the inhabitants of Cyprus are slaves to the Venetians, being obliged to pay to the state a third part of all their increase or income, whether the product of their ground, or corn, wine, oil or of their cattle, or any other thing. Besides every man of them is bound to work for the state two days of the week wherever they shall please to appoint him: and if any shall fail, by reason of some other business of their own, or indisposition of body, then they are made to pay a fine for as many days as they are absent from their work ... The common people are so flayed and pillaged, that they hardly have wherewithal to keep soul and body together.*

* Martin von Baumgarten (1473–1535). In *Excerpta Cypria*.

The main military aim of the Venetians in Cyprus was defence. Due to the revolutionary discovery of gunpowder, the great Byzantine and Lusignan fortifications had become obsolete. The new armaments policy was destructive as well as constructive. Not only were the serviceable castles, such as Kyrenia and Famagusta, rebuilt, and strengthened by double walls filled with earth and rubble but free-standing buildings which might have interrupted the field of fire were ruthlessly razed, irrespective of their merit. Nicosia was completely encircled by a great wall and bastions, and memorable buildings outside the perimeter destroyed to the point of annihilation. Such castles as did not enter into the modern scheme of defence – St Hilarion, Buffavento, Kantara – were dismantled and abandoned.

The Ottoman Empire was the arch-enemy against whom all these defensive preparations were made. The Turks had become incensed at the annexation of an island which was under the suzerainty of their sultan. Also, they considered that the safety of their pilgrim ships *en route* for Mecca was threatened by a Venetian base so close to the shores of Asia Minor. Both sides prepared for the inevitable war. Though Venice appealed to the European powers for assistance, more approval than concrete assistance was forthcoming. When the Turks formally demanded the cession of Cyprus, war was declared.

The first invasion came on July 1st, 1570, at Larnaca. The Turks were immediately welcomed by the local population, the reason being dissatisfaction with the poor standards of life under Venetian government. It became immediately clear that there would be no resistance to the Turks in the country, and that defence was practicable only from the fortresses of Nicosia and Famagusta, and possibly from the small garrison in Kyrenia Castle.

After a bloody siege which lasted six weeks, Nicosia was taken, by cutting earth from under the bastions and breaching the walls. Total resistance brought total atrocity. Twenty thousand people were massacred, shiploads of slaves were removed from the island and a great quantity of loot dispatched to the sultan in Constantinople. Kyrenia, disheartened and without support, surrendered without a fight, to be followed by the remainder of the island with the exception of Famagusta, the greatest defensive system of the great Venetian engineers.

The Turkish commander, Lala Mustapha Pasha, put a strong garrison in Nicosia, and pitched camp to the south of Famagusta. But as the season was already far advanced, he decided to winter his troops and defer serious operations until the spring, by which time he would have received reinforcements by sea. This aid arrived from Syria in April 1571, and he immediately moved against the city, which was commanded by Marcantonio Bragadino, a Venetian of exceptional heroism and cool decision. The offensive tactics were similar to those which had been successful in Nicosia. Trenches and traverses were dug, leading to the undermining of the bastions. The Turks had overwhelming numbers of soldiers, and succeeded in placing batteries within close range on a line which ran from the Arsenal to the Land Gate. The Venetians refused to accept terms . . . 'Tell your pasha to continue his enterprise and we will reply with fire, muskets, cannon and swords.' The siege, a succession of vicious assaults countered by heroic defence, lasted until August 1st, when terms for surrender were agreed.

The defending forces were to be spared and permitted to embark for Crete, while the civil population was to go unmolested. But four days later Bragadino complained to Mustapha that, though the soldiers had been allowed to leave, the inhabitants were suffering violence. The two leaders met, but what had been intended as a rational discussion flared into dispute. Bragadino was imprisoned and tortured for fourteen days before being humiliated in public by being forced to kiss the ground at Mustapha's feet, after which he was flayed alive. His skin was then stuffed with straw and put on exhibition in Famagusta and later in Syria and Constantinople.

But Lala Mustapha Pasha was denied a triumphal return to Constantinople. Spurred by the news from Famagusta, the European powers acted at last. In October a great fleet met the Turks in a naval battle in the Gulf of Lepanto, and defeated them decisively. It is memorable as the last major engagement to have been fought from ships propelled by oars. It also marked the close of European interest in the Holy Land. And with the Crusading spirit lost, the plight of Cyprus dwindled into insignificance.

TURKISH RULE (A.D. 1571–1878)

At first the new administration was welcomed by the inhabitants of Cyprus, both as a relief from Venetian harshness and because of two very popular measures. The Turks re-established the Greek Orthodox Church of Cyprus, restored the archbishopric which had been in abeyance and accorded the people the right to worship unmolested. Such privileges did not, however, extend to the Latins, who were deprived of their property, while their churches were converted into mosques, warehouses, stables and other secular uses. The second popular measure was the removal of the feudal system and the freeing of serfs. At last the people were allowed to own their own land, although in doing so they became taxpayers. Some 30,000 Turkish settlers from Mustapha's soldiery were given land, and their numbers were augmented from time to time by immigration from Asia Minor. There was little differential treatment, but as there was no intermarriage between races and religions, the population became sharply divided into two.

Taxation was severe, and began to cause exceptional hardship when dearth of seed and the closure of mines lowered earning capacity. The population declined, until after two years of famine and pestilence only 25,000 native Cypriots remained out of a number which according to the first census of the Turkish administration had been 150,000. The Sublime Porte showed awareness of the manner in which the peasant population was being bled beyond all legitimate standards by local tax-collectors, and, though malpractice was not greatly curtailed, it is of great significance that in 1660 the Grand Vizier began to recognize the archbishop of Cyprus and his suffragan bishops as spokesmen for their compatriots.

From that time onward the archbishop became more and more powerful as a representative of the people. He engaged as mediator with the Turks on all matters, particularly those connected with taxation, and was also successful in tempering repressive measures after several abortive revolts.

The Turks by this time had come to look upon Cyprus less as a colony than as an investment. In fact, at one stage the island was presented to the Grand Vizier, who promptly farmed out its revenues in exchange for a fixed annual payment. This system made for the extortions which the bishops tried to combat. In fact, they did this so effectively that by the end of the eighteenth century they became so powerful, and so much money passed through their hands, that the resident Turks became envious and rose against the bishops. Hostilities were avoided solely by the intervention of the

European consuls appointed to the island, most of whom were resident in Larnaca.

Yet in the end outside forces contributed to the fall of the bishops. In 1821 the Greeks in Morea rose against Ottoman rule, and their revolt was to lead to the Greek nation's independence. Seeing an analogy in Cyprus and wishing to forestall it, the Grand Vizier summoned Archbishop Kyprianos, the bishops of Paphos, Kitium and Kyrenia, the abbot of Kykko Monastery and other leading clerics to Nicosia. Here they were hideously slaughtered. Some influential Christians were given asylum by the foreign consuls at Larnaca, but the power of the hierarchy had come to an end.

When Greece gained independence many Cypriots went to Athens and acquired Greek nationality. Greece, liberated by her own efforts, more than ever became the ideal of the Orthodox Greeks of Cyprus.

Conditions began to improve in the reign of Abdul Mejid I (1839–61), during which time the sultan undertook to accord equality of treatment to Ottoman subjects of all creeds. Tax-farming in Cyprus was abolished, and the governorship of the island was made by appointment, rather than by auction as in the past. Local courts were set up in 1839.

In spite of this the British Parliament of the day continued to show concern about the treatment of Christian subjects of the Ottoman Empire, and in 1867 the British Government called for a report from Mr T. B. Sandwith, British Vice-Consul in the island. The resulting report showed that Christians and Muslims alike suffered from maladministration. The opening of the Suez Canal in 1869 brought Cyprus still further into the British sphere of interest. Cyprus, in fact, was once again prominent on the trade-route map. Following the Russo-Turkish War of 1877, Britain became alarmed at Russian encroachments in Asia Minor and negotiated a defensive alliance with the Turks which included terms for the British occupation of Cyprus. The agreement contained various safeguards for the Muslim population of the island, financial adjustments between the two governments, and a clause guaranteeing that if Russia returned her recent territorial gains, then the British Government would hand back Cyprus to Turkey.

BRITISH RULE (A.D. 1878–1960)

One of the reasons behind Britain's occupation of Cyprus had been that it should constitute a base for safeguarding the newly opened Suez Canal. But military operations of 1882, led by Sir Garnet Wolseley, brought Egypt under the military control of Britain, and this meant that the strategic importance of Cyprus became substantially less.

In the late Victorian and Edwardian period, Cyprus remained an anomaly. The island had not ceased to be part of the Ottoman Empire. According to the treaty, surplus revenues were paid to Turkey, so that there was no longer any question of the island being a money-making concern for its administrators. On the contrary, after the annual payment was made to Turkey, expenditure was in excess of revenue. However, the national income was boosted by British funds and the country benefited considerably. It is true to say that the British régime, though not disinterested, was the first one in the whole history of Cyprus to be in any way benevolent, and this is admitted by even the most fanatical anti-British factions which arose after the First World War. Much money was spent on trade, public works, afforestation, agriculture and antiquities. At the same time the island was not governed by consent or according to the expressed wish of the people. The British occupation was something which had occurred solely through the pressure of international politics. And the Greeks of Cyprus continued to look towards Greece, a country to which they considered themselves bound through race, language, religion and culture. The movement for Enosis, or union with Greece, was ardently fostered by the Greek Orthodox Church of Cyprus.

The outbreak of war in 1914 brought a great change. When Turkey came in on the German side Britain annexed Cyprus, putting an end to the arrangement made in 1878. The island was now completely at the disposal of the United Kingdom, and in 1915 she offered it to Greece on condition that she entered the war on the Allied side. When Greece refused, the offer was withdrawn, and Cyprus continued as a British possession, which included a strong but numerically inferior Turkish population which had every reason for opposing Enosis.

D

In 1925 Cyprus became a Crown Colony, with a governor taking the place of the earlier high commissioners. But this change of status did nothing to appease the Greek-speaking Cypriots, who continued to demand self-determination, and deplored the element of uncertainty in British intentions. The year 1931 saw widespread riots and the burning of Government House, Nicosia. The movement was repressed by military measures and by deportation of the most active leaders.

The Second World War was no time for realignment, and the future of the island remained in abeyance until 1947, when Archbishop Leontios went to London in the hope that the post-war Labour Government would show greater liberality than its predecessors. But the Colonial Secretary, Creech-Jones, stated that he understood that 'people in the grip of nationalism are impervious to rational argument', but that he hoped they would co-operate in the matter of a new constitution which would bring self-government closer and bring with it the possibilities of economic aid. When these new proposals were made to the Cyprus Constituent Assembly in 1948 they proved unacceptable.

The year 1948 saw the growth of power inside the Church. In July Archbishop Makarios II (who as bishop of Kyrenia had been one of the 1931 deportees), Cleopas, bishop of Paphos, Kyprianos, bishop of Kyrenia, and Makarios, bishop of Kitium, formed the Ethnarch Council which was to lead the national struggle. A plebiscite in January 1950 purported to give a majority of 96 per cent in favour of Enosis, but this unofficial poll was unrecognized by the governor and by the British Government. The matter was closed, they said.

In October 1950 the aged Ethnarch, Makarios II, died, and Makarios of Kitium, then aged thirty-seven, was elected as his successor. A period of great political activity followed. United Nations delegates in New York were canvassed and a Panhellenic Committee for Cyprus was formed in Athens. This Committee organized demonstrations and secured sympathetic press coverage, with the result that in November 1954 Greece claimed self-determination for Cyprus at the United Nations. The appeal was turned down.

The immediate result was a well-directed campaign of violence which began in April 1955, and was run by an organization which went by the name of EOKA, standing for Ethniki Organosis Kyprion

Agoniston – the National Organization of Cypriot Fighters. The self-appointed leader of guerrilla operations was General Grivas, born 1898 in Trikomo, who was inspired to assume the name of Dighenis Akritas, the hero of the Byzantine saga which dramatized the resistance of the Greeks to Arab incursions. He withheld his identity from most of his followers, and his feats of undoubted heroism lifted him to almost mystical heights in the popular imagination.

While violence continued, a second appeal to the United Nations failed. Archbishop Makarios III was exiled to the Seychelles, as it was no secret that the Church was strongly on the side of EOKA, preaching propaganda from the pulpits, financing the import of arms, sheltering guerrillas and organizing resistance.

In 1957 Archbishop Makarios was released from the Seychelles, although he was not permitted to return to Cyprus. Agreement was at last reached at a tripartite conference at Zurich on February 6th, 1959, when the Prime Ministers of Greece and Turkey met the British Foreign Secretary and prepared the document which became the basis for the final agreement signed in London on February 19th, 1959, by Mr Harold Macmillan for Britain, Mr Karamanlis for Greece and Mr Menderes for Turkey, and agreed to by Greek and Turkish Cypriot representatives.

The Republic of Cyprus formally came into being on August 16th, 1960, and became a member of the British Commonwealth.

REPUBLIC OF CYPRUS (A.D. 1960–the Present Day)

The new republic was, of course, founded upon its constitution, and this constitution was based upon the agreement reached at Lancaster House in February 1959. Twenty-seven articles incorporated in the agreement were accepted as fundamental parts of the future constitution. The first twenty of these distributed the power of government between the Greek and Turkish Cypriot communities in a proportion of 70–30 per cent. The President was to be Greek, the Vice-President Turkish. The House of Representatives was to be drawn in like proportions from the two communities, and this applied also to the civil service, police and gendarmerie. A standing army of about 2,000 men could be 60 per cent Greek and 40 per cent Turkish. Rules were laid down for the establishment of a balanced High Court of Justice, and for tribunals to try civil disputes. One article forbade land being taken from a member of one community and distributed to a member of the other. There were to be separate Turkish municipalities in the five largest towns. Other municipalities would follow, as far as possible, the rule of proportional representation for the two communities.

As regards international affairs, a treaty guaranteeing the independence, territorial integrity and constitution of the new republic was concluded between Cyprus, Greece, the United Kingdom and Turkey. This was fortified by a treaty of military alliance between Cyprus, Greece and Turkey.

The Republic of Cyprus undertook to remain independent, and with this intent prohibited any activity aimed towards union with another country or partition of the island. The abandonment of Enosis, therefore, had become the price of independence.

With the exception of two areas to be used as bases (Akrotiri–Episkopi–Parmali and Dhekalia–Pergamos–Ayios Nikolaos) the United Kingdom agreed to transfer sovereignty over the island to the Republic, the principal provision being the protection of the fundamental human rights of the minority communities of Cyprus.

For a short time all went well under the stimulus of self-government, achieved for the first time in the island's long history. But it soon became apparent that the constitution's provisions for internal government aiming at maintaining equilibrium between the two racial groups were too much of a compromise to satisfy the majority party.

In 1963 violence broke out between the Greek and Turkish sections of the population, and when armed intervention by the British during the Christmas season of that year failed the question was referred to the United Nations. By this time the active elements among the Greek and Turkish Cypriot factions were being reinforced and supported by their 'mother countries', and the peace of the eastern section of the Mediterranean – and indeed of the whole world – was in jeopardy. On March 4th, 1964, a U.N. force was formed and dispatched to Cyprus with a mandate to 'use its best efforts to prevent a recurrence of fighting and, as necessary, to contribute to the maintenance of law and order and a return to normal conditions'.

The presence of the U.N. peace-keeping force in Cyprus continues and is renewed periodically. Contingents include the British –

who are mainly concerned with communications and administration – Austrians, Canadians, Danes, Finns, Irish and Swedish military personnel augmented by police from some of these countries, and from Australia and New Zealand. Where necessary they set up barriers and checkpoints between the two opposing factions. U.N. personnel can be identified by their pale-blue headgear. Most checkpoints are manned also by the Cyprus Police Force.

While the peace-keeping function of UNO in the island is discharged effectively and with the minimum of friction, there has been less success in reconciling the conflicting elements. Proposals put forward in 1965 by an impartial mediator appointed by UNO proved unacceptable, and this post is at present in abeyance. The position appears not to have changed in important respects since 1964, when the Turkish Cypriots withdrew from the government, their case being that they were forcibly prevented from taking part. They assert that all acts committed in their absence are unconstitutional. On the other hand, the Greek Cypriot case is that the Turkish Cypriot withdrawal was voluntary, and does not affect the legality of the depleted government, which is increasing in confidence and in the efficient organization of the island's resources, as well as in its aim to extend authority into all parts of the country. In the meantime, dialogues continue between the parties most interested in achieving a solution, and when the time is auspicious the offices of another UNO mediator may be sought in the hope of finding a basis for agreement.

Since 1967, when the Greek colonels initiated rule by junta, the theory of union with Greece has become less attractive to all but the most extreme of idealists. But Cyprus is an island of strong feelings, and fanaticism is frequently divorced from realism, leading to expression by violence, as in the attempted assassination of Archbishop Makarios in March 1970 and other acts entirely incompatible with the aims and beliefs of the majority of Cypriots, who at present enjoy a higher standard of living and a stronger sense of identity than ever before in the troubled history of their island.

Since this is a guide-book, primarily intended for the use of new-comers, it may be remarked here that visitors are welcomed by both communities and all classes, and may move freely in all parts of the island. Such complicated differences as await solution are matters particular to those whom they most concern, and need not affect the visitor.

HISTORICAL MONUMENTS

The history of the island makes it appear truly remarkable that there is any sightseeing at all to be done. From the remotest times invasion after invasion swamped Cyprus, and on each occasion the conquerors carried away shiploads of treasure. They all did it: the Arabs, the Assyrians, the Persians, the Romans, the Crusaders, the Venetians, the Turks. It is not surprising, therefore, that there are very few portable objects left on the classical sites, the interest of which lies in their situations, their layout and some imaginative reconstruction work. In addition, earthquake has been a great destroyer.

Luckily, however, Cyprus is blessed with a famous museum in Nicosia, where many of the valuable things salvaged from the past are beautifully and logically arranged. Again, it is surprising how much there is to be seen in the island's collections, considering that until the Antiquities Law of 1904 was passed excavators were permitted to remove two-thirds of whatever they found. An even greater proportion was taken out of the country illicitly. In this way (comparable to the invaders' shiploads) vast quantities of treasure found its way to foreign museums and private collections. The American, Di Cesnola, was the most controversial figure to engage in digging, and, while many experts doubt his veracity, he was certainly one of the consuls resident in Larnaca during the nineteenth century whose activities approximated more to loot than to research.

Many of the classical sites have not only been plundered but razed to the ground and below the ground, and their stones taken away by the barrow-load for domestic building, and also carried by ship as far afield as Port Said and Alexandria for use in the construction of nineteenth-century harbour works. Much of Famagusta was built of stones from Constantia, formerly Salamis, and this building material was later transported to Suez when the town lay ruined. But there is still a lot to see, and more is being uncovered every year. In fact, it is hardly exaggerating to say that Cyprus is one vast archaeological site, the surface of which has barely been scratched.

In addition to the Neolithic, Bronze Age, Mycenaean, Hellenistic and Roman sites, and the many historical monuments left by the

Crusaders, the Venetians and the Turks, there is one flourishing form of art in Cyprus which is very much a local product, and therefore unique. The little medieval mountain churches, with their steep, snow-proof, barn-like roofs, are not found elsewhere, not even on the Greek and Anatolian mainlands. Their simple, Byzantine structure is a delight, and their mural paintings a revelation. It is always difficult to attribute a reliable date to Byzantine frescoes and icons, because many have been repainted in their original form, so that the design may be antique, but the workmanship inferior. But this perpetuation of early art is most interesting and inspiring, and the 'modern' forms are seldom negligible. Damp and neglect in a few cases have already mellowed paintings which Jeffery, in his *Description of the Historic Monuments of Cyprus* (1918), dismissed as crude and vulgar.

Greek Orthodox churches in Cyprus are laid out according to a set pattern, and even the icons on the iconostasis (equivalent to a rood screen) have a prescribed arrangement above and on either side of the central Royal Doors. The space beyond the iconostasis, the *bema*, is an area forbidden to women, except in special cases, as at Kiti, where there is something immovable and of special importance in the apse. Most priests in charge will willingly bring out an icon or a relic so that it may be viewed in the body of the church. Many village churches are kept locked, but the whereabouts of the keys can always be discovered at the nearest *kentron*, or coffee-shop, and someone will usually volunteer to find the custodian, who is probably the village priest. It is customary to leave an offering in the church. If the offertory box is not obvious the priest will accept money when it is made clear that this is for the church, rather than for his personal benefit.

Secular buildings of the Byzantine period have not survived to the same extent as the churches, partly due to the fact that most defensive works were rebuilt and replanned whenever war techniques changed, and partly because of the regrettable local habit of covering vaulted roofs with a cheap terrazzo made of small stones, *puzzolana* or rubble and lime, which did not remain rainproof and led to collapse.

THE PEOPLE

The history of Cyprus shows that until recently the island has consistently been occupied by outside powers, usually those with maritime aspirations. Whichever civilizations controlled the eastern Mediterranean, Cyprus was their natural choice as a strategic base for military and naval operations, as well as for commerce. Too small to protect herself, she was repeatedly colonized: by the Mycenaeans, the Ionians, the Phoenicians, the Persians, the Egyptians, the Romans, the crusading Lusignans, the Venetians, the Turks and, last, the British. As the earliest colonists rarely held the whole island, but concentrated on making strong settlements, there is a long history of internal dissension promoted by the struggle of the underdog against those in authority. The Romans, Byzantines, Lusignans and Venetians did not intermarry to any appreciable extent with the inhabitants – neither did the British, nor indeed the Turks, though from the sixteenth century onwards the latter brought in colonists and settled them on the land and in villages and usually well-defined quarters of the towns. It is from these settlers that the present Turkish minority springs. The remainder, except for very small numbers of Armenians, Syrian Maronites, English and Americans, are Greek-speaking, Greek-thinking and live very much according to the present-day way of life in Greece. The total figure of population varies according to emigration, as well as with the influx or departure of U.K., NATO and U.N. servicemen, who are counted in the census. But a rough simplification would be that the population of 622,000 (1968) consists of four-fifths Greek Cypriots and one-fifth Turkish – allowing, if you will, 2 per cent for minorities.

Though some villages and areas are almost completely Turkish in population (the most obvious example of this being the old walled city of Famagusta), there have always been some localities where the two communities live and work together. It seems a pity to an outside observer that the national flag of Cyprus, 'of neutral design and colour' as stipulated in the agreement of 1959 which formed the basis of the constitution, should be uninspired and uninspiring – as are most compromises – with the result that the blue and white stripes of Greece and the crescent and star of Turkey are all too frequently displayed in conscious rivalry. The

1959 agreement provided that the Turkish and Greek communities should both have the right to fly their flags on holidays.

Of the towns, Nicosia has the greatest number of inhabitants, followed by Limassol, Famagusta, Larnaca, Ktima (Paphos) and Kyrenia, in that order.

RELIGION

The population of Cyprus can be divided into Christian and Muslim according to the proportion of Greek Cypriots and Turkish Cypriots, that is, roughly four-fifths Christian to one-fifth Muslim. The Christians should be subdivided into those belonging to the Orthodox Church of Cyprus, with small minorities of Armenian Gregorians and Maronites. The remaining Christians – Roman Catholics, Anglicans and other Protestants – and the small number of Jews are likely to be living in Cyprus for commercial or military reasons, not as natives.

The Orthodox Church of Cyprus is a part of the Holy Orthodox Eastern Church, the distinction being that it is autocephalous, that is, it elects its own archbishop, who reigns as an independent head. This right was granted in A.D. 478 and was a direct result of the discovery of evidence of apostolic foundation (p. 200) at a time when the Church of Antioch was attempting to bring Cyprus under its ecclesiastical jurisdiction.

LANGUAGE

Greek and Turkish are the official languages, and these are spoken in the same proportion as the distribution of the two communities. English is much used in official circles. It will be found that the majority of townspeople also speak English, and sometimes French. Fewer know German. In the more remote villages a spokesman (who may well be the village priest) will often be able to help if there is any language difficulty. Though English is compulsory in secondary schools, and therefore the better-educated sections of the community learn it, visitors should remember that if they are able to return hospitality by a few words or phrases in Greek these will be greeted with more pleasure than such a mild effort deserves. But even in the out-of-the-way corners of the island, where a speech barrier might be expected, it is noticeable that the ability to communicate in foreign tongues grows among acquaintances as loosening influences get to work – a mysterious process which seems to be effective in both English–Greek and Greek–English.

Place names in Cyprus are sometimes confusing, due to latitude in spelling when transliterating the Greek characters into Roman. Spelling in this book (and that generally accepted by the Cyprus authorities) is taken from the *Index Gazetteer* compiled by the War Office Survey Directorate in 1946. The descriptive character of some of these names can be of great use in imagining or remembering the places to which they are attached.

Aspro-	White
Ayia	Saint (*fem.*)
Ayii Pantes	All Saints
Ayia Trias	Holy Trinity
Ayios	Saint (*masc.*)
Kako-	Bad
Kalo-	Good
Kato	Lower
Khryso	Golden
Megalos	Large
Metamorphosis	Transfiguration
Nea	New
Palaeo-	Old
Panayia	The Blessed Virgin Mary
Pano	Upper
Petra	Stone
Stavros	Cross
tou, tis	Of (*gen. sing.*)
ton	Of (*gen. pl.*)
stou, stis	In the
Xero-	Dry

A useful phrase book to cover basic requirements in Greek is *Travellers' Greek* (Jonathan Cape).

CUSTOMS AND LEGENDS

In Cyprus hospitality and generosity will be found to be at the root of most conventions, typified perhaps by the frequent provision in cafés of five chairs for the use of one customer, so that he may have support for each of his limbs as well as his trunk! The generosity of a host can best be returned by a different kind of thoughtfulness: a particular care to avoid the appearance of hurry, especially in the drinking of the ceremonial Turkish coffee, which is produced everywhere for a guest at all times of the day. It is rude to leave before the cup has become cold. Preserved fruit, spoonfuls of jam, or even glasses of water, should also be accepted whenever proffered, for they are gestures of hospitality rather than provision for appetite, or even refreshment.

As in other countries, especially those which have a considerable peasant population, pagan superstitions die hard. Actually, they seldom die but are modified before being incorporated into Christianity – as, for instance, the dedication of wax replicas of afflicted persons or their diseased limbs to the saints who have effected cures, and, of course, the votive rags which adorn trees near wells or shrines credited with miraculous properties. Not only the feast days of the Church but the customs appertaining to them have developed from pagan feasts. The *sesamotá*, or Christ's Bread, which is baked and eaten ritually at Christmas is an illustration – also the *kolliva*, a kind of boiled wheat which at that season is blessed and distributed in memory of the dead. There is also a period of propitiation of evil spirits, the *kalikandjaros*, who are supposed to be at large from All Souls' Day until Epiphany, on which day they can be appeased and banished by an offering of *xerotiana*, a special kind of doughnut.

Cataclysmos is the festival unique to Cyprus, and the one which has least connection with Christianity, although the Church has done its best to appropriate what was originally the Feast of Aphrodite. It has been re-named Cataclysmos in an optimistic attempt to identify it with commemoration of the Great Flood of Noah's time, and it has also been included in the calendar by fixing the date as fifty days after Easter.

Cyprus is the Mediterranean island which has always been most closely associated with the cult of Aphrodite and Adonis. The mysteries of these gods are believed to have been introduced from Egypt by Kinyras, the priest-king, who set up the very famous Temple of Aphrodite, near Paphos, not far from the foamy stretch of beach believed by the ancient world to be the birthplace of the goddess. The spring Festival of Aphrodite consisted of three days of worship, initiation and feasting, during which the goddess was said to reveal herself, riding naked on the waves, to the young people of Cyprus to whom the gods had bequeathed their beauty. During this period of feasting her *alter ego*, Adonis, the bright youth who was killed while hunting in the hills of Cyprus, was allowed by the Olympian gods to return to earth, and his advent, too, was greeted with rejoicing, feasting and musical contests. It is fascinating to find that similar competitions, known as *chattismata* or poetic arguments, persist to this day as an important part of the feast of Cataclysmos. The performances may have deteriorated into doggerel and humorous invective, and they may bear closer resemblance to Aristophanes than Aeschylus, but the evolution will be welcomed by many people, except possibly the classicists, now that some of the polish and the pompousness has worn off. The modern competitions, which usually take place towards the end of the day, and even so are apt to be protracted affairs, are great fun because of their human interest. The whole day is celebrated with a great deal of archaic gusto and sense of happiness, especially that part of it which consists of sprinkling everyone with sea-water, both on shore and from boats. It may be that there is a lingering Venetian influence here, something remaining from the great water carnivals of that seafaring nation. Or the custom may be simply a re-enactment of the birth of Aphrodite from the foam of the sea. But whatever its composite origins, Cataclysmos is a very popular feast, in both senses of the word, and Larnaca, with its traditional fair and junketings, is probably the most lively place for its celebration, as well as for admiration of the smooth manner in which the Goddess of Love has become identified with the Blessed Virgin. Indeed, Aphrodite and the Queen of Heaven are difficult to separate in either belief or legend.

Cyprus has another queen, one who is usually spoken of quite simply as 'Regina', and whose myth has attached itself to the three romantic castles of the Kyrenia range. She is invariably the sweetheart and protagonist of the Greek hero Dighenis, the fabulous figure of Byzantine saga who has become more than ever established as the national hero of Cyprus since General Grivas was inspired to adopt his name (already being possessed of some of his ideals) in the EOKA struggles for freedom. The mythical Dighenis is notable for his heroic deeds – usually achieved by slinging vast rocks from the mountains – in defence of the island at the time of the Arab raids of the seventh to tenth centuries B.C.

These then, are the two folk images of Cyprus: Aphrodite the queen, symbol of the beautiful island itself, and Dighenis the warrior-patriot, whose spirit has resisted thousands of years of occupation by foreign powers. Nothing is likely to disturb their deep influence on the people of Cyprus – not even the adoption of Aphrodite as a brand-image for many of the country's products.

FOOD AND DRINK

FOOD

Greek and Turkish cuisine – those are the obvious ones to look for. Happily, from first playing safe with international cuisine, many hotels and restaurants now include Cypriot alternatives on their menus. At the same time, it is as well to see that olive oil is used sparingly (as it is *not* in the humbler eating-places), because an insidious surfeit of this can be responsible for more stomach upsets than are likely to arise from other causes. As it happens, the restaurateurs of Cyprus know all there is to know about the food preferences of Anglo-Saxon and other northern races, so that when they provide local dishes these are usually tempered and seasoned to suit foreign tastes.

Restaurants in towns may be chosen from the lists available at Tourist Information Offices, but in country districts it is more fun to experiment. There are any amount of wayside eating-places which provide out-of-door terraces shaded by vines, as well as a fascinating glimpse of the comings and goings of local people. Coffee-shops provide excellent fare in the form of *mezé*, a profusion of local dishes which arrive in rapid succession from the kitchen, and which constitute a hearty meal rather than as titbits eaten with drinks, as is more usual on the mainland of Greece. Kebabs, savoury portions of meat grilled over a charcoal fire, are to be found in the most primitive of cafés. For orthodox meals with recognized courses it may be necessary to patronize hotels. Eating-places are plentiful because, as on the Continent, eating-out is a local habit for families, as well as for professional men and manual workers. It is exceptional to see unescorted women in the restaurants or coffee-shops. A comprehensive charge is often made for the main dish inclusive of vegetables and/or salad.

Grapes for breakfast, cut from an overhead trellis, apricots and peaches warm from the sun, figs galore, the rather dull but beautiful pomegranate – there is hardly a fruit in the whole world which cannot be cultivated in Cyprus's varied climate. In fact, fruit and vegetables are so plentiful, and so well spread out throughout the year, that they need no further enumeration. Fish is excellent, but rather scarce (except from the deep freeze), because this part of the Mediterranean is deficient in plankton owing to the very small amount of fresh water which reaches the sea. However, fresh fish is much prized by local people. Mullet – the red and the grey variety – swordfish, octopus and squid are excellent. Lamb is the best as well as the most common meat, and adapts itself well to cooking with herbs. Paphos is the district for pigs and therefore for pork.

The following glossary may be useful:

Ambeloboulia (or beccafico)	A tiny migratory bird caught in the fig season, and sometimes pickled in wine or vinegar.
Aphelia	Pork chops marinated in red wine.
Barbounia	Red mullet.
Bourgourri	Wheaten porridge, a substitute for rice.
Colocasia	Sweet potato having a gastronomic affinity with the turnip.
Dolmas	Stuffed vine-leaves.
Fetta	Cheese made from ewes' milk.
Gliko	Sweet, often consisting of preserved fruit in syrup or Commandaria. Green walnuts are good done in this way.
Haloumi	Salty cheese, much used for cooking.
Hiromeri	Local ham pickled in wine.
Houmous	Chick-pea purée with tahina (sesame paste).
Kalamari	Squid (inkfish).

Kaskavali	Good mild cheese.
Kephalotiri	Cheese with Gruyère-like holes.
Keptedes	Spiced meat balls.
Koupepia	Marrow flowers with savoury meat filling.
Koupes	Fried meat rissoles enclosed in pastry.
Lokmades	Similar to doughnuts.
Lounza	Smoked pork tenderloin.
Mezé	Appetizers served with drinks or as a meal.
Mousaka	Baked custard-like dish of mince, aubergines, peppers and other vegetables.
Moutchentra	Rice and lentil pilaff with crisp onion rings.
Parayemista	Stuffed vegetables or fish.
Patcha	Sheep's head broth (+ brains) flavoured with lemon.
Pitta	Flat unleavened bread.
Ravioli	Similar to the Italian dish, but stuffed with cheese.
Shamishi	Sweet pancakes with honey.
Sheftalia	Grilled spiced sausage.
Skordalia	Garlic-flavoured sauce or dip, based on breadcrumbs, oil and ground almonds.
Snails	A speciality of Boghaz and the Karpas – better boiled than roasted.
Soujoukko	Sweetmeat dried in the sun, sold at fairs.
Souvlakia	Grilled kebabs.
Tahina	Sesame 'dip' popular in Eastern Mediterranean
Talatourri	Salad dressing or dip based on yoghourt.
Yiaourti	Yoghourt.
Zalatina	Highly seasoned brawn.

DRINK

The popular taste for wines in Cyprus is for a sweeter and heavier product than that which appeals to most foreign palates. It must be remembered that Cyprus wines are meant to be drunk with rich, highly spiced and oily meals, and they have developed so as to be gastronomically complementary to local food. But because the export of wines has become an important part of the island's economy, much thought and expert attention has gone into producing something drier and lighter than the traditional village wine. Nowadays quantities of red wine of the Mâcon or Beaujolais type, a dark rosé known as *kokkineli* and a white wine made from Xinisteri grapes (grown principally in the Paphos district) are perhaps the most popular for the northern European market. By far the greater proportion of Cyprus wines is produced by three firms: Keo, Sodap (a co-operative wine factory) and Haggipavulu, a business of long standing which has been reconstituted into the Cyprus Wine Association of ETCO.

The most palatable red wines are Othello, Afames, Dark Lady, Olympus Claret, Cœur de Lion and the justifiably more expensive Domaine d'Ahuera. Sodap's Muscat is recommended as a dessert wine. The white wines Aphrodite, Keo Hock, Arsinoe and White Lady are eminently drinkable and, for a sweet table wine, St Pante-leimon. Rosella and Pink Lady are perhaps the best of the rosé type. Until recently the sherries did not prove so adaptable, due to the high sugar content of Cyprus grapes. However, drier types have now come on the market, notably Juno Extra Dry, Keo Fino and Olympus Pale Dry. Emva sherries are exported in quantity to the United Kingdom. Commandaria is, of course, the most famous of all the wines of Cyprus, because of its association with the *commandarias* (village estates) administered by the Knights Hospitaller from Kolossi Castle. This is a dessert wine, and should be taken with appropriate food, or as a liqueur. *Filfar* is a fragrant orange liqueur, whereas *sourmada*, flavoured with almonds, is a delicious product of the Pitsilia district. Local brandy or *zivania*, where procurable, is very strong and should (as it were) be drunk with open eyes. Other popular drinks are *ouzo* and beer, brewed by Keo in Lima-ssol. Brandy sours, based on the Cyprus spirit, make one of the most refreshing and inexpensive alcoholic hot-weather drinks. In season fresh orange juice is obtainable from street sellers, though not always at the breakfast tables of hotels.

Actually, water comes highest in popularity of all drinks. A glass of it is invariably produced with coffee, other drinks, all food and sometimes simply as a gesture of hospitality. It is apt to be cold and good – in fact, Cyprus, like Greece, has its connoisseurs of water. Coffee comes next in the poll, though French coffee is the exception. Although the instant brands have made their encroachment into eastern Mediterranean drinking habits, it is Turkish coffee which will be produced unless the other is requested. As Turkish coffee is sweetened during the boiling process, the degree of sugar must be stipulated in advance, *glykos* being sweet, *metrios* medium and *sketos* unsweetened.

NICOSIA

Population 112,000.
Information
Tourist Information Bureau: 26 Evagoras Avenue (Tel. 4000) : *Map* **38.**
(Also at Airport)
Public Information Office: Ministry of the Interior (Tel. 4000).
Emergency Telephone Numbers:

>> First Aid : 70–5111 (ex. 6).
>> Hospital : 70–5111.
>> Pharmacies (night) : 62118.

Cyprus Airways and B.E.A. Reservations: Stassinos Avenue (*Map* **40**).
Olympic Airways Reservations: Homer Avenue.
Hotels
De luxe Cyprus Hilton ; Ledra Palace ; Regina Palace ; Saray.
1st (A) Acropole ; Catsellis Hill ; Hilarion ; Louis.
1st (B) Excelsior ; Liberty ; Carlton ; Nicosia Palace ; Cleopatra ; Kennedy and Lido awaiting classification.
2nd (A) Alexandria ; Averof ; Elsy ; Majestic ; Cottage awaiting classification.
3rd   Delphi ; Olympic ; Olympus ; Riverside ; Royal ; Victoria.
4th   Atlas.
Many of the newer and grander hotels are situated outside the walls of the Old Town, and therefore have greater ground space. However, visitors who like to stroll straight from their hotels into the old quarters of Nicosia without using transport may prefer a base nearer the centre, from which both new and old parts of the city may be reached on foot.
Principal Restaurants and Bars
Charlie's Bar, Passiades St.
Corner,* on hill off the old road to airport.
Cosmopolitan,* Demeter Severis Ave.
Cyprus Tavern,* Metachiou Ave.
Flamingo Grill, Athens St.
Fournaki, Strovolos by-pass.
Hadjisavvas, Evagoras Ave.
Makedonitissa, off airport road.
Montparnasse, Grivas Dighenis Ave.
Nea Korytsa, Metaxas Square.
Scorpios, Grivas Dighenis Ave.
Turkish restaurants include Pikpik and Annibal, both in the Turkish sector.
The hotels have restaurants and cocktail bars which correspond to their ratings. Special mention may be made of the Cyprus Hilton's Commandaria Grill, and Ledra Palace's Crystal Restaurant. Many hotel restaurants concentrate upon 'safe' international cuisine, but popular demand is producing local dishes as alternatives. For those who wish to eat nation-wise there are numerous establishments in the main streets. The kebab stalls in the moat, reached by steps southwest of Metaxas Square, are full of local colour.
Night Clubs, Dancing and Cabaret
Among others : Antonakis Bar ; Asteria ; Athina, and those marked with an asterisk in our list of restaurants. Discotheques include La Noche, Salingari and Scorpios.
Churches
Anglican St Paul's, Byron Ave.
Roman Catholic Holy Cross, Paphos Gate.
Principal Embassies, Legations etc.
France   43 Savvas G. Rotsides St.
W. Germany   10 Nikitaras St.

Greece	8–10 Byron Ave.
Israel	27 Androcleos St.
Lebanon	13 Queen Olga St.
U.A.R.	Egypt Ave.
United Kingdom High Commissioner	Alexander Pallis St.
United Nations	Leoforis Ave.
United States of America	Therissos St.
U.S.S.R.	Gladstone St.

Clubs

Field Club (lawn tennis), Egypt Avenue – hard courts in the moat below the walls floodlit on summer evenings. Apply to Secretary for temporary membership.

Nicosia Club, Rupel St (off Osman Pasha Ave). Golf, swimming, tennis, dancing, etc. Membership available to visitors on application to British High Commissioner's Office.

Nicosia Race Club. Meetings in spring and autumn seasons. Membership available to visitors.

Libraries and Institutes

British Council, 17 Archbishop Makarios Ave – lectures, exhibitions, films, etc.

British Information Services, Alexander Pallis St – reading rooms, reference library, etc.

Centre Cultural Français, 4 Costis Palamas St (off Byron Ave) – weekly meetings, lectures, debates, films, etc., all in French language. Subscription lending library.

Cyprus Museum Library, Museum St – reference library specializing in archaeology.

Phaneromeni Library, Phaneromeni St – reference books mainly in Greek, English and French (*Map* **18**).

Sultan Mahmoud's Library – rare books in Turkish, Persian and Arabic (*Map* **8**).

United States Information Service, 33B Homer Ave – lectures, exhibitions, films, reading room, lending library, etc.

Theatres

Municipal Theatre, Museum St (Stage presentations also take place in various cinemas.)

Cinemas

Athineon, Magic Palace, Mimosa; Minerva; Diana nos. 1, 2, 3, and 4 (open-air in summer).

Few city plans are as arresting as that of Nicosia, and few can exert such immediate attraction. For the sixteenth-century walls describe a circle three miles in circumference, embellished by eleven bastions and surrounded by a moat – the whole in an excellent state of preservation and faithful to the original design. From an architectural viewpoint, it is regrettable that the irresistible needs of modern traffic have dictated that the walls should be breached in a number of places, and that the three original gateways to the city have become obsolete. The streets within the city walls are labyrinthine and colourful, with a minimum of modern building. Ledra Street, originally the main shopping thoroughfare, is narrow and crowded. It runs directly north towards the centre of the circle and makes a useful line of orientation to which to return after having been tempted by alleys and courtyards of houses with timbered overhanging balconies. All the worthwhile antiquities are inside this crowded inner part of the city – with the exception of those housed in the Cyprus Museum.

However, dictated mainly by the limitations on growth within the constricting ancient defences, the major part of the life of the capital city has moved outside the walls. Here the government offices, the factories, the newest hotels, the apartment blocks, the supermarkets, the shopping avenues – with adequate parking space – form a lively, if straggling, new city. This is a practical place which allows for freedom of movement and other adjuncts of civilized life. The Old Town, with its fascinating design and narrow streets, has become an anachronism, but as such will retain its historical associations and charm for visitors. Both might have been threatened had modern central development been possible.*

Due to the capital's central position on a plain bounded by two mountain ranges, it has high summer temperatures. The saving grace is a reliable evening breeze.

HISTORY

This is one of the few island capitals which not only is situated inland but is served by no navigable river. In fact, Nicosia's watercourse, the Pedieos river, dries up in the summer months, and strangely, it is this factor which has contributed to the city's establishment as the capital of an island which has very vulnerable coasts. Similarly, because the coastal towns were exposed to depredations from abroad, notably by the Arab pirates of the seventh century A.D., some of these were moved inland to a position of greater strength, and villages and fishing harbours on the coasts remain scarce.

To judge by the large number of tombs in the vicinity of Nicosia, this was a populous region from the Bronze Age to the days of Roman occupation, though the city itself did not play a very important part in the island's history until the Lusignan era.

---

* At the time of going to press, the city is divided by the 'Green Line', manned by the U.N. peace-keeping force.

This line runs roughly from the Paphos Gate along Paphos Street, and three-quarters of the length of Hermes Street before swinging north to its eastern termination between the Flatro and Loredano Bastions. It effectively separates the Greek-Cypriot and Turkish-Cypriot citizens of Nicosia, who live to the south and north respectively. At various places there are checkpoints through which holders of passports other than Cypriot, Greek or Turkish may pass without restriction.

However, it is thought that ancient Ledra, the city-state founded in 280 B.C. by Lefcon, son of Ptolemy Soter, was situated identically with the fortified city as it is known today. At any rate this is a popular belief, and the main shopping street of the old city is known as Ledra Street.

A traveller in 1211 records that 'Cossia' had no fortifications, but that a castle had recently been built to house the rulers of the kingdom. He was very much impressed by the wealth of the citizens, and compared the luxury of their houses with those of fabulous Antioch – the highest standard of the times. The prosperity of Nicosia appears to have lasted until 1426, when the Egyptian Mamelukes invaded the island at Limassol. They defeated King Janus, took him prisoner, burned and plundered his royal palace at Nicosia, and sacked the remainder of the town. By the time the island was annexed by the Venetians in 1489, the boundaries of the city had extended considerably. Then, in view of the likelihood – indeed, the certainty – of attack by the Turks, the Venetian engineer in charge of fortifications recommended in 1567 that the circumference of the city should be reduced by three miles. This resulted in a regular circular plan with eleven bastions and three gates, much as it is today, the main difference being that in places the height of the walls has now been reduced and part of the moat filled in. The massive new defences were constructed in accordance with the technique adopted by the Venetians at this turning-point of strategical defence, when the aim was to withstand bombardment from the newly invented cannon. The walls consisted of vast earthworks faced with stone. The Venetian engineers were ruthless. Any building outside their defensive line had to be levelled for fear it should obstruct the field of fire. Thus vanished many of the splendid manifestations of Lusignan wealth and taste, the greatest loss probably being the Abbey of St Domenico, in which the sovereigns and aristocracy of Cyprus had been buried in splendour. The site of this great monument to a glorious era, which was near the Paphos Gate, is now lost beyond all hope of reclamation.

Despite desperate resistance and the strength of the newest defences, Nicosia was reduced in seven weeks after the first Turkish assault in 1570. Unbelievable atrocities and wholesale massacre followed. Venetians and Cypriots suffered alike.

The rapacious and cumulative rule of terror lasted just over three hundred years, until the signing of a defensive alliance with

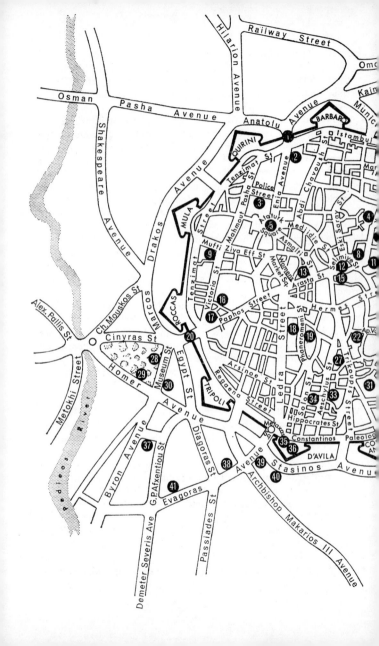

Nicosia – Old City

For route directions out of
Nicosia, see map on page 125

N

0   100 200 300 400 500

yards

Great Britain in 1878. In that year Vice-Admiral Lord Hope landed at Larnaca and raised the Union Jack in Nicosia. Now the city is expanding again; new hotels, blocks of flats, offices, restaurants, factories, gardens continue to spread outward to the south, east and west.

FORTIFICATIONS

For the most part, the walls and moat remain substantially as they were at the time of their construction by Venetian engineers in 1570. The chief changes have been in the interests of modern traffic, in that the Famagusta, Paphos and Kyrenia fortified gates, which at one time were the sole points of entry and departure, have become obsolete, and various other openings have had to be made. Of the three original entries, the *Paphos Gate (Map* **20**) – known originally as the Porte Domenico because of its proximity to the Lusignan palace and abbey – is in the best condition. It was closed in the first year of occupation by the British authorities (1878), and later accommodated the city's chief fire station. The *Famagusta Gate (Map* **21**), or Porta Giuliana, is intact, though closed to traffic. It is surmounted by a curious dome. The *Kyrenia Gate (Map* **1**), the Porta del Proveditore, has suffered worst, having been isolated by a breach in the walls on either side, which, far from preserving its architectural value, has emasculated it.

Parts of the massive walls now form a ring road; other portions may only be reached on foot (see map). It is these less accessible areas which produce the picturesque sights, and which contain an overspill of the teeming life of humbler citizens. One painless concession to the pressures of modern existence has been made by the conversion of several of the bastions into parking lots combined with bus termini. The moats for the most part have been converted for residential and recreational purposes, and provide lively pleasure grounds.

MAJOR CHURCHES AND MOSQUES

Cathedral of Santa Sophia (Selimiye Mosque)
Map **12***; apply to custodian at any reasonable time.*
Though from a Christian point of view this great cathedral has been desecrated by its conversion to Muslim use, which has involved the

removal of all features abhorrent to the Muslim faith, such as representations of the human figure, it remains one of the greatest Christian monuments in the Near East. Building began in 1193, in the form of a small church to be used for the coronation of King Amaury four years later. Marble decoration from this first building is incorporated in the present north doorways. The foundations of the existing building of early French pointed design were laid in 1209, but the cathedral was not consecrated until 1326. Even so, the ambitious western façade could not have been completed by that date, because a papal bull of 1347 granted an indulgence of a hundred days to the men working on it.

The west window between the twin towers made provision for the out-of-door seating of distinguished persons witnessing important celebrations, such as coronations, which were conducted in great processional pomp. Though remains of sculptured figures are still discernible on the exterior, everything of this sort has been banished from the inside of the church. The high altar, the painted screen, the choir stalls and the paintings in the vault were all of renowned beauty. But the Turks should not be blamed for the disappearance of all these treasures, because the cathedral suffered under the Genoese in 1373, the Mamelukes in 1426 and earthquake damage in 1491 and 1547. And a singular advantage is that the purity of the interior design is enhanced by its emptiness. Indeed, the interior is in many respects superior to the exterior, for the unfinished towers, the flat terrace roofs over the church (peculiar to Gothic architecture in Cyprus) and the incongruous minarets on both corners of the west front detract somewhat from the sky-piercing ideal expected of cathedrals.

Of the five chapels incorporated in the cathedral, the one in the north, originally dedicated to St Nicholas, is now shut off, and its apse, where the altar once stood, provides for access to the women's gallery of the mosque. The placing of the chapel's entrance on the north side of the cathedral suggests that it was designed for ceremonial processions from the palace of the archbishop. A smaller chapel, immediately adjacent, was originally the treasury of the cathedral. The lady chapel in the south transept is now occupied by the *mithrab*, which orientates the building for Moslem use, and there is a grandfather clock of no great antiquity which is set to Mecca time. The chapel in the second bay from the west end, still on the south side, was dedicated to St Thomas Aquinas and now contains a collection of tombstones of Crusaders which have been removed from the body of the cathedral.

Bedestan (St Nicholas of the English)

Map **15.**

Opening hours*

The original church is associated with the cult of St Thomas à Becket, who was held in especial reverence in Europe during the Middle Ages. It became the Greek Orthodox Cathedral during the Venetian occupation, and declined into use as a grain store and market (hence its present name) during the period of Turkish rule. Though now ruined, the remains of the church are of interest because of their combination of Byzantine, Gothic and Venetian styles of architecture. The part which is the most imposing and attractive is the great north façade adjoining St Sophia. This contains three doorways, the centre one being an obvious copy in stone of the marble archway of its neighbour. The five orders of this entrance are surmounted by a gable with a circular central opening of tracery, and niches for sculpture on either side.

Armenian Church of the Blessed Virgin Mary

Map **16***; apply to custodian, who lives in the courtyard, at any reasonable time.*†

Previous to the Turkish occupation in 1570 this was a great Benedictine convent dedicated to St Mary of Tyre. After using it for a short period as a salt store, the Turks presented the property to the Armenians in recognition of services rendered during the seven-week siege of the city. The fourteenth-century structure did not suffer excessive damage during that time, and some of the Gothic detail has defied later over-zealous restoration work. A vaulted cloister on the north side, with arches supporting nothing at all, suggest that at some period a scheme for enlargement was abandoned. The tombstone of the Benedictine abbess, Eschive de Dampierre (d. 1340), has been incorporated in the east end of this cloister.

* Admission may possibly be obtained through the custodian of the Selimye Mosque now that the key is no longer available from the Cyprus Museum.

† 1970 Footnote: This church and its precincts, situated just inside the Turkish sector of the City are not open to the public at the time of going to press.

The tracery of the church windows must be studied from outside, because their inner sides have been barricaded with wooden sashes and coloured glass. It is, however, worth while applying to the custodian, who lives in the churchyard, for entry to the church for a view of the medieval tombstones set into the floor. The majority of these are covered by a carpet, which can be rolled back. The best examples are near the entrance to the sanctuary. They are mainly of the fourteenth century, and illustrate most beautifully the dress and armour worn by the aristocracy of the period. The design of the church is also of interest. It has a single nave, two large bays and a polygonal choir, with a large window of eight lights occupying the total width of the east bay.

Church of St Catherine (Haidar Pasha Mosque)
Map 7.
A minaret and windows pierced at ground level have been added to the original Gothic design of two vaulted bays and a three-sided apse built in the late fourteenth century. Above the sacristy to the north of the apse there is a room rising to the height of the church, and believed to have been intended as the lower structure of a tower which was never built. Those carvings in the church which have not been mutilated as a result of its conversion to Muslim use are of great interest. Gothic survivals in Cyprus are few, due to the special aversion the conquering Turks held for the Latin rite.

Church of St John
Map 25.
The church of the Orthodox archbishopric adjoining the modern archiepiscopal palace, is built on the site of the Benedictine Abbey of St John of Bibi, which was deserted when the order left the island in 1426. The early church's most sacred relic, the finger of St John the Baptist, was presumably removed at this time. At an early period of Greek Orthodox use, the dedication was changed from St John the Baptist to St John the Divine. The wall paintings generally date from 1730, though those used in the decoration of the west end are later – in fact, the latest in the churches of Cyprus. The Day of Judgment above the south door is especially graphic and terrifying; the Creation on the north side is the most charming, and the Discovery of the Tomb of St Barnabas (to the right of

the archiepiscopal throne) is considered to be of the greatest historical interest.

OTHER CHURCHES AND MOSQUES

Arab Achmed Mosque
Map 9.
This was built in 1485, and incorporated in its floor are gravestones of the fourteenth century, including that of Louis de Nores (1369).

Ayios Kassianos Church
Map 10.
Many of the icons displayed on the iconostasis were thought to have come from the cathedral of St Sophia, and now form an important part of the collection housed in the Icons Museum (p. 123).

Ayios Yeoryios Church
Map 6.
A simple barrel-vaulted building of the seventeenth-century; a fifteenth-century sarcophagus with coats of arms is built into the masonry over the west door.

Church of the Holy Cross
Map 17.
This is a large modern church built by the Roman Catholics on the site of the Franciscan church destroyed during the siege of Nicosia. It contains a bas-relief of St Mamas, dated 1524, from that building.

Church of the Panayia Chrysaliniotissa
Map 14.
Of different periods from 1450 onwards, it contains a large number of interesting icons.

Church of St Antoni
Map 32.
Restored in 1743, this contains a tombstone of the fifteenth century, possibly rescued from a destroyed Latin church. It also has a curious grandfather clock with a ship on its pendulum.

Church of St Savvas
Map **33**.

Built in 1851, this church contains a painted panel showing a man dressed in eastern furred robes. The inscription is not decipherable, but it is thought that the painting may depict the patron saint of the church. The medium used, probably egg-tempera on gold leaf, is of special interest to artists.

Mosque of the Standard Bearer (Bairakdar Mosque)
Costanza bastion.

This mosque, on its picturesque site on a great bastion, is of greater historic than architectural interest. It marks the spot where the Turkish flag was planted by the first Turkish soldier who breached the defences in the siege of Nicosia. He is buried here with all that remained of his standard.

Omerieh Mosque
Map **31**.

Originally an Augustinian church which was damaged in the siege of the city, the west door and a chapel on the west side (now used by Muslim women) have survived. This almost certainly was the shrine of St John de Montfort. Many tombstones which were suffering from use by the Turks as rough flooring have been removed to museums.

Phaneromeni Church
Map **19**.

The name means 'revealed'. The present church, built in 1872, is probably the most popular in Nicosia for worship.

Tripioti Church
Map **34**.

This is considered to be one of the principal buildings in Nicosia belonging to the Greek Orthodox Church of Cyprus. It was erected in 1690, at a time when the Turks had become more tolerant to the Greeks, though the Latins continued to be suppressed. The church is notable for the number of fragments from earlier buildings which have been incorporated in its structure.

Yeni Djami, or New Mosque
Map 4.

This is another medieval church converted (1571) to Muslim use. In the course of a hunt for treasure in the eighteenth century a Turkish official tore down all except its south-west corner.

MUSEUMS

Cyprus Museum
Map 30.

Opening hours

Mid-May to mid-Sept. Weekdays 8 a.m. to 1 p.m.
4 p.m. to 6 p.m.
Sunday 10 a.m. to 1 p.m.
Mid-Sept. to mid-May Weekdays 8.30 a.m. to 1 p.m.
2.30 p.m. to 4.30 p.m.
Sunday 10 a.m. to 1 p.m.

Because, quite understandably, most articles of portable size and weight have been salvaged from their sites, and as many as possible have found their way here, it is of great value to visitors to Cyprus to spend some time thoroughly inspecting the collections in a museum which enjoys a world-wide reputation. Even for people not fanatically museum-minded, in this special case there is great benefit to be derived from seeing the exhibits before the sites from which they came have been visited – and afterwards, too. The ivory furniture and bronze cauldrons (*c.* eighth century B.C.) and other discoveries from the royal tombs at Salamis are of exceptional interest.

The Cyprus Museum came into being in 1908 as a memorial to Queen Victoria, and was used for housing collections which until that date had been scattered in various institutes in the city. Reorganization was undertaken in 1935, and an extension was built in 1959–61. The museum is in fact a vital, growing concern. The arrangement is good, and designed to lead visitors forward from room to room, beginning at the earliest period, the Neolithic and Chalcolithic Ages (*c.* 5800–2300 B.C.).

Folk Art Museum
Map 23.

Opening hours

Mid-May to mid-Sept. Weekdays 8 a.m. to 1 p.m.
4 p.m. to 6 p.m.
Sundays 10 a.m. to 1 p.m.

Mid-Sept. to mid-May Weekdays 8.30 p.m. to 1 p.m.
2.30 p.m. to 4.30 p.m.
Sundays   10 a.m. to 1 p.m.

Housed in the old archiepiscopal palace, and separated from the modern one by the Church of St John, this museum is excellent of its kind. Village arts and crafts are displayed in stone arched recesses according to the districts of their origin. Bridal costumes, silk sheets and many other examples of weaving and embroidery, pottery and carving give great insight into a vanishing way of life.

Musée Lapidaire

Map **11**; *apply to custodian at Selimiye Mosque.*
An old Venetian house where stone carvings are displayed.

Icons Museum

Map **24**.
Opening hours
Same as Folk Art Museum.

On an upper floor, immediately above the Folk Museum and reached by an outer staircase. Fabulous collection of painted icons from Byzantine churches which created great interest when on a travelling exhibition abroad in 1970.

Tekké of the Mevlevi Dervishes

Map **2**; *open daily, except Sundays, during office hours.*
Originally a monastery of the famous Whirling Dervish sect. This was closed in conformity with Kemal Ataturk's suppression of all such monasteries in Turkey. Now the oriental compound and bathlike domed structure houses a small collection of typical Turkish arts and crafts.

OTHER SIGHTS

The Beuyuk Khan

Map **13**.
An example of a typical medieval Turkish caravanserai designed to shelter travellers and their beasts of burden. Similar to the neighbouring Kourmardjilar Khan, it has deteriorated into shabby but still picturesque housing.

Venetian Column

Map **5**.
This is a pillar of grey granite which stands in the middle of Ataturk

Square; it served the Venetians as a symbol of their ascendancy over Cyprus. It is believed to have come from Salamis, near Famagusta. The Turks overthrew it when they took the city, but it was re-erected in 1915. Unfortunately the lion of St Mark which once surmounted it has been lost. The coats of arms around the base are identifiable as those of Venetian families.

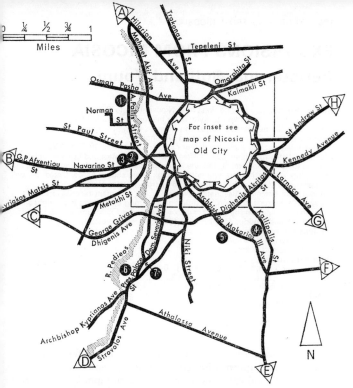

Nicosia – Route Directions

A route to
  Bellapais Abbey (p. 161)
  St Hilarion Castle (p. 165)
  Kyrenia (Direct)
B route to
  Kyrenia (Indirect)
C route to
  Airport
  Peristerona (p. 126)
  Morphou (p. 127)
  Soli and Vouni (pp. 128–31)
  Asinou Church (p. 136)
  Troödos Hill Resorts (pp. 139–42)
D route to
  Tamassos (p. 150)
  Makheras Monastery (p. 151)
  Pitsilia District (p. 247)
E route to
  Nisou for Dhali (Idalion) (p. 152)
  Limassol and Paphos

F route to
  Larnaca
G route to
  Larnaca
H route to
  St Chrysostomos Monastery (p. 132)
  Buffavento Castle (p. 133)
  Kythrea (p. 144)
  Halevka (p. 146)
  Antiphonitis Monastery (p. 148)
  Famagusta

1 United Kingdom High Commissioner
2 Parcels Office and Customs
3 Ministry of Agriculture & Natural Resources
4 U.S. Embassy
5 Ministry of Commerce and Industry
6 Presidential Palace
7 U.N. Office

E

EXCURSIONS FROM NICOSIA
Peristerona, Soli and Vouni

Route Take the road leading west from Nicosia (Route C on Nicosia routes map) ignoring a right fork leading to Kyrenia by the long way round the mountains. Our road to Soli (35 m.) and Vouni (37 m.) diverges from the highway to Troödos just before Astromeritis at a signpost marked Morphou.

On the way back to Nicosia a detour can be made to Asinou Church (p. 136) by taking the Lefka road immediately after passing Karavostasi and continuing left for Kalokhorio and Angolemi. Cross the Troödos road at Kato Koutraphas for Pano Koutraphas and for Nikitari, where the village priest should be contacted. He will accompany visitors to Asinou Church (25 m. from Pendayia).

Should the overnight destination be one of the mountain resorts, fork right as above in Karavostasi, but then fork right again, skirting Lefka and turning right again on the road leading due south via Xerarkaka crossroads to Kalopanayiotis, Pedhoulas, Prodhromos and Troödos (pp. 139–44) (29 m. from Karavostasi).

Ancient Monuments
Soli Theatre and Vouni Palace
Custodians attend offices at both sites.

Opening hours
Soli: summer 9 a.m. to 12 noon, 3 p.m. to 6.30 p.m.
      winter 9 a.m. to 1 p.m., 2 p.m. to 4.30 p.m.
Vouni: same opening hours as for Soli.

Hotels
At Kambos: 4th Kambos.
At Lefka: 4th Istanbul.
At Xeros: 4th Soli Riviera.

The road westwards from Nicosia runs through a fertile plain of unfenced land, green with crops in spring and early summer, baked brown and expectant of rain in the autumn. The two great mountain ranges on either side are at all stages close enough to be seen in detail: the toothed crags of the Kyrenia range to the north, and the Troödos mountains, humped and massive to the south, with the white dome of the Early Warning scanner usually clearly visible on the summit of Mt Olympus.

[13½ m.] **Akaki**, a village once famous for its curious horizontal water-wheels and for the cultivation of flax, is to the left, by-passed by improvements to the road.

[17 m.] **Peristerona**
Also to the left, the *Church of St Barnabas and St Hilarion* stands on

the river bank on the farther side of a bridge. Built of warm-coloured stone, without any external decoration, this church's five domes make it one of the most beautiful and charming of Byzantine remains. The one other comparable church with the same number of domes is St Paraskevi at Yeroskipos, near Paphos. Except for the narthex, which is of a later period, the interior remains very much as it has always been, though unfortunately most of the paintings which originally covered the walls have disappeared. A sixteenth-century icon of the Presentation in the Temple is of particular interest, as well as the iconostasis (1549) and an exceedingly ancient chest, the purpose of which appears to have been the storage of ecclesiastical archives, and which is painted with a spirited scene showing the siege of a medieval castle which has been identified with Rhodes.

[19½ m.] Turn right off the main road about 2 m. from Peristerona for **Astromeritis**, a village famous for the cultivation of water melons. It has been suggested that this village derives its name from a well so deep that at midday the stars can be seen from its bottom, but this probably apocryphal story is not substantiated by present-day villagers.

[24 m.] **Morphou**

As one approaches the town, well-tended plantations of citrus fruits protected by bamboo wind-breaks demonstrate its continuing importance in the economy of the island. It is a district, too, for tulips and strawberries.

The church of the *Monastery of St Mamas*, originally a Byzantine building with Gothic embellishments, was reconstructed after a fire in the early sixteenth century, when a central dome was added. Early 'flamboyant' interior carvings have survived on the columns of the nave, the surrounds to the west window and in the shrine of the saint. But the iconostasis is the most interesting piece of church furniture. It incorporates marble columns crowned with Gothic-inspired capitals, and lower panels in high relief depicting fruits, with Venetian heraldic devices at the corners. These carvings date from *c.* 1500, while the remainder of the iconostasis in carved and painted wood is rather later, being contemporary with a small pair of Holy Doors and the baldachin.

The monastic buildings are no longer occupied, except for the modern west wing, which the bishop of Kyrenia uses when he is in residence.

St Mamas is a very popular and admirable saint, who finds favour for his objection to tax-paying and the manner in which he won relief. When soldiers came to arrest him and bring him to trial, he tamed a ferocious lion and rode on its back to the palace of the Byzantine ruler, who was so amazed by the sight that he granted immediate exemption. His shrine is recessed in the north wall of the church, and can be viewed from both inside and outside. It has been credited with exuding a liquid which has the power to calm tempests.

Take the road leading south-west out of Morphou. The fertile red soil of this district is reminiscent of Devon. Not only is the land red, but the sea is tinged various shades of red and pink from minerals in suspension, the effluent of the mines.

[32 m.] A right-hand turning leads to *Pendayia Hospital*, the property of the Cyprus Mines Corporation of Skouriotissa, which has its headquarters in Los Angeles. For the next few miles the extensive plant is visible from the road.

[34 m.] **Xeros** (hotel p. 126).

[34½ m.] There is a great crushing plant near the ancient port of **Karavostasi**, which has been associated with the export of copper since very early times. The place-name means 'safe anchorage for sailing vessels'.

[35 m.] To the left of the coast road, immediately outside Karavostasi, is the site of *Soli* (opening hours p. 126).

SOLI

This was a great city, traditionally founded in 600 B.C. on the recommendation of Solon, which became of prime importance during the Roman occupation of the island. Unhappily, nothing remains of the temples and porticoes which travellers report as having been in existence as late as 1738, for since then tons and tons of stone have been carried away for building elsewhere, and even transported by sailing-boat to Egypt for use in the construction of the harbour at Port Said. In 1930 the Swedish Archaeological Expedition excavated a *Roman Theatre* of the second or third century A.D. This has now been reconstructed and looks almost uncannily new. However, the theatre justifies its reconstruction by occasionally being used for dramatic performances, and no doubt the stone will weather. The near-by hilltop site of a Temple of Aphrodite and Isis has yielded a frieze (350–300 B.C.) with panels depicting the classic fight of the Amazons and the Greeks. One of these can be seen in the Cyprus Museum.

The site of the ancient city is very large, and so far has been only minimally excavated. A *necropolis* exists to the south, while the ancient port was immediately north. Important ecclesiastical remains are being excavated by the Mission Archaeologique de l'Université Laval, Quebec. The dig continues for a limited period each year. The preliminary findings consist of a medium-sized *Basilica* of the fifth century B.C., superseded by a larger one about a hundred years later, then in the tenth century, by a smaller one built from the ruins of the previous two. The same Canadian expedition has also been responsible for trial excavations of an area north of the Theatre. This has provided evidence that this part of Soli existed throughout periods extending from the Archaic to the Roman. The remains of the Basilica are to the east of the present car park, from which the Theatre is approached by a steep path, but this car park may have to be resited in the interests of further archaeological work.

[38 m.] The conical hill upon which *Vouni Palace* is built is a landmark on the southern shore of Morphou Bay. Turn off the coastal road at a right fork high on the headland, and continue in the opposite direction for about 1 m. to the summit of the site (opening hours p. 126).

HISTORY OF VOUNI

Baffling for the ordinary visitor, but a challenge to the archaeologist, there is no historical record of the Palace of Vouni. Not even its name in antiquity has come down to us. Nevertheless, though the answer to 'Who lived here and why?' may never be known with absolute certainty, much knowledge has been pains-

takingly wrung from the surviving stones since the beginning of
excavations by the Swedish Expedition in 1928–9. The layout of
the palace is extensive and complicated. It can be divided into four
periods of building, all of which probably took place during the
early part of the fifth century B.C. and the following hundred years
– a very short space of time indeed. Vouni was certainly the residence of some local king, who is likely to have been pro-Persian
in an era when the inhabitants of Cyprus were constantly rebelling
against their Persian overlords. He must have been a man blessed
with great wealth (without which the palace and its life could
neither have been initiated nor maintained) and with a taste for
luxury, exemplified by elaborate bath and hot-water systems which
derive more from the oriental way of life than from the Greek.
And the architects of this ambitious complex of buildings must
have felt a great sense of security, because except for traces of an
outer wall, no fortifications have come to light. But even so, disaster
did overtake Vouni on more than one occasion.

There is evidence that in the middle of the fifth century B.C. a
philhellenic dynasty succeeded at Vouni. This is expressed by
Greek-inspired modifications of the state apartments, and by
discoveries of sculptured works of art which indisputably had been
imported from the Greek mainland. This second dynasty is assumed to have occupied the palace for about seventy years, until it
was destroyed by fire *c*. 380 B.C., probably at a time when the
neighbouring city of Soli, turning to the Persian side, regained her
strength and attacked the palace, which in the first place may have
been built for the express purpose of keeping her in subjection.

DESCRIPTION OF SITE

Even if this site had not been so thoroughly excavated, and the
foundations of the different periods of building exposed and well
mapped, it would be worth visiting for its situation alone. This is
one of the beautiful and atmospheric places such as are found all
over the world, with little in common except a quality of magic.

From the custodian's office there is a magnificent view across the
sweeping Bay of Morphou and the anchorage for ore-carrying
ships. The headland to the west ends with the rocky island of
Petra tou Limniti, where Stone-Age finds were made by the Swedes
in 1930. This is another of the island-rocks said to have been hurled
by the national hero Dighenis against the invading Saracens.

From the highest point on the hill of Vouni it is advisable for visitors either to follow the official plan in the guide obtainable from the custodian or to enlist his services, because the remains are intricate, and they naturally have greater impact if their function is appreciated, in conjunction with the effect of certain modifications – as, for instance, when the main entrance was changed to the north-east corner, which detracted from the importance of adjoining rooms and added to the status of others. The wide flight of seven steps leading down to the *Central Court* makes a good vantage point from which to relate the various remains one to another. And throughout the site traces of the palace water system give a good idea of the degree of civilization achieved here in such an early age – not only the domestic supplies in great cisterns under the courts but the caldarium and frigidarium used for bathing – a refinement usually attributed to Romans of a later epoch.

The remains of several shrines adjoin the palace buildings, and it is not known which deities they honoured, except in the case of the *Temple* at the extreme top of the hill not far from the custodian's office, which is known to have been dedicated to Athena. Here was found the bronze cow which is exhibited in the Cyprus Museum. Two companion groups in relief, showing lions attacking a bull are also in museums, one in Stockholm and the other in Nicosia. The discovery of votive offerings in the three smaller rooms of the temple suggests that this was the treasury of the goddess.

St Chrysostomos Monastery and Buffavento Castle

Route Take the main Famagusta road (Route H on Nicosia routes map), turning left after 2 m. for Mia Milea (3 m.), St Chrysostomos Monastery (8 m.) and Buffavento Castle (9½ m. + 1 hr walk).

Instead of returning to Nicosia by the same route it is possible to drive eastwards on the new section of the Forest Road which begins just below Buffavento. This route crosses the mountain and gives wonderful views to the north and south, and also of Pentadactylos from near the level of its peaks, before regaining the southern aspect at Halevka (p. 146).

Ancient Monument
Buffavento Castle
Opening hours
Mid-May to mid-Sept. Daily 9 a.m. to noon
3 p.m. to 6.30 p.m.
Mid-Sept. to mid-May   9 a.m. to 1 p.m.
2 p.m. to 4.30 p.m.

[2 m.] **Turn** left off the Famagusta road, and continue north past **Mia Milea**, which derives its name from the fact that it is one Cyprus mile from Nicosia – a measure, now obsolete, of approximately three statute miles.

[7 m.] **Koutsovendis** is a straggling village set on the southern slopes of the bare eroded foothills of the Kyrenia range.

On the left-hand side of the well-engineered road leading up to St Chrysostomos Monastery are the ruins of a pair of *Churches*. In the smaller, southern church a beautiful and large twelfth- or fourteenth-century painting of Christ in his sepulchre has survived years of exposure to the elements. The colours are especially vivid after rain. On the south wall of the second church there is a delightful painting of St George mounted on a white horse.

[8 m.] MONASTERY OF ST CHRYSOSTOMOS

This monastery, the white buildings of which have been in view ever since departure from Nicosia, belongs to the Orthodox See of Jerusalem, not to the Church of Cyprus. Twin Byzantine churches stand against each other in the centre of the enclosure. In spite of appearances to the contrary, the church standing to the left or south is the older of the two. It was demolished and rebuilt in 1891, and much of its beauty was lost. However, in its present form the church, which according to tradition was built by St Helena after her visit to the Holy Land, is the pride of the monks. It retains the original apse, portions of a marble floor in geometric design and a fine west door beautifully designed in wood and fitted together without the use of nails – a wonderful example of carpentry. The icon of St Chrysostomos, painted in 1589, is especially venerated. Contrary to usual practice, it has been freed from its silver-gilt protective casing.

The church to the north, dedicated to St John Chrysostomos, is in disuse, but is almost as interesting as its neighbour. Until a few years ago, only the sketchiest traces and fragments remained of great wall paintings which once covered the whole of the interior surface. Much plaster had fallen, revealing the original Byzantine structure in the form of courses of brick and stone. But work begun in 1963 by the Center of Byzantine Studies of Dumbarton Oaks,

U.S.A., and the Department of Antiquities, Cyprus, has revealed exceptionally beautiful late eleventh-century frescoes.

The monastic buildings are in the main modern, though a few marble pillars and capitals are left over from earlier buildings, and giant beams in what were used as guest rooms are supported by equally massive carved brackets. Apart from the churches, what is most attractive here is the view across the whole of central Cyprus. Until latterly this was a most hospitable and comfortable religious guest-house. But at the date of going to press the buildings are under military occupation, though visitors are permitted to visit the churches.

The monastery has one tremendous cypress, which is a noted landmark, and also a spring of water credited with power to cure leprosy and other skin diseases. This miraculous property was discovered by a Byzantine princess who was gratified to see that her pet dog was cured of mange after immersion.

Seen from a ridge above the monastery – a fascinating place for echoes – the Castle of Buffavento seems to grow out of the topmost peak of the mountains. Its stonework is only distinguishable from the natural rock by a slightly yellower tinge. The castle appears to hang precariously forward, and seems closer than it in fact is.

[9½ m.] BUFFAVENTO CASTLE

The road goes as near as possible to the castle, stopping at a circular parking place surrounding an olive tree. From here a steep foot-path leads to the castle. Not for nothing is 'zigzag' a word in common usage in Cyprus. Care has been taken to keep the way clear of rock-falls (which are apt to occur after heavy rain), to fix loose steps with cement and to provide metal handrails so that there is no danger, though the climb is a strenuous one, and may take the best part of an hour. But with every upward step the outlook becomes better and better, rivalling that of the eagles which are common birds in these peaks. A good breather may be taken three-quarters of the way up, where a ridge between two heights reveals the very green tree-clad northern slope of the mountains, and the sea displayed far below like an enormous disc. (Plans are under discussion for continuing the road to a higher level.)

As well as being the highest (3,131 ft), Buffavento is perhaps the strangest and most evocative of the three castles of the Kyrenia mountains, probably because it is less frequented and less organized for tourism.

In medieval chronicles this was called the Castle of the Lion, and later referred to locally as the House of a Hundred and One Houses (probably meaning 'rooms') in line with the legend common to all three castles, to the effect that anyone who discovers the hundred-and-first room will disappear into a garden paradise. But probably its present name of Buffavento suits the castle best, on account of its vulnerability to wind from all four quarters.

Apart from legend, the first references to Buffavento date back to 1191, when after his marriage to Berengaria, Richard Cœur de Lion set about conquering the whole island. The daughter of Isaac Comnenus, the despot of Cyprus (1184–91) whom he had defeated outside Limassol, abased himself to Richard's deputy, Guy de Lusignan, and delivered her own person and the fortress to the English king's mercy while her father had fled to Buffavento Castle. Later the megalomaniac Peter I of Cyprus, 1359–69, believing that his wife, Queen Eleanor of Aragon, had been slandered, shut up his friend Sir John Visconti in Buffavento, and allowed him to die of starvation there. During the reign of Jacques I (1382–98) one of two brothers who were political prisoners made a spectacular escape down the northern precipices, but was recaptured, tortured and executed. These northern precipices bear examination in the light of a moonlight escape. Throughout most of its history, Buffavento seems to have been used less as a residence than as a political prison and torture chamber. The Venetian conquerors of the island decided that they had insufficient men to garrison it, and they deliberately 'slighted' it by removing many of the roofs and all of the armaments.

Partly due to this, there are no features of architectural interest remaining, nor much indication of period except for a small amount of Byzantine brickwork such as might in fact have been carried out in a succeeding century. The ruins are fairly extensive within the limitations of a mountain-top and are in such a state of disorder that only a few of the rooms (nothing like 101) can be traced. The site, and the feeling of cruel and unhappy history, are what make the greatest impression.

Asinou Church and Troödos Hill Resorts

Route Leaving Nicosia by George Grivas Dighenis Avenue (Route C on Nicosia routes map), follow the main road westwards to Kato Koutraphas (24 m.), make a diversion to Asinou Church (+15 m.), returning to Kato Koutraphas to rejoin the main road, and continue through Evrykhou to Kakopetria (37 m.), and Troödos (50 m.). Unless you plan to return direct to Nicosia, an overnight stay en route should be arranged. In that case you can continue via Prodhromos (53 m.), and on to Kykko Monastery (70 m.), Cedars Valley (80 m.) and Stavros tis Psokas (87 m.).

You can return to Nicosia from Stavros tis Psokas via Chakistra and Kambos, turning right at Karavostasi to by-pass Morphou and Astromeritis (72 m.). A diversion may be made westwards from Karavostasi to Soli and Vouni (pp. 128–31).

For Paphos continue south from Stavros tis Psokas on twisting mountain roads, passing turning for Pano Panayia, Chrysorroyiatissa and Ayia Moni Monasteries (pp. 274–5) and joining main Polis–Ktima road after Polemi (+ 35 m.)

N.B. Allow plenty of time to cover distances on these mountain routes, as they are tortuous, and the minor roads often have rough surfaces. None of the extended routes indicated above should be undertaken without an overnight break.

Hotels

At *Galata:*	3rd	Rialto.
At *Kakopetria:*		Makris (awaiting classification).
	2nd (C)	Hekali; Hellas; Krystal; Loucoudi (awaiting classification).
	3rd	Kifissia.
		Loucoudi
At *Kalopanayiotis:*	2nd (B)	Loutraki.
	3rd	Kastalia.
	4th	Drakos; Synnos; Heliopolis (awaiting classification).
At *Kambos:*	4th	Kambos.
At *Pedhoulas:*	1st (B)	Pine Wood Valley.
	2nd (B)	Marangos.
	2nd (C)	Christy's Palace.
	3rd	Central.
	4th	Elyssia; Kallithea; Koundouris; Lykavitos.
At *Prodhromos:*	1st (A)	Berengaria.
	3rd	Overhill.
	4th	Alps.
At *Troödos:*	1st (A)	Troödos.
		Pingos (awaiting classification).
	Camping Hotels Jubilee (A); Makhlouf's (A).	
	Restaurant Ben Nevis.	

At *Stavros tis Psokas: Restaurant/Bar.* For *Rest House* see p. 39.

Church

St George's, Troödos (summer only).

[17 m.] **Peristerona** (p. 126).

[24 m.] **Kato Koutraphas.** Immediately after crossing the Elea river, of which the Asinou river is a tributary, turn left at the signpost for *Asinou Church,* famous for its medieval frescoes (there is no longer a village of that name). The minor road climbs through the deserted village of Pano Koutraphas and leads after two miles to **Nikitari**. Here the village priest should be contacted through the café opposite Nikitari Church. He holds the key of Asinou Church, and will accompany visitors in their car, and should of course be returned to his home village afterwards. He is an excellent guide, though he speaks no English.

Except for the holy doors of Nikitari's modern *Church of St John the Baptist*, which originally belonged to Asinou Church and are dated 1610, there is little cause for delay when the supreme example of Byzantine art in Cyprus is only five miles farther on. For a short distance beyond Nikitari the road is cobbled, then the surface improves, though it remains narrow, but is viable even in bad weather. On the opposite side of the little river gorge, whitewashed cairns mark the boundary of the State Forest. Four and a half miles from Nikitari a road comes in from Ayios Theodhorus. Continue for another half-mile, when the church will be seen on a ridge to the right.

ASINOU CHURCH

The church at first sight seems insignificant. It is very small, and a steep protective roof covers the rectangle of the original twelfth-century building as well as the domed narthex, which is a later addition. But it is the church's interior, with its glorious, deceptively fresh paintings, which makes this tiny church notable, not only in Cyprus but in all the Mediterranean countries where Byzantine art has flourished. Visitors from the mid-1960s onwards are particularly fortunate, because during this period the paintings have undergone expert cleaning under the auspices of the Center of Byzantine Studies of Dumbarton Oaks, U.S.A.

FRESCOES

To take the frescoes as far as possible in chronological order, those at the west end of the nave and in the two blind recesses on either side of it belong to the original period of building. The S.W. recess (correctly termed arcade) contains a fresco depicting Nikiphorus Magister, the donor of the church at the time of Alexis Comnenus, with an inscription giving the dates 1105 and 1106. This has been invaluable evidence in dating this portion of the church, because it can reasonably be assumed that the erection of the church would have been followed closely by its interior decoration, and that it is unlikely to have been left unfinished for more than a very short time.

A later painting of the donor in the act of presenting a model of the church to the Virgin Mary appears over the south door, but this is believed to have been painted over an earlier and possibly nearly identical composition, as has been the case with many other early frescoes.

In the matching N.W. arcade the subject is a harrowing representation of the Forty Martyrs of Saint Sebasto bleeding from arrow wounds and about to be thrown into a frozen lake. Almost comic relief is provided by the coward escaping to the right, and the soldier on the left volunteering to take his place, and to whom the fortieth crown of martyrdom is awarded from on high.

The Death and Assumption of the Virgin Mary (*c.* A.D. 1106) above the west door of the church (which leads into the narthex) is perhaps the most important painting of all. It shows Christ holding his Mother's soul in the symbolic form of a swaddled infant.

The narthex is an addition of the fourteenth century, and its paintings are mostly dated as *c.* A.D. 1333. The central subject is the Last Judgment, with Christ the Ruler of the World as the traditional centrepiece. He is surrounded by medallions of the Virgin, angels and saints, and the subjects descend, in fact and in rank, to just men; then, lowest of all, sinners tortured by snakes and by fire, in the narrow arches below. St George occupies the south apse of the narthex. His armour is in gold, and the jewelled harness of his horse is particularly beautiful. Notice where damp has dissolved the pigment in the upper part of the picture, revealing the preliminary outlines made by the artist – a well-known technique of fresco painters.

The Virgin Mary attended by Archangels in the semi-dome apse of the main church is iconographically related to the earlier mosaic at Kiti (p. 207). It is later in date than the paintings of the narthex, while the work in the main vault of the nave are of the fifteenth century.

No description of these paintings or their colours (particularly after restoration – from which the blues and the blacks seem to have benefited most) can do them justice. They should be treated as a giant illuminated book assembled over a span of centuries, with each precious page meriting separate attention. And this of course is right, because the primary purpose of medieval church paintings was educational, aimed at the instruction of illiterate persons.

Apart from the obligation to return the Nikitari priest to his home, it is advisable to continue in the reverse direction as far as Kato Koutraphas, and to turn left there on to the main Troödos road. (Though motorists naturally dislike heading away from their destination, on this occasion little will be missed by not continuing into the mountains immediately above Asinou Church. The road from that point is monotonously tortuous, and very tiring for passengers as well as driver, and the pine trees shut out all chance of a good view. However, should this route be preferred, Kourdhali and Spilia are the objectives. The church of Panayia Khrysokourdaliotissa at Spilia is worth visiting. A right turn at Spilia leading to a further four-mile section of twisting road emerges on the main Nicosia–Troödos highway. Turn right for Kakopetria, a further three miles.)

[32 m.] Continuing straight along the main road from Kato Koutraphas, you come to **Evrykhou**.

[36 m.] **Galata** (hotel p. 135).
As there are churches of greater importance than Galata's *St Sozemenos* in the neighbourhood, it might be advisable to continue towards Kakopetria, which practically adjoins Galata, but turning right before reaching the centre of the second village. Two miles along this side-turning, on the left, is the *Church of St Nicholaostis-Steyis* – 'tis steyis' meaning 'of the roof of planks', describing the original construction, which was of timber set on end in a stone platform. A shed roof now covers the whole of the cruciform layout, including the dome. The interior is completely covered with frescoes of various periods from the eleventh to the thirteenth centuries, while portraits of the donors in the narthex suggest by their costumes that these were painted *c.* 1430. The fourteenth-century icon of the patron saint surrounded by scenes from his life is rare for the reason that it is painted on vellum. It is one of the most interesting in Cyprus.

Not far from the church, an aerial ropeway, the property of the Cyprus Chrome Company, leads from their crushing plant to their mine near the summit of Mount Olympus.

From the church return to the main road.

[37 m.] **Kakopetria** (hotels p. 135) with its straggling houses following the course of the Solea, which runs through a steepening valley, finds favour with visitors who prefer the lower altitudes and yet seek a temperate summer climate. The stream, the poplars and the fruit trees, and the shady central square make it a pleasant and leisurely stopping-place.

There are steeper gradients after Kakopetria. It may come as a surprise here and elsewhere in the Troödos range to see vineyards clinging to the mountain-tops. Some vines grow as high as 4,500 ft.

[40 m.] The road from **Spilia** comes in on the left.

[42½ m.] At the Karvouna Crossroads take the right turn. The road on the left leads to a sanitorium, and **Kyperounda** and **Agros** in the Pitsilia District (pp. 247–9).

[45½ m.] At the *Amiandos Mines* asbestos deposits have been worked since 1907, although local mineral wealth has been exploited in the neighbourhood since ancient times. Visitors may be shown over the quarries and the mine-workings on application to the local offices of the Cyprus Asbestos Mines Ltd or by pre-arrangement with the Hellenic Mining Co. (Tel. Nicosia 2005).

[50 m.] **TROÖDOS**

The resort is 5,500 ft above sea-level and was the summer seat of government during British rule. It is now very popular as a summer resort, with good hotels and camping facilities (p. 135), and is also the winter-sports centre of the island. The highest point of the Troödos range, *Mount Olympus* (6,401 ft) is 2 m. north-west of Troödos crossroads. The observation post on the summit, not unnaturally, gives a splendid unimpeded view stretching to the farthest distances of the island.

It would be unreasonable to expect that there should be many features of historical or archaeological interest on these exposed heights, though according to Strabo the geographer (b. 66 B.C.) Olympus was the site of a temple of Aphrodite Acraia which was not only unapproachable for women but actually invisible to them.

There is some evidence of a Venetian fort, and Poracacchi, a sixteenth-century writer, has mentioned that Cypriot nobles at the time of the Venetian occupation customarily visited the monasteries in the vicinity for summer recreation. In 1881 Rimbaud designed a house on the lines of a Scottish shooting-box which became the summer residence of British governors of the island. The French poet's stay here in an interval between unconventional wanderings is reason enough for interest in his all too conventional Victorian design. For the rest, lovers of natural history will appreciate the flat-topped pines, the springs and the waterfalls. The wild flowers in spring and autumn (some rare elsewhere) provide additional interest when walking or riding.

[53 m.] The right-hand turning at Troödos crossroads leads by an excellent new road to **Prodhromos**, 4,600 ft above sea-level, the highest village in Cyprus. (Troödos ranks as a resort and has none of the qualities of a village.) It has a delightful aspect on the north-western spur of the high mountains, and is the site of the Cyprus Forestry Training College. There is a large hotel, as well as good accommodation in lower price ranges (p. 135). The former *Trikoukkia Monastery*, 1 m. from the village, which has buildings dating from 1761, has been converted into use as a government fruit-growing research station. The locality is especially favourable to apple trees.

[55 m.] **Pedhoulas** (hotels p. 135) is reached by continuing along the descending road. It is a charming village, at 3,600 ft, at the head of the Marathasa valley, in a neighbourhood suitable for fruit-growing and especially good for cherries. The blossom in the spring is deserving of the kind of pilgrimage made by Japanese in their own land. The beauty of Pedhoulas is slightly marred by roofs of corrugated iron – practical in winter emergencies, no doubt, but so are traditional tiles. In summer there is an open-air cinema.

The biggest church is so prominent on its platform-like site, clearly visible from almost every point, that its whiteness, central dome and twin cupolas distract the eye, and perhaps attention, from a neighbour which, though close by, is not at all easy to locate. The tiny *Church of the Archangel Michael* was built in 1474. The interior is dark, for the reason that it has no windows, but it is possible to open the north and west doors and thus admit enough light to reveal the existence of the beautiful but damaged frescoes which are contemporary with the church. The iconostasis is interesting in being similar in design to a Latin rood screen, unlike those of Orthodox churches, which aim to exclude the congregation from the altar and the officiating priests. Note the Lusignan coat of arms, and those of lesser nobles, on the upper division of the screen.

[57 m.] High above the village of **Moutoullas** there is a tiny *chapel* dedicated to the Blessed Virgin Mary in 1279. It has an interesting fresco of the donors, John Moudoulas and his wife Irene, as well as good carved doors. This diversion is not recommended if time is short, because Kalopanayiotis is a very short distance down the main road, and its famous church is more accessible. Moutoullas mineral water is bottled and sold all over the island.

[58 m.] The sulphur springs of **Kalopanayiotis** (hotels p. 135) are used in the treatment of digestive disorders, debility, skin affections and certain types of rheumatism. The waters may be drunk or used in the form of thermal baths. Medical supervision is recommended, especially in the case of the baths, which are liable to affect the action of the heart and the circulation of the blood.

The most interesting of the churches – some say the most interesting in the whole of Cyprus – is undoubtedly *St John Lampadistes*, which is reached by a picturesque path and a bridge across the river ravine. Apart from the moving beauty of this church belonging to a deserted monastery, it is especially interesting because it consists of three churches covered by a single steeply-pitched tiled roof which reaches almost to the ground – the traditional barn-like structure developed to withstand heavy snow-fall. The interior is apportioned between the Latin and Greek Orthodox rites, and services are conducted by rota. It is entered from the south, at the part which is a cross-in-square domed church of the eleventh century dedicated to St Heraclides. This has paintings of the fourteenth and sixteenth centuries, the most notable being a Triumphal Entry into Jerusalem, also thirteenth century paintings in the south and west vaults which have recently been exposed and treated. The central church is dedicated to St John

Lampadistes, about whom little is known. It has been greatly restored, and contains the tomb of the patron saint, as well as fifteenth-century paintings, also much restored, in the narthex, which it shares with the southern, Orthodox, church. The Latin chapel to the north was expressly built for the celebration of the Latin rite, and is covered with paintings of the early sixteenth century which are remarkable for their Italian cinquecento beauty as well as for the fact that experts consider them to be true frescoes (unlike the majority in Cyprus), that is, painted on the original plaster while it was still damp. The iconostasis in the Orthodox part of the church was once the Latin rood screen. Note the west doors of the Latin chapel as a particularly fine example of sixteenth-century wood-carving.

Kalopanayiotis has many interesting small chapels in the neighbourhood. It should be borne in mind that in all probability their keys will be obtainable in the village and not near the chapels themselves.

[59 m.] A short distance down the main road, opposite the village of **Nikos**, take a turn to the left which leads via Yerakies in the direction of *Kykko Monastery*. This is a mountain road with little in the way of habitation, and which is joined on the left after about 6 m. by the direct road from Pedhoulas.

[67 m.] At Xistaroudhi Junction take the right-hand turning.

[70 m.] MONASTERY OF KYKKO

As well as being the richest monastery in Cyprus, Kykko enjoys prestige throughout the whole Greek Orthodox Church, the abbot ranking with bishops of the church. Throughout many centuries, the monastery amassed great and profitable property abroad, largely due to associations with Tsarist Russia. Since the Russian Revolution, Kykko has come to depend solely on its estates and investments inside Cyprus. Fame abroad began with its foundation *c.* A.D. 1080 when the Byzantine governor of Cyprus, being grateful for a cure by the local hermit Isaiah, procured from the emperor in Constantinople the miraculous golden icon of the Virgin which is one of the three reputed to have been painted by St Luke. This precious icon has survived fires which have several times destroyed the monastery. It is now covered with silver-gilt, and by a cloth decorated with seed pearls, and stands in the monastery church in an elaborate shrine of mother-of-pearl and tortoise-shell. It is especially venerated as a bringer of rain. Processions of pilgrims traditionally gathered to carry rain-working images to curious outdoor thrones or chairs on the mountain slopes. The windswept trees of this exposed ridge can be seen to be permanently bowed as though in respect – a feature which is observed with awe by the crowds who throng to the monastery on its feast day.

Ever since medieval times, Kykko Monastery has been regarded as a sanctuary. It fulfilled this function as late as the period of the British occupation, as well as being so actively concerned with EOKA operations that at one time its buildings had to be occupied by Commandos and the Gordon Highlanders (1956).

Due to repeated destruction by fire, and to pillage by the Turks in 1821, nothing of great antiquarian interest is on view, except of course the icon described above, a curious relic or two and some ancient books which are kept in the church's treasury. The layout of the conventual buildings is roughly triangular in form, following the shape of the site. There are two principal courtyards with cloisters, and several ranges of buildings which provide hospice accommodation for a large number of guests.

[73 m.] About 3 m. farther along the Kambos and Xeros road, before reaching Chakistra, take a left turning.

[74½ m.] Another left fork about 1½ m. further on leads to *Cedars Valley*. This route keeps to the south of Mount Tripylos (4,619 ft). The cedar of Cyprus (*c. brevifolia*) is indigenous. It is outstandingly beautiful in these mountain areas, which are otherwise rather monotonously covered with pines, or dotted with low-growing scrub. The unproductive growth, however, is gradually being replaced by plantations. The cedars were until recently threatened by extinction by fire, and by the depredations of goats and the need for firewood, but they are now strictly protected. It is relevant that the Department of Forests issues a map of Cyprus showing vast areas where the keeping of goats is prohibited.

[87 m.] The tour should be continued as far as **Stavros tis Psokas Forest Station**. This is the headquarters of the Paphos Forest

District, which maintains a rest house for visitors (p. 39). A feature of Stavros tis Psokas is the *Moufflon Enclosure*, where this strange breed of wild mountain sheep may be seen in its natural habitat. The males and the females occupy separate ranges. They are fawny brown in colour, and the males have huge archaic curled horns. These animals are re-establishing themselves at free range in the surrounding forest, after a critical period when their numbers had declined to the verge of extinction. But the wild moufflon are indeed wild, and prefer inaccessible places. The best way to be certain of seeing them is to walk the perimeter of the enclosure, which provides a more realistic environment than can be simulated in zoological gardens.

A short distance beyond the point of access to the moufflon enclosure, at a higher level, are terraces providing a *nursery* for forest trees, principally the giant *C. brevifolia*, where these may be inspected at their different stages of growth.

Kythrea, Halevka and Antiphonitis Monastery

Route take the main Famagusta road (Route H on Nicosia routes map) and after 6 m. turn left at signpost for Kythrea (which can be by-passed by the better road leading up to the quarries which are clearly visible on the mountain slope). Continue northward past Kephalovryso Spring to Halevka (14 m.), making a diversion to Sourp Magar Monastery (+1½ m.) and Mount Pentadactylos (+2 m.). Return to the Forest Road and continue eastward to Antiphonitis Monastery (21 m.).

One way of returning to Nicosia is to continue east along the Forest Road to the Mersiniki Pass. Turn right for Lefkoniko, and continue south to the main Famagusta road, turning right before reaching Prastio. A short-circuit may be made by following the new section of the Forest Road to below Buffavento Castle and thus returning to Nicosia (see p. 131, directions in reverse).

For Kyrenia take the road west of Antiphonitis, and descend to the coast road via Ayios Amvrosios (+22 m.).

For Famagusta turn left at this crossroads (+11 m.).

Kantara Resort and Castle (p. 206) can also be reached by continuing along the Forest Road beyond Mersiniki Pass (junction ½ m. to the north) passing Mt Olympus on the way (+ 25 m.).

Hotels

At Kantara Resort:	3rd	Regina.
At Aya Marina, (near Akanthou):		Glaros (awaiting classification).
At Dhavlos:	2nd (C)	Tony's.
	4th	Louis.

[8 m.] **KYTHREA**

The key to beauty in Mediterranean countries tends to be the presence of water, and, due to its situation on both sides of a river, Kythrea is a pretty place – or, in actual fact, four pretty villages linked into one. The houses straggle up the lower slope of the Kyrenia range almost as far as the river's source at *Kephalovryso Spring*. They are set in luxuriant gardens of fruit trees and flowers, and fields of cauliflower, a vegetable which originated here and was introduced to Europe in 1604. This is one of the localities where travellers might well make some excuse for halting, even when reason argues that it is too early for coffee or drinks and there is more to be seen elsewhere.

Kythrea cannot be considered separately from the water supply which has been responsible for so much of its development. Some inhabitants believe that this flows under the sea-bed from Asia Minor. A legendary old woman who had migrated from Anatolia is said to have recognized a silver vessel which she lost in a stream near her old home, and which now came floating into her hands. Whatever the geological possibilities of such a phenomenon, it is a fact that water from Kythrea was channelled across the island to the city of Constantia, the successor of Salamis, where remains of the aqueduct are still in evidence. And because Nicosia was in later days dependent upon the flour which was ground by Kythrea water power (some of the mills are still in use), it became part of strategy in local wars for attackers of the capital to take Kythrea and its mills first, before laying siege to the great city.

The name Kythrea has developed from Chytri, as the settlement was called in the twelfth century B.C. when it was colonized by Greeks under Chytros, grandson of the Athenian, Akamas. In A.D. 806 marauding Saracens captured the entire population with their valuables and movable stock, and transported them in bondage to Syria, whence they were eventually repatriated through the intercession of their bishop, later to be canonized as St Dimitrianos. Near the ruined *Church of St Dimitrianos* there is a large carved sarcophagus thought to have contained his body.

An acropolis and traces of the sanctuary of Aphrodite Paphia were excavated by Dr O. Richter in 1883, and about the same time a necropolis of the Bronze Age came to light near the spring-head. But the most important finds in the vicinity have been in the near-by village of **Voni**. The site of a Bronze-Age temple on the north side of the village was ransacked in 1883, and the archaeological finds dispersed. It was here, also, that the statue of Septimus Severus (now in the Cyprus Museum), a fine statue of Apollo and other pre-Roman objects were found. The situation is delightful, but what is left on the scattered sites is of minor importance.

Out of Kythrea follow the roughly surfaced side road which climbs up towards the mountains past the Kephalovryso Spring, and joins the Forest Road near Halevka.

[14 m.] **Halevka**

This is the headquarters of the Northern Range and Plains Division of the Forestry Department. Here there is a restaurant and a café, and car parking space from which there are pleasant walks through the plantations (chiefly *pinus brutia* and *cupressus sempervivens*) which flourish against the limestone crags of this dolomitic range. The pattern of plantations follows the contours wherever there is soil for roots, giving a welcome touch of green which is offset by the misty distances of the Mesaoria Plain. In spring and autumn cyclamen and anemones carpet the ground, and sheltered corners and crevices in the rocks harbour narcissi, ground orchids and rare alpine plants.

At Halevka a turning leads north and downwards for about $\frac{3}{4}$ m. to the Armenian **Monastery of Sourp Magar.** In the Middle Ages this was inhabited by a Coptic community of Egyptian Christians who dedicated their monastery to St Makarius the Hermit (A.D. 309–404), a saint thought to have no great connection with Cyprus. Since 1425 the monastery has been in Armenian hands, and a small brotherhood ministered to pilgrims and visitors from Nicosia. It was used as a summer resort for orphans of the Armenian massacres in Turkey of 1895–7. The former guest-house is no longer in use. On the saint's feast day, the first Sunday in May, this became a place of pilgrimage and feasting for the Armenian community of the island. The original church was built, according to general practice, in the centre of the enclosure, but it was ruined, probably by earthquake, and its walls now form part of a terrace. The exterior east wall of the enclosure contains remnants of medieval building work, and the room used as a guest chamber at the north-east corner, which has a roof supported by a central pillar, probably dates from the fifteenth century. The present church, built 1811–14, is without character. It is the courtyards and the peace of the enclosure with its trees and gardens, and the atmosphere of shelter, which are of value.

The Forest Road continues westwards towards the mountain known as *Pentadactylos*. This place-name, meaning five fingers, is one of those which assist foreigners to memorize useful Greek words, because the crags of this peak of 2,430 ft really can be imagined as five rather blunt fingers. The legend is that a village beauty or 'queen' set a suitor the difficult task of fetching a capful of water from remote Cape Andreas. When he miraculously succeeded she went back on her word, and refused to marry him. Whereupon he threw the water on the ground, scooped up a handful of wet soil and threw it at her. It missed, but sticks to this day to the very top of the range, clearly showing the impress of human fingers. A rival legend insists that the imprint was made by the hand of the great hero Dighenis as he vaulted the mountains in pursuit of the Saracens. The paths below the steepest crags lead to good vantage points with a choice between looking south over Nicosia to the Troödos range or north across the sea to Asia Minor.

Returning to the main route, the road eastwards from Halevka towards Antiphonitis Monastery is perhaps the most spectacular section of the Forest Road, which continues along almost the whole length of the northern range and has been constructed partly as a tourist attraction and partly to facilitate forestry work. It gives views on both sides of the mountain with their contrasting characteristics: to the north steep slopes and very green pockets of vegetation established by the superior rainfall, dropping to a narrow, fertile littoral and then the sea; to the south exposed limestone crags, plantations wherever planting is possible, but altogether stonier, harsher and more eroded than the other side. Instead of sea, the plain. The hairpin bends of the road reveal first one aspect and then the other. Inexperienced drivers should take great care, because though there is little traffic, passing places are few and far between.

[21 m.] ANTIPHONITIS MONASTERY

The monastery is tucked into a narrow wooded valley which falls steeply to the coastal strip. Its patrons were the all-powerful, regal Lusignan dynasty. When during the Turkish occupation there was a likelihood that the church was to be converted to Muslim use, a Cypriot bought it as his personal possession. In 1906 the property was sold to the Monastery of Kykko. It is now uninhabited. The church is constructed in twelfth-century form, with a large dome supported by eight columns. The dome is not a true circle, and this fact, taken in combination with the irregularity of the pendentives, suggest local workmanship. A narthex at the west end and a loggia to the south were added towards the end of the fifteenth century. This loggia, which has pointed arches springing from octagonal columns, originally supported a flat wooden roof which has now disintegrated, but the stone workmanship is elegant and shows a fine simplicity of conception. Though the paintings in the interior of the church have been dismissed by one expert as 'mechanical Byzantine of a very rustic kind', they have the charm of decay. Originally the whole of the interior was painted. The most complete survivors of these frescoes are an enormous head, shoulders and hands of Christ Pantokrator in the dome, and a beautiful Stem of Jesse (both *c.* fifteenth century) painted on a dark-blue ground in the centre of the south wall. The buildings are open to the public on Sundays, otherwise the key is obtainable from Ayios Amvrosios Police Station. This entails a descent almost to sea-level and a return journey, so that a better approach on weekdays is from the Kyrenia direction (see chart).

Tamassos and Makheras Monastery

Route Leave Nicosia by the suburb of Strovolos (Route D on Nicosia routes map) for Kato Lakatamia (5 m.), Tamassos site (13½ m.) and Makheras Monastery (25 m.).
  You can get back to Nicosia by continuing through the hill villages of Lazania and Gourri (traditional window and door carvings), joining a first-class road soon after Kalokhorio and returning via Pano and Kato Dheftera and Lakatamia (+29).
Ancient Monument
Tamassos tombs
Opening Times Summer, daily, 9 a.m.–noon. 3 p.m.–6.30 p.m.
Custodian lives at Politico; winter daily at reasonable times.

[2 m.] **Strovolos** has now become a suburb of Nicosia. The *Church* *of the Blessed Virgin Mary* was rebuilt in 1817 with care to retain the apse and the dome of the original Byzantine building. It possesses a delightful and incongruous example of French Empire furniture, origin unknown, in the form of a chair. A chapel on the south side of the church has an interesting column as part of its outside wall, with an archiepiscopal crown forming the capital. It is believed that this is an anonymous memorial to Archbishop Kyprianos, who, in company with many other prelates and ecclesiastics, was massacred by the Turks in 1821.

[5 m.] A right turning near **Kato Lakatamia** leads in 2 m. to the *Monastery of the Archangel Gabriel*, which is on the farther side of the Pedieos River. The monastery belongs to the famous and wealthy Monastery of Kykko but has fallen into disuse. The monastic buildings and the church which served them are remarkably ambitious in conception, especially in view of their having been erected in 1636 very soon after the Turkish Conquest. Note the vast fresco of the Archangel (1785) and the iconostasis (1650), the tomb of the founder, Archbishop Nikephorus, in the narthex, and the *graffiti* near the north door. This records the years when it was necessary to bring the famous rain-working icon from Kykko to put an end to intolerable drought.

[8 m.] At **Kato Dheftera** a side road to the right leads in 1 m. to the unique *Chapel of the Chrysospileotissa*, which is also situated on the far side of the Pedieos. This consists of a natural cave in the cliff which has been enlarged to 30 by 24 ft. Time and damp have taken toll of the interior plasterwork and paintings, but the little church is worth visiting, especially now that it has been made more accessible by local people grateful for the rain-working powers of their Virgin. They have replaced the original precarious draw-bridge by an iron-girdered structure.

[9 m.] At the far end of **Pano Dheftera** turn left on to a secondary road.

[13½ m.] The site of the great ancient city of *Tamassos* extends between four villages, but is best reached from the southernmost, **Politico.**

HISTORY OF TAMASSOS

Tamassos is believed to have been in existence four thousand years before Christ. It owed its later importance in the ancient world to the discovery of copper, whereupon it became the centre of population of the island. Many deities were worshipped here, and Venus in particular. According to legend, her temple was built round the sacred tree from which came the three apples she presented to Hippomenes. The site of the Temple of Apollo has been identified. Except for two royal tombs (*c.* 600 B.C.) there is not a great deal to interest the unlearned sightseer. In the last century a life-size bronze of the god came to light. Accounts suggest that it was of supreme beauty. Unfortunately, due to fear of the Turks, who were then in power, coupled with great poverty, the finders sold it piece by piece for the price of the metal, making bad bargains at that. One discovery which has survived, and which is on show in the Cyprus Museum, is a sword which can be assumed to bear a close resemblance to the one described by Homer as in the possession of Agamemnon.

Phoenician settlers of the sixth century B.C. came to Tamassos from coastal Kitium and Salamis. Towards the end of the fourth century B.C. the mining rights were awarded by Alexander the Great to the king of Salamis in reward for his support at the Siege of Tyre. When St Paul and St Barnabas visited Cyprus they were conducted here by Heracleidos, who was ordained first bishop of Tamassos, and held the see until his martyrdom. The mines had by that time been rented by King Herod, who brought in Jews from Palestine to work them. In A.D. 115–16, as part of a widespread revolt, the Jews turned against their Roman masters. Fatal casualties during the initial massacre and the reprisals which followed, here and at Salamis, have been estimated at close on 250,000.

DESCRIPTION OF SITE

Evidence of this long history doubtless lies untouched in the rocky ground. Not much modern excavation has yet been done, but the two *Royal Tombs* should without doubt be visited. They are not unlike others discovered by Di Cesnola at Amathus. Slabs of stone form ridged roofs, and architectural detail in the form of moulding and pillars with Ionic capitals make them impressive. The larger tomb has an inner doorway surmounted by carvings of an oriental pattern. The cover of the sarcophagus in the inner chamber has disappeared, and a hole in the roof shows where robbers and violators broke in to remove what is certain to have been great treasure.

The *Monastery of St Heracleidos* lies to the south of the confines of the ancient city not far from Politico. It was rebuilt in 1759. The skull of the patron saint is preserved in the church. A small medieval domed chapel, now in use as a reliquary, is of exceptional interest. Note especially the curious iconostasis formed of stone slabs which were subsequently covered with plaster, and the floor of hexagonal tiles in which there is an aperture leading to what is undoubtedly a Roman tomb, but which local piety insists was the burial place of the saint and his friend St Mnason, 'an old disciple', with whom St Paul lodged (Acts xxi 16). There are remains of a mosaic floor to the east of this chapel, and to the south the outlines, at ground level, of the first Byzantine church to be erected on this site.

To continue for Makheras Monastery, follow the road south from **Pera**, the village to the east of Tamassos, which climbs and winds through lovely foothills.

[16 m.] Kambia

[25 m.] MAKHERAS MONASTERY

This was named the 'Convent of the Sword', either because of the cutting winds which in winter blow from Mount Kionia or because of a belief that the miraculous icon of the Virgin Mary which the founders of the monastery discovered in a cave was guarded by a naked sword. As a result of divine revelation, the hermits Ignatius and Neophytos began building in the twelfth century. (This Neophytos is not to be confused with the saint of the same name who formed his enclosure near Paphos.) Ignatius and Procopius, the successor to Neophytos, were dismayed at the slowness of their labours, so they journeyed to Constantinople in quest of funds. Here they petitioned Manuel Comnenus, Emperor of Byzantium 1143–80, who awarded them fifty pieces of gold from the imperial treasury, a grant of a large tract of mountain and a promise of absolute independence in perpetuity. As soon as the travellers returned to Cyprus and news of the icon spread abroad, numbers of monks and aspirants flocked to Makheras, and work proceeded fast. Nilos, a foreigner who arrived in 1172, was the first abbot. Legend relates that Queen Alix, the wife of Hugues IV, being a d'Ibelin and of the Latin faith, and therefore disdainful of Orthodox rulings, forced her way into the church though it was forbidden to women, whereupon she was struck dumb, and did not recover her speech until under duress she was forced to testify to the authenticity of a fragment of the True Cross.

The monastic buildings and the church were totally destroyed by fire in 1892, resulting in complete replanning, reconstruction and loss of early architectural features. However, the site itself is superb, with views north across the Mesaoria. The immediate surroundings of wooded valleys and hill-side vineyards are very beautiful indeed. Below the high buttressed walls of the monastery is the renowned Holy Well, possessing an endless flow of water, near which the original icon was found. This icon miraculously escaped the fire which destroyed the monastery, and it is preserved in the new church, covered with repoussé work on account of its extreme antiquity and sanctity.

The Monastery of Makheras was very active in the EOKA troubles, and harboured many fighters, one of whom, Gregory Afxentious, second in command to Grivas, has been adopted as a national hero in memory of the battle he put up against overwhelming odds. His mountain hide-out, where he at last fell, has become a place of pilgrimage.

Perakhorio and Dhali (Idalion)

Route Leave Nicosia by the Limassol road (Route E on Nicosia routes map), and continue as far as Nisou (11½ m.), turning off after that village (signpost to Dhali) (14 m.).

By returning from Dhali to the Limassol road, emerging opposite the village of Perakhorio, the expedition can include Kornos, Pyrga and Stavrovouni Monastery (pp. 224–6) on the way to Limassol or Larnaca.

For Larnaca continue eastward from Dhali, to join the Nicosia–Larnaca highway after 4 m.

There are low hills to the south and south-east of Nicosia from which Turkish batteries bombarded the city in 1570. Traces of these military earthworks are still in evidence on either side of the road running due south, which passes on the right first the masts of the Cyprus Broadcasting Corporation and then the headquarters of the Experimental Station of the Agricultural and Forestry Department at **Athalassa**. Visitors interested in these subjects are welcome, but should they require expert attention, should first contact the Ministry of Agriculture (Tel: Nicosia 4000). The public is allowed free access to the fields and woods.

[11½ m.] The modern mosque at **Nisou** is probably built on the site of some ancient church, but the main source of interest is a curious *Hellenistic Rock Tomb* near the top of the hill immediately north-east of the village. The interior is reached by a flight of modern steps. It measures approximately 33 by 13 feet, and contains a marble sarcophagus, on the lid of which a large cross is carved. This is accepted as the tomb of St Epaphras, who is the object of special veneration on his feast day, December 9th. He has been identified with the bishop of Tamassos who attended the Council of Chalcedon in A.D. 451, rather than with his namesake, the first bishop of Paphos, an envoy of St Paul.

[12 m.] The village of **Perakhorio** to the right is by-passed by the main road. The principal church here, dedicated to *St Marina*, was built in the nineteenth century, but materials from some very old building were used in its construction. To the south-west, on a hill, stands the more interesting medieval *Church of the Twelve Apostles*, which may be considered as being typical of Cyprus village churches, with a cruciform plan and a small dome which terminates externally in conical fashion. What makes this church chiefly remarkable is a painted frieze of angels in procession round the lower part of the dome. They carry gifts to the Madonna and Child, and are surmounted by a large representation of Christ. Though these paintings have suffered a certain amount of damage and inexpert restoration since their origin in, probably, the twelfth century, they are of extreme beauty. Note in particular the hands of the angels. Recent work under the auspices of the American Center of Byzantine Studies has clarified the colours. The frescoes on the south wall of the church are of a later date.

[14 m.] A right-angled left turn to the east near Perakhorio leads in 2 m. to **Dhali**. This village, in antiquity known as *Idalion*, is one of the great historical sites of Cyprus. It has been ransacked repeatedly by treasure seekers, yet much of it awaits excavation. Di Cesnola, the American archaeologist about whose veracity controversy still rages, boasted of having opened as many as 10,000 tombs, but he was not the first; as early as the seventh century A.D. barbarian pirates pillaged the Graeco-Roman tombs of the district which were superimposed on Phoenician graves.

The present village of Dhali has a conspicuous modern church. There are two smaller Byzantine churches in the vicinity, *St Dimitrianos* and *St George*. The structure of the former church was consolidated in 1964. It contains an interesting painting over the west door. This represents the donor, one Michael Castouroubes, in 1316 presenting a model of the church to Christ. The latter church has fragments of the ancient city built into its walls. The Latin *Church of St Mamas* dates from the sixteenth century. The moulded Gothic arches are of architectural interest, as are the wall shafts which almost certainly originated as columns of some pagan temple. This church is currently in use as a Greek Orthodox cemetery chapel.

IDALION

References to ancient Idalion occur in many classical writings, both before and after Virgil's appreciation (*Aeneid* i 691) of its shady gardens and bright herbage. The district was, and is, connected with the death of Adonis. The city was founded by emigrants from Salamis or Alasia, and occupied later by Phoenicians, who owed allegiance to Persia, and who settled also in the neighbouring city of Tamassos.

There is no official custodian, and at the present time it is difficult for the casual viewer to reconstruct the shape and extent of the ancient city, but the knowledge that it lay between two limestone hills will be of assistance. Gabriel's Peak to the east was crowned by the chief sanctuary of Aphrodite, below which remains of the city wall are still evident. A sanctuary of Athena stood between these twin heights. At a greater distance, and outside the city boundaries, two further sanctuaries have come to light. At one of these, that of Aphrodite Kourotrophos, many fascinating stone statuettes of votives and models of the participants in temple life were found in 1883. These are now in the Cyprus Museum.

Idalion as it now stands has a feeling of desolation, despite its proximity to the vestiges of the idyllic gardens admired by the classical writers and Venetian usurpers. But the site should not on that account be by-passed on the way from Nicosia to Limassol.

KYRENIA

Population 4,000.
Hotels
De luxe Dome, and Seaview annexe.
1st (A) Rock Ruby.
1st (B) Cœur de Lion; Hesperides.
3rd   Acropole.
Chrysallis Seaside Apartments (Kyrenia 3 m.).
Awaiting classification: Bristol; Dolphin; Dudley Court. The Dome is the doyen of Kyrenia's hotels. It has now grown almost beyond recognition. Other establishments are more intimate. The tendency has been to site the newer hotels to the west, many having direct access to the sea (see also p. 170).
Restaurants and Bars
Theo's, Bishop Laurentios St.
Top Town, Hellas St.
Harbour Club, Nikiforos St.
Three Stars (Night club, Greek dancing), Catsellis St.
Freddie Kerr's, Harbour.
Clito's Bar, Rigas Fereos St.
Pachyammos beach restaurant.
As usual, the hotels have restaurants and bars corresponding to their grading. For the others, it is difficult to distinguish between their functions, since they frequently combine elements of restaurants, bars and evening entertainment. The tables of coffee-cum-drinking bars line the edge of the inner harbour.
Churches
Anglican St Andrew's, Helena Palaeologos St.
Roman Catholic Terra Santa, Themistocles St.
Clubs
Country Club, off 28th October Avenue.
Harbour Club.
Cinema
Katzelis.
Bathing and Water Sports
Though swimming is permitted in the area between the Dome and the harbour, better facilities are provided by the Country Club, the Dome and Rock Ruby Hotels, and in the small cove opposite the Hesperides Hotel. Otherwise it is necessary to go farther afield, to Pachyammos (6 m. east), or west to Snake Island (2 m.), 5 mile or 6 Mile Beaches, at all of which there are modest restaurants. Equipment for water ski-ing and skin-diving may be hired, and lessons can be arranged. Good sailing centre. Regattas held every summer weekend.
Entertainment
Cypriot theatre, dancing and singing every summer weekend.

The life of modern Kyrenia centres around the harbour and the sea, whereas in earlier days it was indivisible from its great castle. It would be difficult to find another place in the Mediterranean which is so close to the English ideal.

The mountains backing the town have fantastic shapes, reminiscent of fairy-tale illustrations; the slopes are well watered and fertile, producing a profusion of fruit and wild flowers. The high buildings around the horseshoe harbour are little changed from their original functional design as warehouses into which carob beans and other local produce could be tipped at street level and removed three or four floors below on the quayside. And the campanile of the church and minaret add to the pattern. The great Venetian walls of the castle, mellow and golden, squat protectively to the east, while across the open sea, on clear days, the harsh outlines of the mountainous Asian coast break the horizon. In recent years the unsatisfactory north entrance to the harbour has been closed. Extensive construction work and dredging have restored the original all-weather entrance to the harbour east of the castle, the ultimate aim being to provide Cyprus with a valuable port on the north of the island.

Kyrenia is no longer a backwater retreat for retired, excessively clubbable Empire-builders. It is gay and full of life. Sailing, fishing, water ski-ing and a warm sea attract visitors, and combine with the very special night life of the little town. The hotels are popular at week-ends with members of the armed forces and their families stationed elsewhere on the island. Kyrenia has an atmosphere as highly coloured as its picture-postcards.

HISTORY

In the main, the history of Kyrenia is the history of its castle. The extent of ancient fortifications is not known to any degree of accuracy, but it is likely that Achaean colonists founded the town in the tenth century B.C., and that it was a fully fledged city-state until ceding to Salamis in 312 B.C. Though the town is certain to have been walled at the time of the Arab raids of the seventh century A.D., it did not take an important place in history until 1191, when Isaac Comnenus, despot of the island, sent his wife and daughter to the early Byzantine castle for shelter against the invasion of Richard Cœur de Lion. However, while Richard was delayed by illness in Nicosia, he sent Guy de Lusignan into the attack, and the castle surrendered. During the following decade it enjoyed a great period of building and reconstruction, while during the minority of Hugues I the Regent John d'Ibelin converted it into a royal palace. It was then that Kyrenia and its castle attained its greatest grandeur and prestige, despite being involved precariously in the power politics of the Crusading years. After a siege during which the castle was occupied by the supporters of

Frederick II, it was held for the Crown by a Chief Castellan. Re-arrangement of the defences was undertaken after the loss of Acre in 1291, and this work probably continued sporadically until the late fourteenth century. The ultimate strength of the building then caused it to be used as a prison.

After the Genoese had seized Famagusta and sacked Nicosia in 1373 they proceeded to lay siege by land and sea to Kyrenia. The Castellan remained loyal, and withstood attack by the most powerful and vicious machines of war of the period. As soon as the Genoese troubles were over, in 1385 this Constable (now Jacques I) made Kyrenia Castle his favourite residence, and improved the amenities of the living-quarters.

During the Venetian occupation of the island the conquerors set about bringing the defences up to date and making them capable of withstanding heavy artillery fire. They rebuilt the west side by covering the existing Lusignan wall, and they placed great towers at the north-west and south-east corners. On the south side they filled the space between the Frankish and Byzantine walls with earth and rubble, to make for greater strength. In spite of mammoth building, the fortress was surrendered to the Turks in 1570 without a struggle when the garrison had become demoralized by the loss of Nicosia.

Under the British regime Kyrenia Castle was used as a prison and a police training school. It passed in 1950 into the charge of the Department of Antiquities, but was reoccupied by Security Forces during the EOKA troubles, and again used as a prison. It is now maintained by the Antiquities Department as an Ancient Monument.

KYRENIA CASTLE

Opening hours
Mid-May to mid-Sept. 7 a.m. to 7 p.m.
Mid-Sept. to mid-May 7.30 a.m. to dusk.
The official leaflet available from the custodian's office at the entrance contains an excellent map.

Although the exterior of the castle presents a bold geometric outline, the almost quadrangular interior is unexpectedly complicated, due to successive stages of occupation and reinforcement to the original fortifications, which entailed adding to them at many different levels. It can best be understood by following the route recommended in the official leaflet on sale at the custodian's office.

F

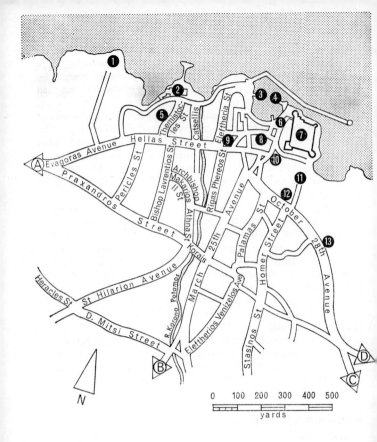

Kyrenia

1 Rock Ruby Hotel
2 Dome Hotel
3 Customs House Jetty
4 Ancient Lighthouse
5 Roman Catholic Church
6 Folk Art Museum
7 Kyrenia Castle and
   Shipwreck Museum
8 Mosque
9 Market
10 English Church
11 Country Club
12 Post Office
13 Hospital

A route to
   Lambousa (p. 171)
   Lapithos (p. 172)
   Cape Kormakiti & Ayia Irini (p.173)
   Soli and Vouni (pp. 128–31)
   Nicosia
B route to
   St Hilarion Castle (p. 165)
   Nicosia
C route to
   Bellapais Abbey (p. 161)
D route to
   Ayios Amvrosios
   Antiphonitis Monastery (p. 148)
   Kythrea (p. 145)
   Famagusta

0 100 200 300 400 500
yards

However, should time not allow for such a detailed inspection, the following are among the most interesting features:

Byzantine Chapel. This part of the twelfth-century construction stood outside the wall of the castle until it came to be encompassed by the Venetian wall and employed as part of their fortification in depth. At this period the dome was removed (it has recently been replaced), but the four marble columns, which probably come from an earlier basilica on the same site, were retained.

Gatehouse. The fourteenth-century structure of the Frankish period had one gate reinforced by a portcullis. The Lusignan coat of arms above the gate is contemporary, although it has been fixed into the structure in modern times. At the corner of the entrance passage there is the tomb of Sadik Pasha of Algiers, the commander of the Turkish fleet, who died in the year he took Kyrenia Castle.

The *Royal Apartments* of the later Lusignan kings may have occupied the west range of buildings. In the middle storey there is a palatial vaulted room with large windows which suggest that the outer Frankish wall at that point must have been of sufficient height to afford protection. Dungeons occupy the space below. There was a small Latin chapel and a sacristy on the upper storey.

The South-west Bastion illustrates the Venetian principle of fortification, whereby the south and west sections of the moat could be enfiladed from three levels. A postern gate leading back into the courtyard is decorated by three lions sculptured in relief. These and parts of a column used in a near-by wall suggest that they have been taken from a Roman building.

The space between the Byzantine and the Frankish walls of the south range was filled in by the Venetians, but in recent times these structures have been uncovered. A good part of the Frankish east range is in good condition. A large proportion of the buildings on this side of the courtyard were occupied by domestic offices.

The *North-East Tower*, which rises sheer above a glacis descending into the harbour (not far from the opening to the sea used in earlier days and now again made navigable), consists of two lofty chambers one above the other, with loopholes opening from arched recesses. This was a strictly military part of the castle, and held an important salient position.

The *North Range*, which has been used variously during this century as prison cells and naval barracks, can be prospected from roof-level, where the great battlements have recesses the size of sentry-boxes for the protection of the defenders.

The top of the *North-West Corner Tower*, reached from ground-level by a ramp, should not be omitted as a place of final appraisal, because from here is obtained the best view of the town and mountains, as well as demonstrating the immense field of fire of the Venetian fortress. It is also the best place from which to prospect the remains of the fortifications of the town itself.

MUSEUMS

Shipwreck Museum (in Kyrenia Castle)
Same Opening Hours

Exceptionally interesting remains of a fourth-century B.C. Greek ship salvaged off Kyrenia under the auspices of the University Museum of Pennsylvania in 1968. Items from its cargo are housed in a room near the entrance to the castle courtyard. This included numerous *amphorae* – twelve of which contained almonds, giving evidence of their original contents – and some very interesting grain mills. Certain other articles are presumed to have come from the ship's two galleys, and therefore have been of assistance in determining the construction of the vessel. It is estimated that the rebuilding of the ship, which owes its fine condition to having been entirely covered by sand, will take seven years. Meanwhile the timbers of its hull are on exhibition in the opposite range of castle buildings, enclosed in tanks of preservative liquid. The tanks are glass-topped, and their contents may be viewed from a gallery.

Folk Art Museum *Map* 6.
Opening Times
Mid-May to mid-Sept. 8.30 a.m. to 1 p.m.
4 p.m. to 6 p.m.
Mid-Sept. to mid-May 9 a.m. to 1 p.m.
2 p.m. to dusk.

Can be approached by stairs from the harbour, or from the higher level. Contains examples of needlework, bridal costumes, wood-carving, kitchen utensils, etc., donated by the late Lady Lock, whose house this was.

HARBOUR AND FORTIFICATIONS

In the centre of the inner horseshoe harbour stands a small tower which was either an ancient lighthouse or the pier to which a defensive chain could be attached at night-time. Of the medieval towers which protected the town on the south and west sides, only three remain, one on the western edge of the harbour, another in the main street near the municipal market and the third a little to the east. These must have been linked by walls, but most traces of them have disappeared.

EXCURSIONS FROM KYRENIA
Bellapais Abbey

Route Leave Kyrenia by the coast road which runs east (Route C on Kyrenia map) and almost immediately fork right for Bellapais Abbey (4 m.). A track maintained by the Department of Forests leads up from the village to Buffavento Castle (p. 133), a strenuous walk for the really energetic traveller, but donkeys may be hired in the village. The castle is reached more easily from Nicosia and the south side of the mountain range.

An alternative route back to Kyrenia is to keep to the upper road, which joins the main Nicosia–Kyrenia highway (+7 m.). (Not open at time of going to press.)

For Nicosia turn left at this junction (+16 m.).

St Hilarion Castle (p. 165) can be visited by turning right about ½ m. along the Nicosia road. But an excursion combining these two sights is not recommended unless unavoidable – because a thorough inspection of St Hilarion can be tiring if too hurried.

Accommodation
Studio Flats: Ambellia Village.
Ancient Monument
Bellapais Abbey
The custodian has an office near the entrance to the abbey.
Opening hours
Summer 7 a.m. to 7 p.m.
Winter 7.30 a.m. to dusk.

Almost immediately after leaving Kyrenia, fork right off coast road.

[3½ m.] The village of **Bellapais** has such a beautiful situation and aspect on the gentler slopes of the Northern range that a visit to it would be memorable even if it did not possess the great Gothic abbey which is considered to be the finest of all the monuments of the Lusignan dynasty (opening hours above). This village became Lawrence Durrell's home when he came to Cyprus in 1953. He has written charmingly of its life in *Bitter Lemons*. The Tree of Idleness still exerts its insidious influence on all who sit in its shade, while oranges and lemons grow magically on a single tree in the forecourt of the church. New buildings in the village square and the more obtrusive Ambellia development scheme at a higher level will merge into the scene in due course, if only because trees and gardens establish themselves rapidly where there is no great shortage of water.

HISTORY OF BELLAPAIS ABBEY

Gothic architecture is a rarity in Cyprus, and Bellapais Abbey is a superlative example. The design is worthy of its foundation and patronage over a long period by the Lusignan kings. It was founded, in all probability, by Amaury de Lusignan, who succeeded his brother Guy in 1194, and was crowned king of Cyprus in Nicosia three years later. When Jerusalem was lost, King Hugues I granted these lands to displaced Augustinians, who were joined by Norbertine or Premonstratensian canons of the French order founded at Laon in 1120. The entire community adopted this latter rule early in the thirteenth century and donned the white habit which is the origin of references in fifteenth- and sixteenth-century documents to the 'White Abbey'. Hugues III (1267–84) and his successors increased the size and wealth of the abbey, and awarded the abbot the privilege of wearing a mitre, also a gilded sword and spurs in knightly fashion when riding abroad. The zenith of the abbey's influence occurred before the arrival of the Genoese in 1373, when the church and monastic buildings were looted. Yet during the subsequent period of government of the island by the Venetians, the position of Abbot of Bellapais was still greatly prized, and on a number of occasions there were rival claimants. But decline had set in before the Turkish occupation of 1571; a delegate of the Venetian Senate concerned in making a report on Cyprus revealed that some of the brethren had as many as three wives, and that the abbey's revenues were being misappropriated for the benefit of their families. The structure of the abbey began to deteriorate and fall from the sixteenth century onwards, though the Turks, who had seized the abbey's property, permitted the villagers to continue using the church.

DESCRIPTION OF ABBEY

The original simple arch of the *Gateway* had good carvings on its corbels. These are understood to have comprised the symbols of the four Evangelists, but two have been concealed by a fourteenth-century tower built to house the mechanism of a drawbridge. The *Church*, which is across a forecourt and immediately opposite the entrance, is the oldest surviving part of the abbey buildings, being either thirteenth- or fourteenth-century. Jeffery points out its similarity to the contemporary Much Wenlock Abbey in Shropshire. The porch has recesses at the north and south ends. These may have been intended to contain the tombs of King Hugues III and Seneschals of the d'Ibelin family. Faint fragments of painting are attributed to the Italian cinquecento period, though some may be earlier. The church has the architectural distinction of being provided with a flat roof. This was covered with local terrazzo – an economical finishing technique which has resulted in the disintegration of many ancient monuments in Cyprus.

Adjustments to the interior of the church have had to be made in accordance with its conversion to the Greek Orthodox rite. The provision of an iconostasis where none was intended cannot help but detract from the good proportions of the design, but it is still a lovely and graceful building. Note in particular the 'French' capitals of the thirteenth-century pillars, and the fragmentary painted medallion of the Apostle James on the west wall. The night stair, now blocked, in the wall of the north transept provided access from the dormitory. There was also a smaller spiral staircase to the west of this, by which the treasury and the roof were reached. The remainder of the monastic buildings and the cloister should be approached through the forecourt outside the west entrance to the church.

The *Cloister* is a place of obvious beauty, greatly embellished by four pencil-slim cypresses and a show of brightly coloured flowers which go well with the stone and the herbs which are traditionally associated with community life and cookery. The delicate tracery of the arcades, the fascinating and varied detail of the corbels which support the rib vaults and the central bosses should all be closely scrutinized. A most interesting feature in the north-west corner of the cloister is a marble sarcophagus of the second century A.D. which has been adapted to form a marble lavabo decorated by attractive swags of carving in high relief. It was here that the monks washed their hands before proceeding through the main entrance to the *Refectory*. This great vaulted room is in excellent condition. It has a staircase set in the thickness of the north wall which leads to a jutting pulpit from which the Scriptures were read during meals. Six uniformly spaced windows in the north wall provide a wonderful view of the sea and, on clear days, the opposite coasts of Asia Minor.

The *Chapter House* adjoining the undercroft, both of which are to the east of the cloister, has interesting carvings which include a central marble pillar thought to have formed part of an early Byzantine church in Lambousa. The monks' *Dormitory*, which originally extended over the whole of the undercroft and chapter house, is reached by the night stair on the south side of the cloister. Each monk was provided with a window and a wall cupboard at the head of his bed, in which he could keep his few personal possessions. These can be seen in the surviving west wall.

The *Treasury*, which is above the north aisle of the church, is reached from the roof over the south side of the cloister. Damage to wall cupboards suggests that these were forced by the Genoese invaders who violated the church at the end of the fourteenth century. The *Cellarium* and the *Kitchens* were situated on the west side of the cloister and refectory. Near the ruins of these domestic offices a narrow flight of stairs leads down into two *vaulted rooms* which extend the full length of the Refectory immediately above them. These were once used as storehouses for the community's agricultural produce.

St Hilarion Castle *

Route Follow the main Kyrenia–Nicosia highway (Route B on Kyrenia map) turning right before reaching the highest point of the mountain pass for St Hilarion Castle (7 m.).

For Nicosia turn to the right when regaining the main Nicosia–Kyrenia road (14 m.). Alternatively continue west after descending from the castle, and connect with the Forest Road to Larnaca-tis-Lapithou, from which a secondary road leads to Kondemenos and the excellent new road to Nicosia (+28 m.).

Bellapais Abbey (p. 161) is reached from St Hilarion by taking a right turning after rejoining the direct Nicosia–Kyrenia highway about ½ m. in the Kyrenia direction, although a combined excursion to both these sites should be avoided if the most is to be got out of them. At the time of going to press, however, the linking road is closed.

Ancient Monument
St Hilarion Castle
Official leaflet available from the Cyprus Museum.
Opening hours
Mid-May to mid-Sept. 9 a.m. to 1 p.m.
       4.30 p.m. to 6.30 p.m.
Mid-Sept. to mid-May 9 a.m. to 1 p.m.
      2.30 p.m. to dusk.

[4½ m.] Turn right off main road.

[7 m.] A further turn to the right leads after a series of bends to the main guard of *St Hilarion Castle*.

This most glamorous of castles stands splendidly 2,380 ft above sea-level, yet appearing to be within a giant's stone's throw of the mountains of Anatolia.

HISTORY OF ST HILARION CASTLE

The first habitation here was the cell of a hermit – either the St Hilarion known to have been a native of Palestine or else a lesser recluse of the same name. Whoever he was, he attracted pilgrims and devotees in numbers; so that a monastic foundation was the logical outcome. It seems probable that this mountain-top was first put to a secular use late in the eleventh century, at a time when it was imperative that the northern coast should be fortified against

* This is a strongpoint of the sector of the Kyrenia mountains which at the time of going to press is held by the Turkish Cypriots. Though holders of neutral passports will have little difficulty in gaining access to the castle, it may be that certain strategic points on the heights will be out of bounds to them. They may also find themselves put in the charge of a not too disturbing military escort. No photography is permitted.

the Turks, whose practice it was to despoil the outlying provinces of Asia Minor. The new overall defensive scheme linked St Hilarion with Kyrenia at the foot of St Hilarion's peak, and Buffavento and Kantara to the east.

These four strong castles were the last to be reduced during the campaign of Richard Cœur de Lion in 1191. At the time when Richard was ill in Nicosia, Isaac Comnenus ordered the Castle of St Hilarion to be surrendered to Guy de Lusignan. The defences were strengthened and reorganized in 1229, and during the four ensuing years the castle was a key position in bitter struggles, first for the regency and then for total sovereignty of the island. A peaceful period of 140 years followed these troubles, and during this time improvements were carried out with the object of making the place attractive and comfortable as the summer residence of the Lusignan royal family. But violence broke out again in 1373, when the Regent, John, Prince of Antioch, held out against the attacks of the Genoese. He was able to do this by means of the assistance of Bulgarian mercenaries, but when he was falsely persuaded that these Bulgarians intended treachery he caused them to be thrown out of a window over a sheer drop, defeating his own interests because he was thereafter without a guard. Soon after the occupation of the island by the Venetians in 1489, the castle was 'slighted' – dismantled and rendered of no account – as an economy measure.

DESCRIPTION OF CASTLE

It can be seen to this day in what respects the Lusignans improved the castle's defences, as well as converting it to the standard of comfort necessary for a royal residence. The fortifications consist of three wards, the uppermost perched on the double-crested summit of the mountain, known originally as Didymus (the twins), a name which was later corrupted by the Franks to the even more charming 'Dieudamour'.

The castle is approached through an outer gate; the gatehouse to the right has been restored and is used for the display of post-cards, souvenirs, etc. The custodian's office is situated immediately to the left after entering the main gateway to the *Lower Ward* (*Map* 4). Unless in possession of unlimited time, with perhaps the prospect of a second visit, it is advisable for newcomers to follow the recognized upward route which begins by turning at an angle around a building used in the Lusignan period as stables. (The surrounding outer wall of Byzantine construction, with its jutting semicircular towers, can be explored later, should time permit.) The function of this lower ward, of course, was to accommodate the castle's soldiery, horses and equipment. The buildings contained in it were entirely functional.

The entrance to the *Middle Ward* is through a vaulted passage cut by the Lusignans in the Byzantine bailey, and above what was a secondary defence in the form of a drawbridge. There is access to the *Church* (*Map* **13**) on the right. This is built in the form of a parallelogram with pillars which originally carried a dome. (The one similar church in Cyprus is at the Monastery of Antiphonitis.) Near to the church and the annexes which relate to it, there is a graceful *Belvedere* (*Map* **14**) built in the peaceful period of Lusignan rule, with the intention not of being a defensive look-out, but for the sole purpose of affording a beautiful view – as its name implies. This is part of an extensive group of mainly domestic rooms. The more palatial buildings at the north-east corner are likely to have been royal quarters in the thirteenth century, previous to the provision of grander accommodation in the upper ward for the Lusignan royal family. Part of this Byzantine section has recently been converted for use as a restaurant equipped with panoramic views.* The red roofing tiles appear inappropriate, though this may have been the type of material used in the original buildings. Experts differ. It has also been suggested that the roofs were thatched – a theory borne out by the total absence among the remains of any less perishable roofing material.

The *Upper Ward* is approached by a winding and steep path above a large open cistern to the right. Approach paths here and farther up the slope have been affected by landslides and earthquakes, and their original courses are in doubt. To the left, and in front of the entrance, another steep path and flight of steps leads to what is known as *Prince John's Tower*. It is perched precipitously above sheer drops on three sides, and has been identified as the scene of the violent death of the Bulgarian mercenaries. (This additional climb should be attempted only by the adventurous and cool-headed.) The upper ward is entered through an arch guarded on the right by a tower similar in design to those of the outer defences. The courtyard is contained by the twin moun-

* At the date of going to press, only basic refreshments are on sale.

Postern

UPPER WARD

Summit
▲ 2577 ft

Entrance through arched gate

St Hilarion Castle

Lower Ward
1 Gatehouse
2 Barbican
3 Custodian's Quarters
4 Custodian's Office
5 Cistern
6 South Tower
7 South-west corner Tower
8 Stables
9 Cisterns
10 Gatehouse
11 Byzantine Baths
12 Postern

Middle Ward
13 Byzantine Church
14 Belvedere
15 Hall
16 Buttery
17 Kitchen Block
18 Castellan's Quarters
19 Royal Apartments
20 Terrace
21 Vaulted Chambers
22 Postern
23 Open Tank

Upper Ward
24 Frankish Tower
25 Frankish Tower
26 Tower
27 Service Buildings
28 Lusignan Royal Apartments
29 Closet

0 10 20 30 40 50
yards

N

MIDDLE
WARD

Prince
John's
Tower

LOWER
WARD

Gate

Passage

Tunnel

footpath

parapet walk

Main
Entrance

Entrance
(outer gate)

tain peaks to the left and right, while immediately opposite the entrance there are the romantic remains of the royal residence, built in two storeys and looking west over an impregnable precipice towards Lapithos and the high mountains tapering away in the direction of Cape Kormakiti. The elegant windows in the upper storey are more sophisticated than any previously encountered. One, with tracery and side-seats, is known as the *Queen's Window*. The upper ramparts of the castle, and two square towers which evidently replaced Byzantine round towers, are to the south. They are reached from the courtyard by another steep path.

Lambousa, Cape Kormakiti and Ayia Irini

Route Follow the coast road leading west, (Route A on Kyrenia map) which has been engineered as an excellent and scenic but circuitous link between Nicosia and Kyrenia. This now by-passes Karavas (7½ m.), Lambousa and Akhiropiitos Monastery (+1 m.) and Lapithos (8½ m.). Fork right (20 m.) before Myrtou for Cape Kormakiti (28 m.) and return to Dhiorios, 1 m. west of Myrtou, for Ayia Irini (+ 9 m.).

For Nicosia rejoin the main road near Myrtou. This approaches the city by way of Skylloura and Yerolakkos.

Soli and Vouni (pp. 128–31) (+30 m.) can be reached from Dhiorios (1 m. west of Myrtou) via Morphou (p. 127), but an overnight stop is recommended if many or all of the suggested detours are made.

Hotels

At Karavas:	Mare Monte (luxury self-contained accommodation, restaurant and bars, etc.).
	3rd Klearchos, Zephyros (awaiting classification).
At Lapithos:	4th Romantzo.
At Vavilas:	4th Avro.

The road west from Kyrenia keeps in touch with bays and headlands where there is good bathing. Most of the villages are a short distance inland.

[3 m.] **Ayios Yeoryios** is famous for pottery. The fossilized bones of pigmy hippopotami have been found in quantity not far from a tiny chapel near the sea. In the belief that these were the remains of their patron saint, Ayios Phanourios, the villagers consumed them in powdered form as a sovereign remedy for various diseases.

[7½ m.] Though the village of **Karavas** with its luxuriant orange and lemon groves lies to the left of the road, the hotels are on the right, or sea, side. The *Shrine of Panayia Galaterosa*, cut into the rock, contains a fragmentary wall-painting depicting St John the Baptist.

A right turn below Karavas leads in about half a mile to the coast through an area of ruins which is all that survives of the old city of *Lambousa*.

LAMBOUSA

This was founded in the latter part of the eighth century B.C. and reached the height of its power during the Roman and Byzantine periods. Though, due to its vulnerable seaboard position, Lambousa was sacked by the Arabs in the seventh century A.D., it regained its status in the Middle Ages.*

The disused *Monastery of Akhiropiitos* presents a melancholy and blank-looking façade on the brink of the sea, not far from the ruins of a Byzantine lighthouse and fishponds. The name signifies 'Built Without Hands', to perpetuate the tradition that the Blessed Virgin translated the monastery in its entirety from Asia Minor in order to prevent its desecration by heathens. Inside the enclosure, surrounded by two-storeyed cloisters and old buildings at present accommodating a family of caretakers and their farm animals, there is a very beautiful church which is of special interest owing to its combination of different periods of architecture, starting with the central double-domed and cruciform main construction of the fourteenth century. At the end of the fifteenth or beginning of the sixteenth century, an apse of absurdly large dimensions was substituted for an older one which had fallen into disrepair, and which belonged to the early Christian basilica, the eastern portion of which has been excavated by the Department of Antiquities. The existing large apse is seven-sided externally and semicircular within. A narthex and exonarthex were added at the west end in the fifteenth century. The gypsum tomb of the donor of these improvements – Alessandro Flatros, who died in 1563 – shows him in the court dress of the period. The iconostasis is mainly seventeenth-century workmanship, but it contains a lower panel fashioned from a Byzantine plaque. The majority of the icons were painted in the eighteenth century. The oldest and the most revered, which represents St Veronica and the Holy Handkerchief, was covered

* A military installation occupies part of the area, and at the time of going to press access is allowed only to the Monastery (afternoons only).

with silver-gilt in 1814. This is the object of great veneration, supported by an unsubstantiated legend that the wonder-working handkerchief or shroud was kept here before being taken to Turin by a princess of the House of Savoy.

A great number of sculptured stones from the Roman and Byzantine cities have been brought for safe keeping into the enclosure. Outside, in the midst of a desolation which a combination of circumstances has made a characteristic of many sites in Cyprus, there are two interesting churches absolutely distinct from the monastery. The nearest is the *Chapel of St Evlambios*, which presents a peculiar aspect because of its original form as a hole hewn in the rock which later was quarried away, leaving the cave-chapel standing in one detached block of stone. It is here that beautiful sixth-century silver plates depicting the life of King David were found. Some of these are in Room VII of the Cyprus Museum, the remainder being apportioned between the British Museum and the Metropolitan Museum of New York. They are of additional interest because they bear the signs recognizable as the earliest examples of the hall-marking of silver. The prominent *Church of St Evlalios*, nearer the sea, dates from the sixteenth century.

[8½ m.] The pretty village of **Lapithos** (hotel p. 170) is about a mile beyond Karavas, high above the main road. A second left turn leads up to a perpetual spring which issues from the rock at *Kephalovryso*, 850 ft above sea-level. This generous water supply is responsible for the verdancy and the flourishing fruit farms below. It also affected the choice of Lapithos as a Greek settlement, as one of the four principal capitals of the Romans and as a town of ten thousand inhabitants under the Lusignans. Lambousa and Lapithos were not so much one town as two poles between which the population alternated in obedience to the demands of different centuries. Pottery and weaving are traditional industries in the present-day village, but the manufacture of silk cloth is being driven out of existence by the popularity and cheapness of synthetic fibres.

The churches of Lapithos contain very little of particular interest, with the possible exception of the modern *Church of St Anastasia* which has in its *bema* an elaborate Roman sepulchral monument to a certain Seleukios. It has an attractive design of vine-leaves carved in high relief in limestone.

[12½ m.] You could make a short detour (right turn) to the fishing village of **Vavilas** (hotel p. 170).

[13½ m.] Five miles beyond Lapithos the road turns inland, about 1 m. beyond the turning off to the **Vasilia** and the scenic but rough route to **Larnaca-tis-Lapithou** and what was planned to be the western end of a continuous Forest Road.

[16½ m.] Three miles of well-engineered gradients climb through the western foothills of the Kyrenia range. Fork right just before **Myrtou** is by-passed, and take the road to the Maronite village of **Kormakiti**, which is 6 m. distant from *Cape Kormakiti* at the north-western extremity of the island. The one feature of interest is the lighthouse at the tip of the promontory.

Return to the fork near Myrtou, turning right, then right again in **Dhiorios**. This branch road leads after 5 m. to the village of **Ayia Irini**, 1 m. inland from the dunes which border the wide sweep of Morphou Bay. It was near Ayia Irini that the fascinating collection of terracotta figures in the Cyprus Museum was discovered. They come from a temenos excavated by the Swedish Expedition of 1929 on a site in use from the late Bronze Age (*c.* 1300–1050 B.C.) to the end of the sixth century B.C.

FAMAGUSTA

Population 41,000.
Information
Tourist Bureau: 58 Evagoras Ave ; *Map* **11.**
Old City Antiquities Office: Othello Tower; *Map* **4.**
Hotels
De luxe Cypriana ; Grecian.
1st (A) Constantia ; Florida ; King George. Awaiting classification : Esperia Tower ;
         Golden Mariana ; Marina ; Salaminia Tower ; Venus Beach ; Sandy Beach ;
         Golden Plage ; Asterias ; Trojan ; Aspelia.
1st (B) Famagusta Palace.
2nd (B) Othello. Awaiting classification : Savoy ; Harry's.
3rd   Kantara ; Panorama.
4th   Kastella ; Middle East ; Troödos ; Victoria ; Argentina. Awaiting classifica-
         tion : Harbour ; Byzantium ; New Salamis. (See also p. 187.)
Self-catering: Lordos Hotel Apartments ; Lordos Etoile Court ; Apollo Flats ; Attika
Hotel Apartments ; Regina.
All the hotels are situated outside the Old City, many of them lining the seemingly
limitless stretch of sands to the south. The situation favours skyscraper development
with direct access to the beach, and as such is unique in Cyprus. As new hotels are
in course of construction, while others have reached the drawing-board stage, it is
more than ever necessary to consult the current Hotels Guide before making a selec-
tion. The Golden Sands holiday complex, on a 40-acre site, is due for completion in
1973.
Restaurants and Bars
Avenida Tavern, Miaoulis St.
Boccaccio Restaurant-Café, Franklin Roosevelt Ave.
Edelweiss Café, Franklin Roosevelt Ave.
Famagusta Tavern, Franklin Roosevelt Ave.
Frixos Beach.
Kalamies, Kennedy Ave.
Kamares (Cypriot cuisine), Esperidon St.
Quo Vadis, Altin Tabya Road (Old City).
Chimney Pot Pub, Evagoras Ave.
All the hotels do a lively trade in their restaurants and bars. At the other extreme come
the beach restaurants, particularly those two immediately south of the Florida Hotel,
which serve grills, fish and *mezé* and where midday 'undress' is the norm. As for the
others, there are so many, ranging from the very chic to family establishments, that
our list is inevitably far from comprehensive. Floor shows and dancing feature at some
of these, so that at a later stage of the evening they function as night clubs, as does the
Royal Tombs Discotheque, 92 Evagoras Avenue, and the Perroquet, Franklin
Roosevelt Ave.
Churches
Anglican St Mark's, George V Avenue *Map* **6.**
Roman Catholic and Maronite Santa Maria off Aeolus St *Map* **14.**
Cinemas
Hadjhambis (open-air in summer) ; Heracleon, Idyll ; Olympia ; Rio.
Club
Anchorage Sailing Club (south of Florida Hotel).
Bathing and Water Sports
Besides the popular beaches stretching southwards from the reef opposite the Con-
stantia Hotel to the Golden Sands area and beyond, bathing is possible north of the
port and the Old City. This sandy coast, backed by dunes, extends beyond Salamis
and its new hotels to Boghaz (15 m.), a pleasant small sea-side village with a hotel
and restaurant.

All forms of aquatic sports are catered for from the main beach, which is in fact the playground of the island. A new marina is to be constructed to increase the existing facilities for sail and powered craft.

A preliminary warning should be given to intending visitors to Famagusta. Not only is this two towns – the Old City and Varosha, which spreads to the south – but these are as distinct as they could possibly be. Varosha, which was once almost entirely suburban, now contains everything of modern importance from the point of view of administration, shopping, hotels and transport centres. In fact, its name is largely obsolete, and 'Famagusta' covers both parts of the town. The inner areas of the famous walled city are likely to come as a shock even to people familiar with the words of H. V. Morton: 'Medieval Famagusta is one of the most remarkable ruins in the world, and it could be made one of the wonders of the world by one millionaire in search of immortality.'*

The important word here, although not immediately recognizable as such, is 'ruins'. The great Venetian walls and bastions stand firm, as does the citadel to which the story of Othello has attached itself, but within their ring there is more desolation than is conceivable from an outside standpoint. Except for one new housing area, the inhabitants crowd into the habitable areas of winding streets intersected by narrow alleys, surrounded on all sides by acres of fallen stone. The cathedral is the best-preserved ancient building, and without doubt it owes its continued existence to the fact that it has been converted to Muslim use as a mosque. In the absence of H. V. Morton's millionaire, no efforts have been made to rebuild and repopulate the Old City, which is traditionally Turkish. Though the inhabitants were integrated into the Republic as Turkish Cypriots, they retained their sense of nationality as regards language and way of life, and the Old Town remained under the local government of the Turkish section of the island's community.†

In spite of the fascination of the history, architecture and life of the Old City, visitors will not fail to appreciate the modern amenities of the sprawling southern half of Famagusta which has developed from the 'suburb' of Varosha. As in the case of Nicosia, the new development fulfils modern needs in a way that would not

* *In the Steps of St Paul* (Methuen & Co., London).
† At the time of going to press Greek Cypriots do not go into the Old City, though its Turkish inhabitants have greater freedom of movement. Holders of foreign passports experience no difficulty in entering through the Land Gate.

FAMAGUSTA
OLD CITY

Salamis Ave

Land Gate

Arsinoe Street

Maria Singlitiki Street

Gladstor

Anexartisias Avenue

3

Anexartisias Street

Aeolus St

St Helen

14

Famagusta/Varosha

1 Constantia Hotel
2 Municipal Stadium
3 Police Station
4 Salaminia Tower Hotel
5 Florida Hotel
6 St Mark's Church (Anglican)
7 Aspelia Hotel
8 Golden Mariana Hotel
9 Gymnasium Stadium
10 King George Hotel
11 Tourist Information Bureau
12 Gymnasium
13 Public Gardens
14 Roman Catholic and Maronite Church
15 Municipal Market
16 Post Office
17 Esperia Tower Hotel
18 District Museum (p. 186)

A   route to
     Enkomi/Alasia (p. 201)
     Salamis (p. 187)
     St Barnabas Monastery (p. 199)
     Trikomo (p. 205)
     Kantara Castle (p. 206)
     Karpas Peninsula (pp. 209–13)
B   route to
     Nicosia
     Kyrenia via Lefkoniko
C   route to
     Larnaca
     Limassol and Paphos via Larnaca
D   route to
     Dherinia
     Paralimni
     Ayia Napa Monastery (p. 207)
     Cape Greco
E   route to
     Golden Sands & Marina, Sandy Beach,
     Grecian, Louizianna & Cypriana Hotels
     (p. 174)

N

0   100   200   300   400   50

yards

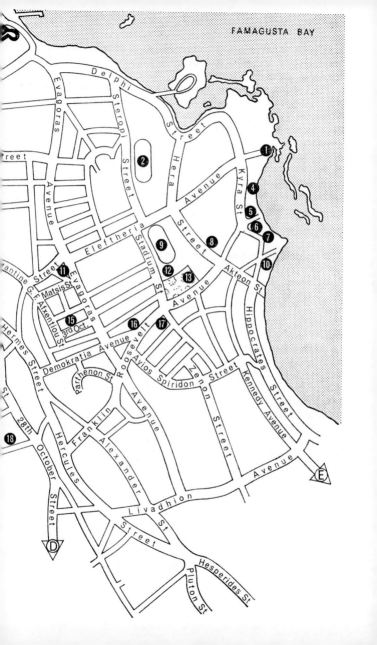

have been possible in a circumscribed area. Hotels, shops, public buildings and, above all, safe beaches make the perfect antidote to strenuous sightseeing programmes.

The beaches for the most part are south of the best deep-water port in Cyprus, where ships lie alongside the quays immediately below the Venetian sea-defences. Substantial recent harbour works have increased the capacity of the port, which is of supreme importance to the country's export and import trades. There are plans for a yachting marina immediately north of the Constantia Hotel. At present the main anchorage for sailing boats and the headquarters for water ski-ing and other sports is in the small bay within the reef to the east of the Florida Hotel.

HISTORY

Famagusta's rise to prominence began in 1291 when the merchants of Acre fled to Cyprus after the fall of their city had brought the last Crusade to an end. During the following years the prosperity of the city became fabled throughout Europe. It was in Famagusta's Cathedral of St Nicholas that the Lusignan kings were crowned as Kings of Jerusalem until 1372, when the continuing rivalry between Genoese and Venetians flared into open fighting as a result of a quarrel over precedence at Peter II's coronation.

When the Venetians took over the island in 1489, the abdication ceremony of Caterina Cornaro having been carried out in St Nicholas Cathedral, Famagusta was converted into the fortified city that can be seen today. As a result, in 1570 the city was able to hold out for five months against the Turks and only surrendered on honourable terms, which were, however, subsequently broken (p. 89). The present desolation of the Old City is largely the result of the fierce fighting that took place at that time, augmented by earthquake and later by the removal of building material for the construction of the Suez Canal.

FORTIFICATIONS

Except when otherwise stated, all map references to Old City map.
The Old City of Famagusta is totally surrounded by walls which remain remarkably complete. They average 50 ft in height and at

certain points are 27 ft thick, and form a rough rectangle, the easternmost side of which follows the line of the shore. Originally there were two gates, the Sea Gate and the Land Gate, but two additional openings have had to be made to cope with modern traffic. Of the ten bastions, the greatest and most impressive is the *Martinengo Bastion* (*Map* a). Following the circuit east of the Martinengo, the other bastions are named the *Mozzo* (*Map* b), the *Diamante* (*Map* c), the *Djamboulat* (*Map* f), the *Camposanto* (*Map* g), the *Andruzzi* (*Map* h), the *Santa Napa* (*Map* j), the *Diocare* (*Map* l), the *Moratto* (*Map* m), the *Palacazaro* (*Map* n) – most of them such good descriptive Italian names for typically Venetian fortifications that it is unnecessary to bother with the Turkish equivalents. The tomb of Djamboulat Bey, the Turkish general who in 1571 lost his life while charging the most vicious of Venetian engines of war used in the defence of the Arsenal, is in the bastion near where he fell, and which now carries his name (p. 185).

Another salient point of fortification which deserves special attention is the *Land Gate* (*Map* k) with its original arch of 30 ft (no longer in use as a gate) which was protected by the existing Ravelin, which comprises a complex of guardrooms and dungeons.

Citadel (Othello's Tower)
Map d.

Opening hours; also for Antiquities Office
Mid-May to mid-Sept. Daily 9 a.m. to 1 p.m.
3 p.m. to 6 p.m.
Mid-Sept. to mid-May Daily 9 a.m. to 1 p.m
2.30 p.m. to dusk.

The Citadel is a square fourteenth-century building with four circular towers at the corners. It was remodelled by Nicolo Foscarini in 1492. His name appears alongside the winged lion of Venice above the main entrance. Famagusta may well remain identified with the 'seaport of Cyprus' described by Shakespeare in *Othello*. But the Lieutenant-Governor of Cyprus from 1506 to 1508, one Christoforo Moro, had nothing of the Moor about him, except possibly his name, which may have given rise to a misapprehension on the part of Shakespeare – unless he was taking literary licence. In any event, the literary licence or the misapprehension is likely to be perpetuated. People enjoy identifying the Citadel with Othello's tower.

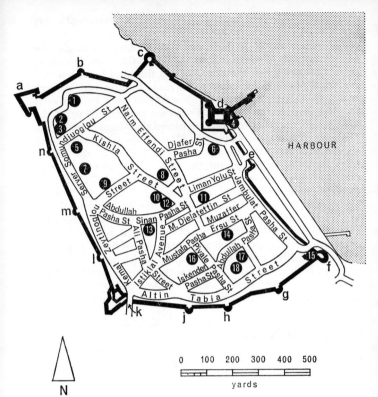

Famagusta – Old City

CHURCHES AND MOSQUES*

All map references are to Old City map.

Cathedral of St Nicholas (Lala Mustafa Mosque)
Map 11.

In 1298, at a time when the importance of Famagusta had increased considerably as a result of the influx of Christians of wealth and importance from Acre, it was decided that the city deserved a magnificent Latin cathedral. The edifice was consecrated in 1326. It is a complete example of Gothic architecture of the early fourteenth century, owing to its lack of any of the subsequent modifications usual in comparable Continental cathedrals. The side chapels are the only additions to the original design. In many respects the plan resembles that of St Sophia in Nicosia, the main difference being that the gallery of circulation around the upper parts of the church, instead of being internal as in St Sophia, follows an external passage at the level of the buttresses. The western face, and indeed the whole structure, is more imposing than that of its counterpart in Nicosia. It has been provided with a single minaret, of no great prominence.

As in the case of St Sophia, the church's conversion to Muslim use entailed the removal of all ornaments and church furnishings, especially those bearing any representation of the human figure. Some tomb slabs in the north aisle have escaped destruction. Frescoes have been covered with whitewash, stained glass has been shattered and the altars demolished. But one compensation is that the architectural conception can now be viewed as a dignified whole, without clutter. Much damage was done to the structure by Turkish bombardment in 1571, and by earthquake in 1735.

The west front is the greatest glory of the cathedral. This has three shallow doorways of four orders surmounted by gabled canopies. It is interesting to remember that the balcony above these doors was used until 1372 for coronation ceremonies. In fact, it was here that the Lusignan kings of Cyprus, who had already been crowned in Nicosia, came for their second coronation as Kings of Jerusalem, a celebration which attracted great pomp and public notice but which conferred nothing more than a token sovereignty. At that time the piazza in front was larger than it is now, and held

---

* Since 1963, when the Turkish citizens of Famagusta took on exclusive occupation of the Old City, many of the ruined and half-ruined churches have been used for secular purposes. When once more these come under the care of the Department of Antiquities a complete reappraisal may have to be made.

huge crowds. The great rose window of six lights in the west front has been compared to the more ornate west window of Lichfield Cathedral, and the twin towers to those of Rheims.

PARVIS

One of the most interesting features of the cathedral precincts is the *Parvis* or square where the coronation crowds assembled. This had the reputation of being the largest in Europe. It is now bounded on the south by a *Loggia* in the Venetian style, which is thought to have been used as an open-air grammar school attached to the cathedral. A wide central doorway of four orders is flanked by circular windows surmounted by coats of arms sculptured in marble – probably those of the builder. Under the twin windows, forming marble seating, there is a fragmentary sculptured frieze, believed to have once been part of the cornice of a Roman temple. The subject, animals chasing each other through a spiral of foliage, is most attractive. The vaulted hall of this open-air building, which appears at one time to have had a second storey, now houses a fountain used for Muslim ablutions.

Greek Orthodox Cathedral (St George of the Greeks)
Map 14.

The original Byzantine cathedral dedicated to St Epiphanios was retained in its entirety when, in emulation of the new Latin cathedral, a vast Gothic structure was added to its north side. The simple, original building of two aisles, each terminating in a semicircular apse, probably owed its survival to having been the burial place of St Epiphanios, though the saint's remains had long since been removed to Constantinople. Both the Byzantine and the Gothic structures suffered tremendous damage in the Turkish bombardment. But it has been suggested that some of the damage done to the larger building was due to the weakness of the outer walls, because they were provided with a great many spaces for the tombs of founders, and these may well have affected the stability of the fabric. It is worth mentioning that the object of this late fourteenth-century building practice was to produce endowments, and therefore it is ironic if it should have, literally, contributed to this church's downfall.

St George of the Latins Church
Map 6.
Very little survives of the earliest example of Gothic architecture in Famagusta. The church is believed to have been built during the time that St Louis, King of France, established his base in Cyprus for the military operations known as the Egyptian Crusade. Fallen masonry suggests that this must have been a very fine and well-decorated building.

Franciscan Church
Map 10.
The altar in the ruins of the south chapel was an interesting survival of a church described by Nicolai Martoni, a fourteenth-century notary and traveller, as 'a house of St Francis, passing fair, with a fair cloister, a dormitory, many cells and other rooms, with a fine garden, and a quantity of conduits, wells and cisterns'. He adds that the guardian informed him that the friars lived badly and received indifferent alms.

Church of SS Peter and Paul
Map 13.
This church, which was originally dedicated to St Catherine, is thought to have been built by a merchant in the middle of the fourteenth century from the proceeds of a successful trading venture. It escaped damage during the Turkish occupation by its conversion into a mosque. The north doorway, decorated with coats of arms which are partially erased, has a fine thirteenth-century door which is likely to have been brought from some earlier church.

Armenian Church
Map 2.
This was built in 1346 for the use of Armenian refugees. The acoustic vases in the walls are of interest. Unfortunately the original wall-paintings have disappeared. In earlier days the Paschal Lamb used to be roasted inside the church, and the Armenian bishop consumed the first piece.

Nestorian Church
Map 9.

This is believed to have been founded in 1359. It once declined into use as a camel stable. The Greek community, who at one period took over the church, preferred that it should be known as Ayios Georghios Xorinos, or St George the Exiler. There is a belief that if dust from the floor of the church is placed in the house of an enemy he will either die within the year or leave the island. The Nestorians used the Chaldean language in their liturgy, and believed in the dual nature of Christ.

Other Churches and Mosques

Other churches may be visited, but rather in the way of pilgrimage to ruins than for their architectural value. There is the *Carmelite Church* (*Map* 3), notable for the coats of arms painted on its walls; the *Tanner's Mosque* (*Map* 5), believed to have originated as a Christian church of the sixteenth century, and with walls containing acoustic vases; *St Anna's Church* (*Map* 7), for mural paintings with Latin inscriptions; the twin *Templars' and Hospitaller's Churches* (*Map* 8), of which the larger and earlier is that of the Knights Templar, the Church of the Hospitallers being distinguished by sockets at the eaves for banner staves; the *Church of the Holy Cross* (Stavros) (*Map* 16), which has been used as a mosque and as a warehouse; *Ayia Zoni* (*Map* 18), or the Holy Girdle, dating from the fifteenth century; and the *Church of St Nicholas* (*Map* 17), a ruined Byzantine building originally surmounted by two domes. It is said that the sites of a hundred churches can still be pointed out in Famagusta.

OTHER SIGHTS

Underground Chambers
Map 1.

An underground cavern discovered in 1966 is reached from the road running parallel to the wall connecting the Martinengo and Mozzo bastions. This consists of two huge chambers, roughly at right angles to each other and carved out of the natural rock, leaving pillars of stone as supports. It is estimated that the area could have accommodated 2,000 persons. Ventilation shafts provide a constant temperature and dry atmosphere. There are signs of domestic fires, recesses for storage and mangers for horses, as well as seating for some of the occupants. The present sandy floor gives a false level, and a depression near the angle between the two chambers indicates that cisterns for water storage may exist below. Though coins of the Venetian period were discovered during the preliminary clearance of the caves, and suggest that this was a place of refuge during the siege of the city, the original date may well go back to the period B.C. The key is kept at the Antiquities Office at the entrance to Othello's Tower, and an escort will be provided.

Turkish Museum and Tomb of Djamboulat Bey
Map **15.**
Opening hours
Winter   8 a.m. to 1.30 p.m.
          2.30 p.m. to 5 p.m.
Summer 8.30 a.m. to 1.30 p.m.
          3.30 p.m. to 6 p.m.

Small collection of Turkish costumes, etc., in the Djamboulat bastion, leading to the plain tomb of Djamboulat Bey, which is second in importance only to the shrine of Ummul Haram (pp. 221–2) as a place of sanctity for Cypriots of the Moslem faith.

Palazzo del Proveditore
Map **12.**
The Venetians made use of granite pillars brought from Salamis to support the three arches in the façade of their provincial governor's palace. The coat of arms which appears over the central arch is that of Giovanni Renier, Captain of Cyprus in 1552. The main interest lies in the front of the palace, and in quarters used as a prison during the Turkish occupation of the city.

Two granite pillars in the square, to the west of the Cathedral, and also from Salamis, were originally furnished with the winged lion of St Mark and the statue of St Theodore, who is much venerated in Venice for his martyrdom by being thrown to alligators. The modern bust at present in the square is that of Namik Kemal Bey, the Turkish poet (1840–88), who was exiled from his homeland for defiance of the sultan, and who was imprisoned in Famagusta near this site.

District Museum
Map **18** (*New Town*).
Opening hours
Mid-May to mid-Sept. weekdays 8 a.m. to 1 p.m.
4 p.m. to 6 p.m.
Sundays 10 a.m. to 1 p.m.
Mid-Sept. to mid-May weekdays 8 a.m. to 1 p.m.
2.30 p.m. to 4.30 p.m.
Sundays 10 a.m. to 1 p.m.

Situated off 28th October St in the new town, this houses a collection of local antiquities.

Police District Headquarters
Map **3** (*New Town*).
Railway enthusiasts may view the steam engine which operated on the Nicosia–Famagusta line until its closure.

EXCURSIONS FROM FAMAGUSTA

Salamis, St Barnabas Monastery and Enkomi/Alasia

Route At the roundabout immediately beyond the Land Gate of the Old City take the third turn to the left, ignoring the main routes to Larnaca and Nicosia. The principal entrance to Salamis (4½ m.) is on the right, immediately after a turning leading to the Royal Tombs, St Barnabas Monastery and Enkomi/Alasia.

After visiting these, return to Famagusta via Engomi village, to rejoin the main road 1 m. south of Salamis.

For Nicosia (32 m.) head west from Engomi and join the main Famagusta–Nicosia road about a mile beyond Styllos.

For Kyrenia by an indirect route, continue northwards from Salamis, turning left at Trikomo (p. 205) for Lefkoniko, Mersiniki Pass and the north coast road (+55 m.).

Hotels
De luxe Evagoras Court; Mimosa Beach (awaiting classification).
2nd (C) Boghaz (12 m.)
All situated on Famagusta Bay with access to its sandy shore.

A new holiday complex to include a 4-star hotel, self-catering flats and convention facilities is due to be completed late in 1972.

Ancient Monuments
Salamis
Resident Custodian; official leaflet available.
Opening hours
Mid-May to mid-Sept. Daily 7 a.m. to 7 p.m.
Mid-Sept. to mid-May 7.30 a.m. to dusk.

Royal Tombs
Custodian in attendance.
Opening hours
Mid-May to mid-Sept. Daily 9 a.m. to 12 noon.
                                     3 p.m. to 6.30 p.m.
Mid-Sept. to mid-May Daily 9 a.m. to 1 p.m.
                                     2 p.m. to 4.30 p.m.

Enkomi/Alasia
Resident Custodian; official leaflet available.
Opening hours
Mid-May to mid-Sept. Daily 9 a.m. to noon.
                                     3 p.m. to 6.30 p.m.
Mid-Sept. to mid-May Daily 9 a.m. to 1 p.m.
                                     2 p.m. to 4.30 p.m.

[4½ m.] Some way past the turning to Engomi village, the entrance to the main site of *Salamis* will be seen on the right. The site is approached by the custodian's office and a barrier.

HISTORY OF SALAMIS

The history of Salamis is such a long one, and so full of major events, that for the present purpose it is best reduced to the barest detail. This should help in relating the remains which are found scattered over a very large site.

B.C.

c. 1180   According to legend, which has been substantiated by recent discoveries, the city of Salamis was founded by Teucer, son of the king of Salamis on the Greek mainland, after his return from the Trojan War.

707   The king of Salamis submitted to the Assyrians.

668   An Assyrian clay tablet is believed to refer to tribute paid to Assur-bani-pal by the king of Salamis.

560–25   King Evelthon, mentioned by Herodotus, is the first named king of Salamis.

411–374   Independence from Persian rule was obtained for almost the whole island by the great patriot king, Evagoras. The powerful city of Kitium (Larnaca), which had remained on the Persian side, was reduced with the help of an Athenian fleet in 387 B.C. There followed a period of offensives and counter-offensives between Evagoras and the Persians. By the time Evagoras was assassinated in 374 B.C. he had accepted terms limiting his rule to Salamis alone.

332   King Pnytagoras transferred allegiance to Alexander the Great, and by assisting him at the Battle of Tyre put an end to Persian domination. He was given Tamassos as a reward.

323   The death of Alexander led to a struggle for power between Ptolemy, king of Egypt, and Antigonus, ruler of Syria.

310   The royal house of Salamis came to an end with the suicide of Nicocreon, the military ruler of the island who had been appointed by Ptolemy.

284   Cyprus was abandoned to Ptolemy after the capture of Athens. Salamis was superseded by Paphos as the chief city of the island.

58   Cyprus was proclaimed a Roman colony. Public works and a programme of major rebuilding began at Salamis.

A.D.

45–6   The Christian community was founded by Paul and Barnabas.

c. 76   Devastation by earthquake.

116–17   Great Jewish insurrection.

A.D.

332, 342   Earthquakes, followed by a tidal wave. The great damage
resulted in the city having to be rebuilt on a smaller
scale under the Emperor Constantine II, and renamed
Constantia.

368–403   Constantia took from Paphos the title of Metropolis of
the island, under St Epiphanios, bishop of Salamis and
Constantia.

647   Saracen raids spread over a period of years brought
siege, sacking and massacre to the city. It was rebuilt and
refortified, but had to be abandoned after further devastation by raiders and earthquake, and because the harbour
had become silted up and unusable. Famagusta became
the chief town of the region. Not only did it take over the
power of Constantia, but many of her stones, using her as
though her only importance was as a convenient quarry
on the doorstep of the new town.

DESCRIPTION OF SITE

Because the remains of the city are scattered, it is inadvisable for
any attempt to be made to look at them in chronological order,
since this would involve a great deal of retracing of steps. All
features of interest in the area are accessible to motorists, though
the distances are quite manageable for average walkers unless the
weather is excessively hot. Incidentally, a long beach of shallow
water stretches in both directions. Fragments of ancient pottery
and marble discarded by the excavators litter the shore. The two
luxury hotels, built low so as to be unobtrusive, are to the north of
the main site. Otherwise the beach, without changing facilities other
than bushes and sandhills, is reached from the Tourist Pavilion or the
car park opposite the Gymnasium. The remains of the ancient harbour will be of interest to underwater swimmers with an eye for
treasure-seeking, though collecting is not permitted. It can be
reached either by walking along the sands or from the newly
discovered Kambanopetra site.

After passing through the main entrance, it will be possible to
recognize the *Walls and Fortifications* of the city to the left and
right. These are of a late period in its history. They continue
roughly north-east to the left of the present track, and may have

G

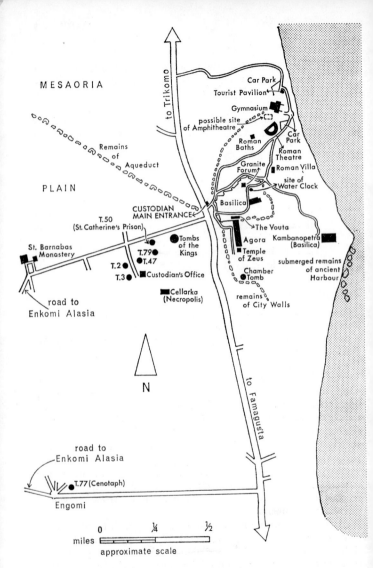

Salamis and Neighbouring Sites

been erected by Constantine II when he rebuilt Salamis in a contracted form, though some experts believe that their purpose was as an extra line of defence against the Arab raids of the seventh century A.D.

Remains of *Roman Baths* are to the left, a short distance off the tarred motor road after it passes through trees, diverging from the line of the walls, and before a similar road comes in on the right. This site has not as yet been thoroughly excavated.

Farther on, immediately after the road junction, and plainly identifiable on the left, is the *Roman Theatre*. Excavations which began in 1960 revealed this to be one of the largest of its kind in the Middle East. It dates back to the early imperial period, probably to the reign of Augustus Caesar, and repairs and alterations were executed in the first and second centuries A.D. when Salamis continued to be under Roman domination. An earlier Hellenistic theatre may have existed on the same site. Earthquakes in the fourth century A.D. destroyed the Roman Theatre, at the time when great damage was done to the rest of the city. A full description is contained in the official guide to Salamis, which no visitor should be without. This guide describes the extent to which the lost portions of the auditorium have been reconstructed for the presentation of Greek classical drama. The actors' dressing rooms and ancillary buildings have been the subject of subsequent phases of excavation.

Gymnasium and Baths
See plan on page 193.

The most important group of remains, the Gymnasium and Baths, has direct access from the car park, a few hundred yards south of the Tourist Pavilion. Its most spectacular feature is what is commonly known as the 'Marble Forum', the great Palaestra surrounded by four porticoes, which was the exercise ground for the athletes. Its principal allied buildings are to the south-east and contiguous. They are of great interest, as well as being of a complexity which is best resolved by reference to the plan, and by following the prescribed route in the official guide which begins by way of steps into the South Portico.

The existence of a Hellenistic gymnasium on the same site is documented by several inscriptions, the most important being a dedication to Ptolemy V Epiphanes (205–180 B.C.) which is set into a step between two columns at the entrance to the South Portico.

The Palaestra belongs mainly to the period of rebuilding by Constantine II. The columns when first discovered were fallen (in fact all over the site there is evidence of violent upheaval) and they were re-erected between 1952 and 1955. The most important statuary from the site has been transferred to the Cyprus Museum in Nicosia, but a collection has been assembled in the North Annexe. Perhaps the most appealing statue is a draped figure in dark marble, believed to represent the mournful Persephone. Her face, hands and feet, which were of inset white marble, are missing. Work is continuing on the excavation of rooms behind the south and north porticoes of the Palaestra. These were destroyed in the fourth century A.D., but partly reconstructed as public baths at a later date. Of particular interest is the semicircular set of latrines at the south-west corner of the Palaestra. These provide stone seating for forty-four persons facing a colonnade, complete with drainage and water system.

The main buildings adjacent to the East Portico have a façade about 12 ft thick. This has withstood the earthquakes which shattered so much else. The large North Hall at the north-east corner of the group of buildings has walls of corresponding thickness and an apsidal east end, both of which have only partly survived.

Many of the buildings, including baths for use of the athletes, which form a complex series at this end of the site, show traces of Roman methods of construction. Excavation work proceeds here and elsewhere in Salamis, and the discovery of mosaics has added to the architectural and functional interest attached to this complex of buildings. In a niche in the South Hall, which functioned as a sudatorium, may be seen a representation of the River God Evrotas alongside an upturned jar from which water flows, and presided over by Zeus in the form of a swan. Another niche contains detail of a picture of Apollo and Artemis in conflict with the Niobids. The mosaics are late Roman in style, and probably form part of a scheme of decoration of the early fourth century. A similar recess in the North Hall also shows mosaic work, but in fragmentary condition.

At present the Gymnasium and Baths are the most northerly of the ancient monuments on the site, though at any time this statement may become incorrect, as it is reasonable to believe that an almost unlimited amount of exciting things will come to light and

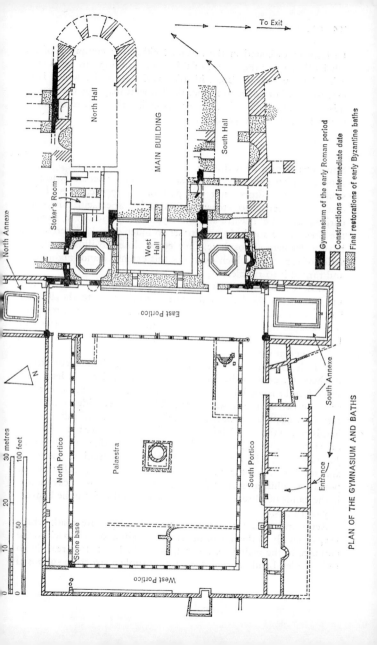

PLAN OF THE GYMNASIUM AND BATHS

North Hall

MAIN BUILDING

South Hall

Stoker's Room

West Hall

North Annexe

East Portico

South Annexe

Entrance

N

30 metres
20
10
0

100 feet
50
0

North Portico

Palaestra

West Portico

South Portico

Stone base

To Exit

Gymnasium of the early Roman period

Constructions of intermediate date

Final restorations of early Byzantine baths

be fully investigated in the future. Neither the compilers of the official leaflet nor the author of this guide can hope to keep their printed matter up to date with discoveries on a site which is so extensive in both area and time. Be that as it may, for the present this forms a turning-point, or else a stopping place for refreshment in the Tourist Pavilion and time off by the sea.

Southern Group of Ruins

For a complete survey of ruined Salamis it is now necessary to turn south. Many visitors omit this part of the inspection as being chiefly of interest to archaeologists and unspectacular in comparison with the Theatre and the Gymnasium. However, because the sites to the south do not attract so much popular interest and have a desolate atmosphere, they come closer to illustrating the series of calamities which overtook this extensive and mighty city and turned it to rubble.

Those visitors with energy and interest should now turn south and branch to the left on the tarred road opposite the Roman Baths. This fork leads past the *Roman Villa*. There is not much to see, because little has been done on the site since excavations in 1881, and its walls and the bath house attached to them are very much overgrown.

A little farther on, the estimated centre of the ancient city is reached at a crossroads. Take the left track, which will lead after several right-angled bends to one of the most newly excavated sites, known as the *Kambanopetra*. This has been identified as an early *Christian basilica*, the most complete of its kind so far discovered in this part of the world. It bears a striking resemblance to the Church of St Sepulchre which was built by Constantine the Great in Jerusalem and fully described by the historian Eusebius. The north and south sides of the church are bordered by long galleries and porticoes, while an atrium faces the sea. The work of excavation is in the hands of a French archaeological expedition from the University of Lyons.

Returning to the crossroads, ignore the opposite road, which keeps roughly to the line of the late city walls and leads back to the entrance to the main site. Instead, turn left. Just before reaching a right-angled bend you will see a round sunken structure supposed to have contained a *Water Clock*. The area at the corner is known as the *Granite Forum* because it contains numerous overthrown pillars of Egyptian granite, many of which are approximately 18 ft in length.

The next sight of importance is also on the left of the road: a second great *Basilica* measuring 190 by 140 ft, which is thought to have been the metropolitan church of St Epiphanios, bishop of Constantia (A.D. 368–403), after the rebuilding of the city. Most of the church was subsequently razed to ground-level – probably during the period of the Arab raids of the seventh century. The foundations show signs of building at different periods, but the original design consisted of a central nave and three aisles on either side, two of which were subsequently united. The drums of columns used in rebuilding have come from some very much earlier Roman construction. Annexes extend on the outer walls of the main church, and remains of staircases suggest that these originally led to internal galleries. A feature of the central apse is a semicircular flight of steps leading to the synthronon, a raised bench for the clergy set against the apse wall. This could have been added in the sixth century. A marble-lined tomb in the most central of the southern apses was almost certainly constructed to contain the relics of St Epiphanios, but these are thought to have been removed to Constantinople by the Byzantine Emperor, Leo the Wise, A.D. 886–912.

A large *Annexe Church* immediately to the east of the saint's tomb was in all probability converted from existing buildings at the end of the seventh century after the destruction of the Basilica. Its narthex and porch were extended to take in the tomb of the venerable patron saint. Later, probably in the ninth century, three domes were added over the nave and chancel. This church was in use in the Middle Ages, long after the city was abandoned in favour of Famagusta. Inferior additions inside the shell of the main church suggest that some part of this continued to be in use during the Lusignan period.

The motor track veers west soon after the Basilica. The great water reservoir which has come to be known as the '*Vouta*', from the vaulting which covered it, lies just off the road to the south. It was built between A.D. 627 and 640 for the storage of the water supply brought from the northern mountains above Kythrea. The Italian traveller, Nicolai Martoni, who came here in 1394, mentions 'a vault raised on thirty-six columns and with apertures above whence the water was drawn'. Comparison may be made with the famous underground water cisterns of Constantinople.

The Vouta is situated immediately north of the *Agora* or '*Stone Forum*'. Inscriptions record the restoration of this market-place during the reign of Augustus in the first century B.C. The remains are mainly of this period of rebuilding. The Agora consisted of a central open space approximately 750 by 180 ft, enclosed on its two longer sides by colonnades formed of stone drums finished in stucco and filled fluting. These columns were set at intervals of 15 ft and crowned with Corinthian capitals. The shops were entered through the porticoes. The main entrance was on the north side, in the area subsequently overbuilt in the construction of the Vouta. Four of the original five columns which formed this entrance have survived in part.

The *Temple of Zeus* at the southern end of the Agora may be approached either on foot or by a track running parallel with the west side of the site, and which peters out soon afterwards. The high podium is the most prominent part of the ruins, which are certainly those of the Temple of the Olympian Zeus, though this has not yet been proved identical with the shrine of Zeus Salaminios, one of the island's three traditional shrines which were granted the right of asylum for fugitives in A.D. 22.

Farther to the south there is an area excavated in 1965 by another expedition from the University of Lyons, where a chamber tomb produced a great deal of interesting material from the eleventh century B.C., mainly vases and jewellery. This discovery was of the first magnitude, since it provided evidence, soon to be augmented by that of the Royal Tombs, that the history of Salamis went back to the Late Bronze Age.

This concludes a full tour of the visible remains of a city which once covered a wide area, and which was successively built over after each major disaster, so that any square yard – now seen chiefly as scrub, stones, trees and sand – could cover a clue to buildings perhaps as interesting as anything yet discovered. Excavation work by the Department of Antiquities proceeds methodically, subject of course to the limitation of funds and the availability of specialist workers. This is most certainly the pet site of the authorities and of the island's archaeologists. Meanwhile, for the lay visitor, a programme of afforestation – pines, acacias, eucalyptus, mimosa, etc. –

begun as early as 1882, has done much to reduce the heat of the site in full summer.

To leave the main site, rejoin the road which runs to the north of the Vouta. This completes a circle at the main entrance. Cross the main Famagusta road by turning left, then almost immediately right on to a secondary road. This is the verge of the Mesaoria plain, and the country is flat, so that the features soon to be visited are easily recognizable. While halting here, look north to the remains of the *Aqueduct* which carried water from the generous springs of Kythrea to the storage tanks of the Vouta.

ROYAL TOMBS

Opening hours p. 187.

[5 m.] Passing, for the moment, a mound traditionally known as St Catherine's Prison or Tomb, take the first turn to the left. This will lead to the office of the custodian, and the most important of the royal tombs are then within walking distance.

The existence of at least one subterranean chamber had been established as early as 1896 by a British archaeological expedition, and the pillaging of others by robbers and vandals, notably the neighbouring villagers of Engomi, had become a part of local folk-lore. But until recently it had been assumed that whatever tombs existed had been thoroughly plundered, and that except for details of their construction, full-scale investigation would be unrewarding. The contrary proved to be the truth when in 1957 the Department of Antiquities undertook systematic excavation of what has come to be known as Tomb 1 of the royal necropolis. Its lower layers were found to be undisturbed, and contained two burials, one of which was equipped with a bronze cauldron used to contain the remains. A necklace and some sheets of gold obviously formed part of the ornamentation of the deceased, a Cypriot princess of some consequence. Another, but no less important, development was the exhumation of the bones of two horses from the *dromos* or entrance to the tomb.

The results of this first operation were now seen to justify the employment of full-scale resources by the Department of Antiquities, though it could not be assumed that the contents of the known burial chambers would have been left undisturbed by the plunderers and collectors of the past, whose activities elsewhere resulted in so much of value being scattered abroad and lost. The most that could be expected was to find that though the tombs had been robbed of everything of intrinsic value, they would yet provide inestimable archaeological and historical findings. The site in effect proved to be the hitherto missing royal necropolis of Salamis. It provided all-important evidence of what hitherto had been legend: that the city was founded by Teucer on his way home from the Trojan War, and that it succeeded Enkomi as early as the eleventh century B.C. The contents of the tombs are Homeric in a literal sense, as they conform to that classical narrator's account of the funeral of Patroclos in the *Iliad*. Among the evidence of sacrificial burial which has come to light are the skeletons of slaves, and of asses and horses in their prime, the chariots of their dead sovereigns and various vessels such as would have contained honey and other funerary food, and which correspond to those used in Mycenaean rites, and ivory furniture of unique splendour. Complete documentation is contained in Dr Karageorghis's book on Salamis (see Bibliography).

Though the priceless contents have had to be removed for restoration and safe-keeping, even the most uninitiated of visitors cannot fail to regard the royal tombs as far more than holes in the ground – largely because the skeletons of horses have been left *in situ* (in fact where they fell under the bludgeons of their executioners) and can now be seen under glass erected for their protection. A gruesome and realistic touch is added by the fact that in many cases it is apparent that whereas the first of a pair of horses was struck down in its harness, still yoked to the chariot, the second had in panic escaped to a far corner of the approach to the inner tomb, before dying from a broken neck. In fact, both because of their antiquity and their substantiation of Homeric legend, these remains constitute one of the most fascinating relics in the entire island, coupled as they are with the more valuable exhibits on permanent exhibition in the Cyprus Museum.

Tombs 47 and 79 to the left of the track and 1 and 2 to the right may be taken as representative. But the site should not be left without returning to *St Catherine's Prison*, now known also as Tomb 50, where a similar ritualistic killing of horses occurred at the entrance to the burial chamber. The particular interest of this tomb lies in the fact that it was at an early age converted to use as a Christian chapel dedicated to St Catherine. Blocks of stone used in its construction are as large as $14\frac{1}{2}$ by 8 ft, and slabs of the same material form its roof. It possesses an inner chamber with an altar, used as the holy of holies. (The tomb and its approach is fenced, but the custodian will produce the key.)

The area under consideration cannot be left without mention of a scattered site known as the *Cellarka*, a word meaning cells or empty chambers, not far to the south-east of St Catherine's Tomb. This takes the form of a congested necropolis, though the burials were in no way grand, nor comparable to those in the royal tombs. But quantity makes up in some measure for quality, and three years' excavation exposed some hundreds of rock-cut tombs within a small area. Most of them had been looted, and contained little of value, save evidence that the site had been used continuously from about 700 B.C. to the end of the fourth century B.C., and also adding to existing knowledge of the funerary customs of that period.

[$5\frac{1}{2}$ m.] The right turning to *St Barnabas Monastery* is a short distance farther on.

HISTORY OF ST BARNABAS MONASTERY

The monastery and its church, together with the mausoleum which has been built over the tomb of St Barnabas, are of greater historical and religious significance than architectural. It is known from the New Testament (Acts iv 36, 37) that St Barnabas was a native of Cyprus who became one of the foremost of the first seventy disciples. He accompanied St Paul to Cyprus (Acts xiii) and later returned with St Mark (Acts xv 36, 39) to see how the converts from this earlier visit had fared. It is believed that St Barnabas was killed by Jews at Salamis, and that St Mark secretly placed his remains in a rock-tomb outside the city boundaries. This tomb was forgotten until A.D. 477, when the saint communicated its whereabouts to Archbishop Anthemios of Constantia (as Salamis was called at that time). When the tomb was opened the identity of the dead occupant was established beyond all doubt by the fact that a manuscript of St Matthew's Gospel, written in St Barnabas's own handwriting, lay near the human remains. Archbishop Anthemios forthwith took the Gospel to the Emperor Zeno in Constantinople in the expectation that the narrative of the miraculous revelation would resolve the prevailing long-drawn-out arguments about the status of the church of Cyprus. His hopes were realized. The church was granted independence, and became the Autocephalous Greek Orthodox Church of Cyprus. Its archbishop was invested with the right to wear a cloak of imperial purple, carry the imperial sceptre and sign his name in red ink. These privileges, which have survived to the present day, are a favourite subject for the holy pictures painted in the Monastery of St Barnabas by the three monks, brothers, who have lived here since 1917 and are in charge of the small community. They produce and sell a large number of icons, and have learnt to speed up their output in the same tradition as early icon-painters, by each specializing in a particular aspect of the painting: one perhaps doing the robes, another jewels and haloes, and the third concentrating on faces and hands. They have created in their own lifetimes something of a legend. Basil, one of the freshest and most evocative of herbs, is cultivated in the courtyard of the monastery. There is also a very old stone mill.

CHURCH AND MAUSOLEUM

The original monastery of A.D. 477 was destroyed by the Saracens. The present church was built by Archbishop Philotheos in 1756. As with many another church in Cyprus, it incorporates in its structure the mutilated remains of earlier buildings – in this case a spirally fluted column of dark-green marble embedded in the wall on the south side of the present *bema*. Some authorities have expressed a tentative hope that this is a survival from the shrine built for the sacred relics by Anthemios on his return from Constantinople *c.* 478. The icon of the patron saint painted in 1762 depicts him as the founder, or at least the originator, of the Autocephalous Church. A small chapel at the east end has been used for the Latin rite. The bell tower was added in 1958, and was paid for out of the proceeds of the work of the three brothers, Chariton, Barnabas and Stephanos, the youngest of whom was born in 1894.

The modern *Mausoleum* which has been constructed over the empty tomb of St Barnabas is about a hundred yards to the east of the church. The tombs are similar to pagan tombs of the Salamis necropolis – which accords with the legend of the saint's death and burial. The mausoleum covers the marble arch which until recently was the sole protection for the tombs. A very old icon shows signs of having been kissed by the devout over a long period of years. There is also a holy well to which is attributed the power of curing skin diseases, and which is reached by a flight of fourteen steps.

[6 m.] Returning to the secondary road, continue on to the Bronze-Age city of *Enkomi/Alasia* (opening hours p. 187) by turning right at the signpost to Nicosia. The site is then immediately on your left.

ENKOMI / ALASIA

The second part of this name was added in 1952 after the site had been identified by the late Professor René Dussaud of the Académie des Inscriptions et Belles-Lettres as the ancient city of Alasia, which gave its name to Cyprus at the beginning of the island's history. Two pieces of circumstantial evidence which support this identification are that the Egyptian Tell-el-Amarna tablets refer to consignments of copper from Alasiya, and it has been proved beyond all doubt that Enkomi at one time was a busy industrial city of metal workers.

The site had been recognized for a long time as that of an extensive necropolis which had been robbed at different periods, and in the tombs of which English and Swedish archaeologists had found great treasure of gold, ivory and fine Mycenaean pottery. But it was not until 1934 that Professor C. F. A. Schaeffer, investigating under the auspices of the Académie des Inscriptions et Belles-Lettres, discovered the first building to prove definitely that an important town had existed in close association with the cemetery. In fact, excavation revealed that the dead and their valuables were buried beneath their dwelling-houses. The French professor's second series of excavations, resumed in 1946 after the Second World War, was carried out on behalf of the French Centre of Scientific Research. A joint undertaking with the Cyprus Department of Antiquities under Professor Dikaios subsequently produced very important discoveries. Work on the site continues under the direction of Professor Schaeffer, and it is hoped that one day this will result in the discovery of the city's Palace, which may well contain archives of incalculable importance.

Due to the incompleteness of archaeological work on the site, visitors are requested not to trespass into the excavated sections, nor to walk too near their edge. Photography is not at present permitted. The site is complex, both in its layout and its chronology, and should an informed guide not be available, reference should be made to the official leaflet which can be purchased from the custodian, and which gives directions. However, some form of identification of the various streets and other topographical features would be to the great benefit of visitors.

HISTORY

Enkomi/Alasia existed in the Middle Bronze Age (2000–1700 B.C.), but its period of prosperity began c. 1550 B.C., when it is known that it contained a stockpile of metal from the copper mines of the island, as well as being a specialized metal-working industrial town. Expensive building techniques which have been exposed by excavations may be taken as an index to the wealth and high standard of living of the city's merchants. Their considerable trade was conducted through the agency of the Mycenaeans, and involved an interchange of goods between Cyprus and the Syrian and Aegean ports. In 1946 Professor Schaeffer uncovered wall fortifications of about the fourteenth and thirteenth centuries B.C. This is the period of the richest tombs. Soon afterwards decline set in primarily as a result of invasion from Greece and Asia Minor. Then in the twelfth century B.C. a large part of the city was destroyed by fire. Soon after it was rebuilt it was shattered at least twice by earthquake, leading eventually to total abandonment in the eleventh century B.C. The city, all of which is below present ground-level, had a walled perimeter of about 1,200 yards. It covered approximately one square mile, while at the height of its importance its population may have reached the figure of 15,000.

DESCRIPTION OF SITE

A comprehensive tour of the site takes in the *House of the Bronzes* (c. twelfth century B.C.), where a hoard of bronze articles was unearthed by Professor Schaeffer in 1934 – his first exciting proof of the existence of the city he felt certain was there. Vestiges of streets suggest that the town plan was on the grid system. The *House of the Pillar* to the north has been identified as a public building. The *Tomb* (known as No. 18) which yielded the greatest finds in the course of Swedish excavations in 1930 is to the left. Beyond, continuing in a northward direction, there is an area of buildings, the most central of which has been named *The Sanctuary of the Horned God*, because it was here that the bronze statue of that description was found. It is 2 ft in height, and is one of the most prized exhibits in the Cyprus Museum. Evidence as to the worship of this god has come to light in the form of skulls of bulls and other animals used for sacrifice, which have been found near the statue. Further excavations below the floor of the sanctuary have yielded remains from the sixteenth to the thirteenth centuries B.C.

The *Wall Fortifications*, which had gates to the west and north of the city, included projecting rectangular towers and a larger square fortress of the sixteenth to fifteenth centuries B.C. in which there have been found traces of copper smelting. Superimposed on these, there is further evidence that copper-smelting continued here in the early fourteenth century B.C., until this, too, was covered by flooring subsequent to fire and upheavals at the end of the thirteenth century and the beginning of the twelfth.

In case lack of time, or excessive heat, makes the route outlined in the official leaflet impracticable, a modified view of the city can be achieved by proceeding first to the North Gate, then turning south down the main street to make a circuit of the House of Bronzes, and then returning to the custodian's office. This has the effect of leaving out the West Gate and sections of the town wall, but gives a rough outline of the scope of the city.

[6½ m.] Keep right on leaving the site, and continue to the village of Engomi, on the further outskirts of which a fenced area to the left is observed.

The Cenotaph (*Tomb* 77), an artificial mound built on a rocky platform, is outstanding. This obvious target yielded few results to old-time plunderers and archaeologists, but has now been thoroughly excavated to reveal plastered steps leading up to a platform which contained a funeral pyre. Because the mound was built off-centre, the contents, lime-stone statues, wine jars from Rhodes and an archaic bronze shield had remained undiscovered, as were the pyre and its contents, human figures and the head of a horse moulded in clay, as effigies placed there in default of bodies and sacrifices. It has been assumed that this is a cenotaph, or empty tomb, erected in memory of Nicocreon, last king of Salamis. In 311 B.C. he and his family committed themselves to the flames of their palace rather than submit to Ptolemy, and the bodily remains were therefore destroyed. This theory, unsubstantiated yet highly probable, does much to enhance the mystery of this prominent and mysterious site overlooking the level plain between Engomi and the remains of Salamis.

Continue eastwards to the main road (1 m.) and then turn right for Famagusta.

Trikomo and Kantara Castle

Route Take the north road out of Famagusta which is signposted for Salamis and the Karpas (Route A on Famagusta map), and which by-passes the Old City. Fork left after 11 m. for Trikomo (13 m.) and Kantara Castle (25 m.).

One way to return to Famagusta is by following the Forest Road westwards as far as Mersiniki Pass, passing Mt Olympus (2,427 ft) on the way. Turn left here for Lefkoniko, joining the main Nicosia–Famagusta road north of Prastio.

For Nicosia turn right in Lefkoniko (+25 m.).

For Kyrenia see Chart of Excursions.

Alternatively, an overnight stay can be made at Dhavlos (+5 m.) near Phlamoudhi on the north coast, or Boghaz, via Trikomo, and the excursion continued eastwards for Kanakaria Church and Apostolos Andreas Monastery (pp. 209–13) (+52 m.).

Ancient Monument
Kantara Castle
Custodian in attendance.
Opening hours
Mid-May to mid-Sept. Daily 9 a.m. to noon.
                                    3 p.m. to 6.30 p.m.
Mid-Sept. to mid-May Daily 9 a.m. to 1 p.m.
                                    2 p.m. to 4.30 p.m.

Hotels
At Boghaz: 2nd (C) Boghaz.
At Aya Marina: Glaros (new, awaiting classification).
At Dhavlos   2nd (C) Tony's.
                   4th   Louis.
(*5 m. north of Kantara Resort*).

[11 m.] Take left fork for Trikomo.

[13 m.] Trikomo

The charming small fifteenth-century *Church of St James* in the main square is worth visiting. This church so enchanted Queen Marie of Rumania that she built its exact counterpart at her private chapel on the shores of the Black Sea. The porcelain plates let into the vaulting are interesting, and some authorities suggest that these show a Portuguese influence. The paintings are inferior to those in the neighbouring *Church of the Blessed Virgin Mary*, which was restored in 1804 when a north aisle was added to structure dating from the twelfth century. The Byzantine slab in the belfry is the most important of the remains of the original church.

Follow the road due north from Trikomo.

[18 m.] At **Ardhana** the road begins to ascend into the mountains.

[19½ m.] Keep right when the Forest Road comes in on the left.

[23 m.] **Kantara Resort**

A winding road to **Dhavlos** (5 m. north) takes you off the main route, for sea bathing or hot sea-water baths.

[25 m.] **KANTARA CASTLE**

The fortress rears itself on a series of pinnacles similar to those which form the foundation of the two companion castles, St Hilarion and Buffavento. In this case, after several hairpin bends, the motor road goes to within a few minutes' walking distance of the outer fortifications (opening hours p. 205). This is the most easterly and the least in height (2,068 ft) of the three castles, but high enough to look in all four directions: to replanted forest areas to the south, with the Mesaoria and Famagusta Bays in the distance; a good view of the sea and, on clear days, the mountainous coast of Anatolia to the north; a series of dolomitic peaks on the west side; and the long 'tail' of the island diminishing as it extends east.

There are more myths than history attached to Kantara Castle – and as always the story of a mysterious 101st room and of a 'Queen' who has given her name to the topmost chamber of the ruins. Search for legendary treasure has no doubt accounted for further dilapidation since the removal of the Venetian garrison in 1525. The first historical mention of Kantara is a siege by royalist forces in 1228, during which attack the outer defences were so badly damaged by catapult that they had to be completely rebuilt early in the fourteenth century. Unlike the castle of St Hilarion, this was never in use as a palace, but was a watch-tower and prison; and in 1373 it became a place of sanctuary for the Prince of Antioch when with the help of a faithful cook he escaped from Genoese captivity in Famagusta.

The castle is in worse condition than St Hilarion, but better than Buffavento. A point of interest lies in observing how the defenders of these heights took every advantage of the precipitous natural rock, which ruled out the necessity for building a completely encircling wall. Entry is by the *Main Gate* on the east side. This had a small bailey, but the main defences were two flanking towers in the very high wall. The one to the north-east is two-storeyed, with a projecting turret with loopholes, the purpose of which is presumed to have been defence of the great water cistern immediately below, and therefore outside the castle *enceinte*, and also commanding the main gate as well as overlooking the sea approaches. The *Guardroom* on the opposite (south) side of the main entrance is in good condition. This had access to an oubliette through which prisoners could pass without the main gate being opened for them.

The ruins were strengthened and made safe in 1914. There is a vertiginous drop to the ramparts on the north side, which gives the best view of all. The better-preserved parts of the castle may be seen from the path following the southerly perimeter, and leading past three identical square rooms with loopholes, used as military quarters with an adjoining latrine. Then at the south-east angle there are three more vaulted rooms, one of which is equipped with a small gate to be used in emergency, and at right-angles two more which were used for water storage. From that point it is possible to make a choice of paths leading upwards to the roofless upper chamber of the 'Queen', of which a stone window in the south wall survives. This portion of the castle may originally have been equipped with a small drawbridge. But imaginative reconstruction of the buildings according to any theory is difficult due to the degree of destruction and the amount of rocky debris on the site. In spite of this, however, Kantara is one of the most magical and atmospheric of castles.

Ayia Napa Monastery

Route Leave Famagusta by the south road (Route D on Famagusta map) for Dherinia (3 m.), then fork left for Paralimni (5 m.) and Ayia Napa (8 m.). It is possible to drive on to Cape Greco (+5½ m.), returning to Paralimni by the coast road.
Hotel
Nisi Beach Bungalow Hotel (Ayia Napa 2 m.).

[3 m.] Dherinia

[5 m.] Paralimni (by-passed). The southern corner of the island is a district which has assumed local importance for its convenience for the snaring of the tiny migratory birds from the Middle East which figure as *ambeloboulia* or *beccafico* on the menus of Cyprus. (They should be eaten whole, bones and all.)

[8 m.] MONASTERY OF AYIA NAPA

This beautiful monastery has none of the dilapidation characteristic of other religious houses which have departed from their primary use. Architecturally, too, this is different from other monasteries on the island. It is among the last few buildings to be erected by the Venetians before they left the island in 1570. For the usual historical reason the free-standing belfry is of later date. On the strength of a Latin inscription copied by Mr Drummond, the English Consul at Aleppo in 1745, the façade of the church and the ornamental fountain in the centre of the enclosure have been ascribed to 1530. All travellers before and after him have been interested in the monastery's water supply, which flows through an aqueduct built on Roman principles, though the discovery of air-shafts has suggested that the water was at one time brought in by the classic Greek method of tunnelling. It feeds two reservoirs, and the most obvious and beautiful features are a Roman carving in the form of a boar's head spewing out the water, and an ornamental fountain in the centre of the courtyard.

The monastic enclosure is entered through a *Gateway* surmounted by a sculptured coat of arms, so worn as to be undecipherable, with stone sockets for standards on either side. The large rectangular *Gatehouse* of two storeys on the right is Venetian in origin. Each panel of the beautiful octagonal *Fountain* has a heavy floral motif in relief. Animal heads and coats of arms above these have been defaced. A domed structure supported by four pillars is set above the fountain, allowing room for raised seats in the shady interior – a very pleasant resting-place for pilgrims, as was its intention.

The *Church* is entered by its south door, above which there is another mutilated coat of arms. A wide entrance passage inside contains seats, and there is a Latin chapel to the east. The church is partially below ground, having been cut out of the rock. It may well be of greater age than is suggested by the Venetian techniques used in its visible construction.

Pietro de Valle, an Italian traveller writing in 1625, suggested that the squareness of the monastery buildings was intended deliberately as a deterrent to pirates, in the hope that they would be hoodwinked into presuming the place to be fortified. When de Valle visited the community it had recently been decimated by the Turks and by pestilence, but a Greek priest still officiated in the church, a part of which was set aside for the Latin rite.

Kanakaria Church and Apostolos Andreas Monastery

Route Take the northern coast road out of Famagusta, skirting the walls of the Old Town, as for Salamis (Route A on Famagusta map). Continue north-eastwards for Leonarisso (33 m.), diversion to Kanakaria Church (+3 m.), Yialousa (38 m.), Rizokarpaso (52 m.), Ayios Philon (+4 m.) and Apostolos Andreas Monastery (66 m.).

For Nicosia return by outward route to a point 3 m. south-west of Boghaz, turning right for Trikomo (p. 205) and Lefkoniko.

For Kyrenia turn right in Lefkoniko for the Mersiniki Pass and the north coast (see chart).

Hotels

At Boghaz:	2nd (C)	Boghaz.
At Rizokarpaso:	4th	Oasis.
At Yialousa:	4th	Shiambelos.

Very simple accommodation is also available at the Apostolos Andreas Monastery, but this is mainly used by pilgrims from country districts, and is considered unsuitable for tourists.

[11 m.] Take right fork, continuing along the coast and by-passing Trikomo.

[15 m.] **Boghaz,** a very small seaside place with a rustic gaiety in the season which is quite charming, especially when coupled with the opportunity for eating local fish and the snails which are a delicacy of this region. The coast bulges slightly soon after Boghaz, and the road continues north-east, out of sight of the sea.

[22 m.] **Ayios Theodhoros**

[28 m.] A turn right before Koma tou Yialou leads to a new fishing harbour, which is a good place for a bathe.

[33 m.] Fork right at the end of the village of **Leonarisso** on to the road for **Lythrangomi.** In 1½ m. *Kanakaria Church* comes into view on the left side of the road.

KANAKARIA CHURCH

This simple stone-built church of three naves, each with a semi-circular apse, is one of the most interesting in Cyprus because it contains a rare mosaic similar to that at Kiti (p. 223). Some authorities have suggested that the two mosaics may have been executed by the same artist, though the Kanakaria one is considerably less well preserved, due, according to Gunnis, to the local belief that the glass cubes which form the mosaic are a cure for skin diseases, so that they have been removed piecemeal.

The church is approached through a courtyard which originally had monastic buildings grouped around it, but these are now part of a farm. Visitors are expected to ring the church bell (in the belfry to the left of the west entrance to the church) and someone will appear with the key. The naves are barrel-vaulted. Most of the construction dates from the twelfth century and appears to have made use of details from a much earlier Byzantine shrine. The central dome was added in the eighteenth century. Some marble columns with Corinthian capitals have been re-used in the west narthex and south porch. The restoration work of 1779 and 1920 has resulted in a confusion of styles. There are some sixteenth-century wall-paintings, also porcelain plates let into the ceiling of the narthex, which merit attention.

Mosaics

But it is the mosaics in the apse, damaged though they be, which have conferred prime importance on this little church. Their subject is the Blessed Virgin (now shown in outline only) seated with the Child on her knee. This portion is better preserved. Jesus is dressed in white, and has in his hand a parchment scroll. Medallions of the Apostles around the group are in bad condition, and the same applies to the archangels who appear on either side, as they do in the Kiti mosaic. Though some authorities have ascribed this work of art to the ninth or even the sixth century A.D., it is in many respects typical of the Sicilian work of the twelfth century which became popular in the Levant at the time of the Crusades – no doubt introduced by Italian pilgrims. Nevertheless, it has been suggested that the Kanakaria mosaics bear an equally close resemblance to those at Ravenna and in the *Katholikon* of the Monastery of St Catherine on Mount Sinai, which have been attributed without absolute certainty to the sixth century. Whatever the date and affinity of its rare treasures, the Church of Kanakaria is well worth this short detour before continuing on the main road from Leonarisso to Yialousa.

[38 m.] **Yialousa** is a large village, almost a small town, which suffers from depopulation, but where there is a simple hotel (p. 209). There is a remoteness about the Karpas peninsula which is particularly charming when taken in conjunction with the friendliness of the local people, who are often avid for news of the world – and of their many relatives who have emigrated to England. Shortage of water makes this district unsuitable for touristic development. However, emphasis on the growing of tobacco and pistachio nuts has greatly improved the economy of what was hitherto an impoverished part of the island.

The excavations of Yialousa's *Byzantine Basilica* under the direction of Professor Papagheorghio of the Cyprus Museum will be of interest to archaeologically-minded wayfarers.

[48 m.] After running close to the north coast and passing several inviting bays and small promontories, the road swings inland through a small pass in the hills.

[52 m.] At **Rizokarpaso** (hotel p. 209) take a turning to the left, followed by a fork right and then another turn to the left, for a diversion to *Ayios Philon Church*, which is situated about 2 m. north on the coast, and north of the site of the ancient city of *Karpasia*. Karpasia never recovered after being burned by the Saracens in A.D. 802. When the survivors of the city's population were able to return from the hills on the departure of the raiders they transferred to what is now the village of Rizokarpaso.

The district had been converted to Christianity by Philon, metropolitan bishop of the Karpas, who is the patron saint of the ruined Byzantine church on the sea-shore. This may have been his cathedral. Fragments of the old city are in evidence in the church's walls, which are constructed of unusually large blocks of masonry. Rounded arches suggest that this part of the church is of the tenth or eleventh century. But of even greater interest is the site of an earlier ecclesiastical building to the south, where there are particularly good marble floors in geometric patterns. The circular central design in red, yellow, black and white is a thing of great beauty.

This is a pleasant place, on the edge of the sea, and bears another resemblance to Lambousa because there are portions of the old city's *Harbour Works* to be seen below the surface of the sea. The mole to the east, which was built of enormous blocks of stone clamped together with metal, can be followed for 370 ft from the shore.

At the time this book goes to press there are plans for a holiday village (chalets and central service area) on the coast road running north-east from Rizokarpaso to *Aphendrika* (5 m.), where there are remains of four Romanesque churches, and a pre-Christian citadel behind the quarry. It has been suggested that this is the site of the old town of *Urania*. The whole site awaits excavation.

[55 m.] The road eastward from Rizokarpaso, having continued across the narrow peninsula, reaches the south coast, where it comes out of the hills opposite the tortoise-shaped rocks known as the *Khelones*. A succession of wide sandy beaches backed by sand dunes fringes the road.

This north-eastern spit of the island was known to the ancients as *Dineretum*. Its extremity, which is accessible by a four-mile cliff path from the monastery, was marked by a temple of Aphrodite Acraea, the barest traces of which have survived. The site has in fact been so exhaustively plundered of building stone that further investigation is pointless either by archaeologists or the casual sightseer.

[66 m.] APOSTOLOS ANDREAS MONASTERY

The main road leads only as far as this. In actual fact it is not a monastery, though it contains a large hostel for pilgrims. The buildings form a giant square and are reminiscent of an eastern caravanserai. The *Oeconomos*, or resident priest, cares for the pilgrims. These number thousands in the year, but congregate chiefly on the feast days of August 15th and November 30th. They bring offerings of valuables and the fruits of their labours or, in cases where a cure is sought, wax effigies of the patient or his afflicted limb. And because the currents of the sea converge offshore, it is not unknown for flagons of oil consigned to the sea at some distant point of the island to be safely delivered, without human agency, near the shrine of the saint.

According to a legend which appears to have originated some time after the Middle Ages, St Andrew was passing the Cape on his return voyage to Palestine when his ship ran out of water. He thereupon counselled the one-eyed captain of his ship to put ashore, and in this seemingly arid region they found water. This when brought aboard cured the captain of his blindness, whereupon his sailors immediately adopted Christianity and were baptized by the saint. On his next voyage the grateful sea-captain erected a shrine near the well where the miracle originated, and set up a costly icon of the saint inside it.

The fifteenth-century *Gothic Chapel* which houses two of the three wells near the sea-shore is of greater architectural interest than the modern church of the saint. The votive offerings, and in particular the wax models, some of them crude portraits of the sick petitioners, illustrate the powerful belief of the islanders in this holy spot at the most remote corner of their land. Students of history, also, will like to remember that this is where Isaac Comnenus finally surrendered to Richard Cœur de Lion in 1191 after he had failed to procure a ship to carry him abroad.

LARNACA

Population 21,000.
Information
Tourist Office: Democratia (King Paul) Square (*Map* **20**).
Hotel
1st (A) Four Lanterns (*Map* **22**).
To date there is one only, of long-standing reputation but others are to be built to fit into the new pattern of Larnaca as a modern port and resort.
Restaurants and Bars
Ambiance, Gregorios Afxentiou Avenue.
Taverna Loukoullas, (Cyprus food).
Eraclis, in Municipal Gardens (*Map* **16**).
Xenyktis, Galileos St.
Africa Lodge Café, Galileos St.
There are also sea-side restaurants, such as the Savvopoulos and Alamo, a short distance along the Larnaca–Famagusta road. A special feature of the town is the delightful practice of setting out tables and chairs under the palms on the sea-front, for drinks, coffee and (at the southern end) kebabs. The hotel has a restaurant and ballroom.
Churches
Anglican St Helena's, Gregorias Afxentiou Ave (*Map* **15**).
Roman Catholic Santa Maria della Gratia, Terra Santa St (*Map* **2**) ; St Joseph, Makarios III Avenue (*Map* **12**).
Presbyterian (*Map* **14**)
Clubs
Rotary, c/o Four Lanterns Hotel.
Cinemas
Attikeon ; Makrides ; Pallas ; Rex.
Bathing and Water Sports
Swimming is permitted from the pebbled beach opposite the promenade, but this is perhaps a little 'towny'. The best bathing is between the third and sixth milestones on the Famagusta road, where there are several beach restaurants. Regattas, speed-boat and water ski-ing competitions are held every week-end from June to September.

Larnaca has in modern times yielded its position as a main port to Limassol and Famagusta. The town is quite unlike any of the other ports of Cyprus. It has a very pleasant almost French Riviera air, rather old-fashioned, partly on account of its long promenade planted with tall palm trees, which allows ample space for café life in the area between street and sea. Though decline in commercial activity has led to an almost imperceptible seediness, the charm has not abated. But now, from having been the poor relation of all the principal ports of Cyprus, Larnaca is to be revitalized by modern development, both in the sphere of commerce and tourism. Not only is it to have a commercial harbour with deep-water facilities but also a modern marina to accommodate over 100 sailing boats. In addition, there are plans to develop an area between the second and third milestones on the Famagusta road in the interests of tourism, as well as a privately financed scheme for a de luxe hotel and apartment block on the sea-front.

HISTORY

Larnaca is the successor of the Kitium of the ancient world, and the Chittim of the prophecies of Isaiah and Daniel, which is believed to have extended from the south of the present-day town as far as the Salt Lake. It is known that the Mycenaean city was abandoned *c.* 1000 B.C. and removed to a site nearer the sea. Some remains have been exposed in recent times (*Map* **3, 9**). Trading relations with the Phoenicians brought great prosperity and power, so that in the middle of the sixth century B.C. this city-kingdom controlled Tamassos and Idalion. When the bitter struggle between Greece and Persia raged in the island Kitium took the Persian side – motivated no doubt by existing good relations with the Phoenician faction. But a Greek fleet under Cimon besieged the town in 450 B.C. and, though the Greek hero lost his life, Kitium was reduced. Yet the city did not renounce allegiance to Persia until 351 B.C.

Larnaca next came into the picture by being the birthplace, *c.* 336 B.C., of Zeno, the great Stoic who was inspired by the works of Socrates to found a school of philosophy which met for lectures in the Stoa of the Agora in Athens. A bust of Zeno, copied from the one known likeness of the philosopher in Herculaneum, was erected in Larnaca in 1921.

Though much damage and loss of life was incurred at the time of the Arab raids, these did not destroy Larnaca. During the Middle Ages Salines (as the city was then called because of its Salt Lake) had a revival of importance due to Famagusta falling into the hands of the Genoese, and it became the principal point of embarkation for pilgrims to the Holy Land. A hundred years later travellers were reporting the city to be in ruins and almost completely destroyed, though the Church of St Lazarus still stood. But Larnaca made yet another recovery during the Turkish occupation of 1570. The Turks landed here before their attack on Nicosia, and for some time retained the city as the seat of foreign consuls. An English consul in the eighteenth century is reported by contemporary Dutch travellers* as being 'highly respected all over the island, as jointly with his company he advances money to the

* Hon. J. A. E. von Egmont and John Heyman, Professor of Languages in the University of Leyden, in *Excerpta Cypria*.

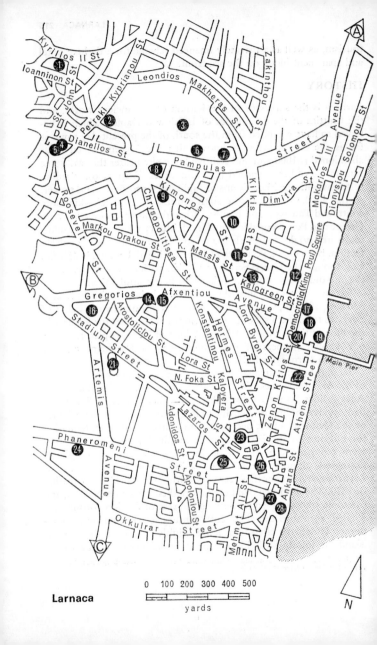

Larnaca

0 100 200 300 400 500

yards

N

inhabitants for getting in their several harvests, in which otherwise they would be at great loss'. English merchants and the companies they represented were indeed responsible for much of the sophistication of the residential quarter. The consuls and merchants are also credited with having indulged in uncoordinated treasure-hunts on the site of the older city, and they may justifiably be accused of being responsible for the dearth of archaeological remains. What escaped their attention, however, were the areas currently being exposed and consolidated by the Department of Antiquities, in particular the large Phoenician temple (p. 219), the site of which was discovered in 1967, in the vicinity of which a variety of ancient objects have been found.

CHURCHES

Church of St Lazaros

This beautiful church was built to enshrine the tomb of Lazarus, who according to legend was expelled from Bethany after his resurrection, and committed by force to an unseaworthy boat in the company of his sisters Mary and Martha. The boat miraculously

weathered the storms and reached Kitium, where Lazarus fell in
with the Apostles who were proselytizing the island, and was consecrated bishop. The saint's remains were discovered in A.D. 890
and removed to Constantinople, whence they were taken by the
French and smuggled to Marseilles. The sarcophagus is therefore
empty, but it is held in great veneration. Descent is by a flight of
steps from the south apse. Some authorities have contended that
the sarcophagus is one that has been brought to its present place
from a local necropolis, but it is generally assumed that the side
hidden from view is inscribed in Hebrew: 'LAZARUS, THE FRIEND
OF CHRIST'.

The church itself is distinguished by its belfry – an unusual concession by the Turks, who advisedly banned campaniles for fear
that they might be used to give a signal for uprising. It has three
aisles, with a roof supported on four stout columns. Several
Corinthian capitals have been re-used in the reconstruction of the
church, which took place in the seventeenth century, when care
was taken that it should preserve its original form. The building
had been repurchased from the Turks in 1589, and was thereafter
used for the celebration of both the Orthodox and the Latin rite.
The iconostasis is a good example of woodwork of the eighteenth
century, and there is a very beautiful rococo pulpit with its staircase
built into the thickness of one of the pillars. The icon of greatest
interest depicts the *Raising of Lazarus*, showing the man opening the
coffin holding his nose for, as Martha said to Jesus: 'Lord, by this
time he stinketh; for he hath been dead four days.' The Royal
Doors, which are dated 1659, should not be overlooked.

Other Churches
Church of St John the Divine – dating from the seventeenth century
and restored in 1850: *Church of Santa Maria della Gratia* (1843).
Chryssopolitissa Church (1815): *Chryssosotiros Church* (19th century).
Phaneromeni Church – constructed from an early tomb.

OTHER SIGHTS

Kitium
Contrary to the fate of the majority of the ancient cities and
settlements of Cyprus, which were abandoned by their inhabitants,
Kitium is covered by the present town of Larnaca, a fact which
hampers systematic excavation. The tombs, which afforded such a

rewarding hobby for the foreign consuls, are widely scattered – and empty, unless any escaped their avarice.

The centre of Kitium is known to have been on the high ground or *acropolis* not far from the present position of St Joseph's Convent. It is here that the temples to the gods were erected. Archaic statues of Hercules discovered in 1930 suggested that this was the site of an open-air temple similar to others located in proximity to Phoenician trading stations.

In spite of difficulties, archaeological survey continued, and work under Professor Karageorghis in 1963 in the area of the Chryssopolitissa Church resulted not only in the discovery of a *Bath House* of the Hellenistic–early Roman period but also evidence that the site had been continuously occupied from the Bronze Age until the Middle Ages. Subsequent projects then concentrated on the north section of the *City Walls*, which also provide a continuous record, of which the Cyclopean portions of the Mycenaean period are the most impressive.

In 1967 and 1968 these sporadic excavations began to yield impressive results – more than enough to justify a greater concentration of the resources of the Department of Antiquities. The work was twofold: to investigate workshops pertaining to the twelfth-century Mycenaean city and, more rewarding still, to uncover an eighth-century B.C. *Phoenician Temple* dedicated to Astarte. This proved to be one of the largest hitherto found, and had a roof supported by two lines of six columns. Whereas it was built subsequent to the evacuation of the city *c.* 1000 B.C., after which it underwent periodic alteration, its own destruction did not come until the end of the fourth century, when in 312 B.C. Ptolemy killed Poumiathion, the last king of Kitium, thus bringing Phoenician dominance to an end. It is anticipated that the site will be open to the public in 1971.

Archaeological Museum
Map **11**.
Opening hours

Mid-May to mid-Sept.   8 a.m. to 1 p.m.
4 p.m. to 6 p.m.
Sunday 10 a.m. to 1 p.m.
Mid-Sept. to mid-May 8.30 a.m. to 1 p.m.
2.30 p.m. to 4.30 p.m
Sunday 10 a.m. to 1 p.m.

Besides recent finds on the various sites of Kitium, the collection includes tools, ornaments, etc., from Khirokitia dating from 5800 to 5250 B.C., also late Bronze Age (fourteenth century B.C.) vases and very 'modern' jewellery of slightly later date. A second room is devoted to statuary, a large proportion having come from Arsos.

Turkish Fort*
Map **28.**
Erected by the Turks in 1625. Compares unfavourably in scope and beauty with Venetian fortifications.

Municipal Gardens and Zoo (*Map* **16.**)

* Not open to the public at date of going to press.

EXCURSIONS FROM LARNACA
Tekké of Hala Sultan and Kiti Church

Route The Tekké of Hala Sultan is situated on the Salt Lake about 3 m. to the south-west of Larnaca (Route C on Larnaca map) and makes a pleasant walk. If transport is available, continue along the main road to Kiti (5½ m.).

[½ m.] Follow the south-eastern shore of the great *Salt Lake* which is the winter habitat of flamingos and wild fowl. When the water evaporates in the summer months this becomes a place of seasonal activity for the gathering of salt, which is hauled from the exposed bed of the lake and piled ready for transportation. The industry is an ancient one. A sixteenth-century traveller records that: ' . . . there is a lake of about nine miles circuit, in which are springs of salt water, which, with waters from the winter rains, and kept enclosed during the summer, by the heat and ardour of the sun, they harden and congeal into a very beautiful salt, white like snow . . .'*

All this is true today, except that mechanization has made the great pyramids of salt awaiting disposal more imposing than ever. The glaring white in summer and autumn accentuates the luxuriance of the oasis-like Tekké of Hala Sultan with its dome and minaret surrounded by palms and cypresses on the opposite shore of the lake.

[2½ m.] A well-signposted right turn leads in ½ m. to the *Tekké of Hala Sultan*.

TEKKÉ OF HALA SULTAN

Tekké means 'shrine', and Hala Sultan is the Turkish form of 'Ummul Haram', which in Arabic stands for 'respected mother'. This is the third most holy site in the Muslim world, ranking immediately after Mecca and the Shrine of Mohammed at Medina. It is visited annually by great numbers of the faithful, who congregate here especially during the Muslim festivals of Sheker Bairam and Qurban Bairam.

* Zuellart, *Voyages*, 1598.

H

Ummul Haram was a female relative of the Prophet Mohammed. As was the custom in the offensives of those days, she was one of the ladies who accompanied the waves of Arabs who invaded Cyprus *c.* 694. Their function was to nurse casualties and encourage assault troops. Unfortunately she met with sudden death here ... 'falling from her beast she broke her pellucid neck and yielded up her victorious soul, and in that fragrant spot was at once buried.'*

The tomb was believed by archaeologists to be a trilithon, with two uprights more than 15 ft in height and a third meteoric stone 16 by 9 ft laid horizontally across them, as at Stonehenge. One popular belief is that the 15-ton meteorite for a long period of time hovered in a state of suspension over the sacred grave, affording it shelter from the elements. Another account testifies that all three stones were brought from Mount Sinai by angels. In spite of these theories, however, it is understood that recent and necessary repair work revealed that the uprights were part masonry and part timber, and not monolithic.

The approach to the shrine is through gardens planted with the tall palm trees that were first seen from the other side of the lake. There are masses of flowering shrubs and trees, and a fountain for ablutions – a real Eastern garden.

The mosque containing the sacred shrine was built in 1816 by Seyyit Mahommet Emin, the Turkish governor of Cyprus. Inside there is a domed structure of 1760 housing the stones over the tomb, which is itself covered by a cloth of rich embroidery. This inner sanctuary is reached through a doorway decorated with dog-tooth moulding of some antiquity. Visitors and pilgrims are allowed to circulate around the tomb. They will also be shown the tomb of the Turkish second wife of King Hussein of the Hedjaz (d. 1929) in the arcade of the mosque, and also a marble slab outside the main entrance. This bears an inscription referring to Baldassare Trivizani, the Venetian lieutenant-governor of the island from 1489 to 1491. The mosque and its minaret are clearly visible from the sea, and it used to be the custom for passing Turkish vessels to dip their flags and fire guns in salute.

[5½ m.] The village of **Kiti** is situated 3 m. farther along beyond the turning to the Tekké. The name is thought to be connected with Kitium, the old city of Larnaca, which did not, however, extend to

* *Journal of the Asiatic Society*, January 1897.

this distance. It is of importance to lovers of Byzantine art for its *Church of Panayia Angeloktisti* – meaning 'built by angels' – which contains the better of the two famous mosaic pictures in Cyprus – the other being in Kanakaria Church (p. 210). The key is kept at a house facing the south side of the church.

KITI CHURCH

The eastern apse and northern chapel of this church are thought to have been erected soon after Cyprus was cleared of the Saracens in A.D. 958. The body of the church was rebuilt in the twelfth century, with a nave and transepts of exceptional loftiness crowned by a central dome. The narthex, which has apses to the north and south, was added later, probably after the thirteenth-century Latin chapel was built. In this chapel, through which the main church is entered, re-laying of the floor revealed a gravestone of the fourteenth century. This bears an inscription showing it to be that of Lady Simone, daughter of Sir William Guers, and wife of Sir Renier de Gibelet, who died at the age of fifty on November 5th, 1302. To the north of the church, and accessible from its interior, there is a small dark chapel of ancient construction which has been used as a mortuary chapel. It shows signs of having had pictures throughout its interior, though many of the frescoes have been partially or wholly obliterated by damp and decay. The darkness, damp and lack of ventilation act as reminders of the chapel's purpose.

MOSAIC

It is, of course, the fine mosaic in the central apse, rather than the various styles of architecture of the church, which draws visitors to Kiti. The picture is remarkable among Byzantine art, and is a work of extreme beauty. The balance of the compositions lifts it above the many designs in other churches which have as their prime function the information and edification of an illiterate congregation. The Virgin stands centrally on a footstool. She is dressed in a long-sleeved tunic and mantle, and supports the Holy Child on her left arm. The Archangels Gabriel and Michael – the latter unfortunately lacking much of his detail – are on either side. They have wings of peacocks' feathers, and carry orbs and sceptres. The

H2

colours are superb, and an attractive border with motifs of rosettes contributes to the unity of the composition.

The date of this magnificent mosaic is doubtful and controversial. Early Russian authorities ascribe it to the fifth or sixth century, Professor Talbot Rice in his *Birth of Western Painting*, published in 1930, favours the ninth century, and other experts argue a later date. But informed opinion now tends to be returning to the early dating, with the additional suggestion that the structure of the central apse where the mosaic is situated is part of a basilica of the fifth century and therefore older than any other part of the edifice, including the mortuary chapel.

Whatever the exact date of origin, and whether or not the mosaic was restored in the Middle Ages, as some believe, it is indisputably a work of great beauty, and should without doubt be seen by all visitors to Cyprus.

Stavrovouni Monastery, Kornos and Pyrga

Route Take the Limassol road (Route B on Larnaca map) and fork back to the right near Kophinou (15 m.) on to the Nicosia–Limassol road for turnings to Stavrovouni Monastery (28 m.), Kornos (24 m.) and Pyrga (24 m.).

On the way back a diversion may be made to Dhali (p. 153) by turning right when rejoining the main road after Pyrga, right again opposite Perakhorio, and joining the main Nicosia–Larnaca road beyond Dhali north-east of Louroujina (24 m.).

For Nicosia continue northwards at the Perakhorio–Dhali crossroads (+18 m.).

Ancient Monument

Chapel of St Catherine, Pyrga

Apply for admission to the custodian in Pyrga village at any reasonable time.

N.B. There is no accommodation for women visitors at Stavrovouni Monastery.

[15 m.] Just before **Kophinou** fork back to the right on to the Nicosia–Limassol road.

[22 m.] Turn right on to a secondary road leading in 6 m. to *Stavrovouni Monastery* by way of the community's farm at the foot of the mountain. Possibly a monk would appreciate a lift up the hill.

STAVROVOUNI MONASTERY

The monastery is a prominent landmark overlooking a wide stretch of country. The summit of the hill upon which it stands is

2,260 ft above sea-level, and it is accessible only by 6 m. of steep road consisting of innumerable hairpin bends. Brakes should be in good order, and special care should be taken after rain. This is no drive for the nervous – or the novice (speaking in lay terms). The lower slopes of the hill are scrub and forest, leading up to more open ground which is the haunt of ptarmigan and partridge. This area is scheduled as a State Forest.

The history of this monastery, which occupies such an eye-catching position that no medieval traveller could resist writing about it, is that it was built on the site of a pagan temple dedicated to Aphrodite, remains of which are still extant. This is the third of the island's mountains to have been given in antiquity the name of Mount Olympus. When St Helena landed in Cyprus in A.D. 327 on her return voyage from Jerusalem to Constantinople, she brought with her the Cross upon which Christ was crucified, and also that of the Penitent Thief. (It is said that she refused to have anything to do with the third cross.) In accordance with a dream, and in thank-offering for having survived tempestuous seas, she donated a portion of the True Cross and the complete cross of the Penitent Thief to a group of monks with the injunction that they should build a monastery here around these relics. Some writers hint that her real purpose was to oust all traces of pagan cults from the summit of the mountain. It was in this fashion that Stavrovouni, the 'Mountain of the Cross', became a renowned place of pilgrimage. Various medieval travellers have testified to seeing the Stavrovouni Cross suspended miraculously in the air without any physical means of support. Following the Turkish invasion, the monastery was deserted until it could be reoccupied in the seventeenth century. The fate of the cross brought from Jerusalem is in doubt, but the devout revere the cross at present in the monastery church. This is a magnificent crucifix of wood on an octagonal base carved with scenes from Our Lord's life. It dates from 1476, but was framed in silver in 1707. A tiny fragment, believed to have formed part of the True Cross, is set into it and protected by gold of seventeenth-century workmanship, and the whole is covered by a 'chemise' of seventeenth-century needlework.

The *Church of the Cross* is mainly modern, though it is constructed on foundations going back to an early period of history. Apart from the famous cross, it contains nothing of greater interest than an inscription carved in the south wall of a corridor of the monastery. This records the prayer of one Philotheos, a monk of the eleventh century. Outside, from balconies which are like ramparts, there is a spectacular view, showing a large tract of country spread out far below as though it were a map.

The way of life of this community of monks is particularly impressive. They keep very strictly to their vows, and spend much of their time working on the land on their *metochi* at the foot of Stavrovouni. They were the pioneers of the dried grape known as the sultana. The honey of their bees is famous. They excel in the painting of modern icons. Their hospitality is well known – and it seems that this is extended to a great number of cats, which are well treated except that their number and their employment as snake-killers result in a hungry look, such as the monks themselves might well have, because their life is a frugal one. Added to this, the monks have the exacting climb to the summit in all weathers and at difficult seasons when there can be little prospect of obtaining a lift. A fairly recent controversy relating to the calendar, which threatened a major schism, has now been resolved. But it is feared that the numbers in the community are dwindling to a figure below the twenty mark, of which a proportion is always on vigil and doing duty at the summit.

[23 m.] Having returned to the main road, proceed in the direction of Nicosia and take the first turning to the right, following it for about another mile to the village of **Pyrga,** at the beginning of which the small *Chapel of St Catherine* comes into view on the right. This beautiful little Latin building was founded by King Janus in 1412 before his capture by the Egyptian Mamelukes at the Battle of Khirokitia. It is built of warm-coloured stone cut roughly and irregularly, and forming a plain barrel-vaulted rectangle with doors on the north, west and south sides. The lintel of the south door has the French surname 'Bazoges' scratched rather than carved over it, and a little above this the belfry has fittings where banner staves would have been supported.

However, the paintings in the interior of the chapel are of greater interest than the architecture. The vaulting of the interior originally had painted panels, the best preserved of which is on the north-east side and depicts the Raising of Lazarus. Of greater importance, high on the east wall under two lancet windows, there are remains of a Crucifixion scene, showing two crowned figures at the foot of the Cross. These are King Janus and his second wife, Charlotte de Bourbon. The king wears a heavy crown and a grey cloak, while his wife is dressed in the French fashion of her time.

[24 m.] Returning to the crossroads, turn right and then, almost immediately, left for **Kornos,** a straggling village on the floor of a valley of red earth. The soil has been found to be excellent pottery clay – hence the enormous jars which are the main industry of the village. The pottery has none of the glazes, decoration and finish of the products of the northern coast near Kyrenia. It is archaic in shape, and absolutely functional, being used for the storage of oil, water and wine. Most of the houses here have an inconspicuous potter's shed attached to them, where the work is carried out with little sign of automation – just the wheel worked by foot, the mass of wet clay within reach and the red hands of the worker (often a woman) fashioning vessels which have not developed in form for many centuries. The giant jars have to be moulded entirely by hand without use of the wheel. It is amusing, though for some reason somewhat alarming, to discover that shops in the cities sell plastic ware identical in design to the old jars and vases.

LIMASSOL

Population 50,000.
Information
Tourist Bureau: On sea-front, opposite Customs House (*Map* **14**).
Antiquities Dept, Administration Office; Anexartisias St (*Map* **3**).
Hotels
De luxe Curium Palace; Miramare (on coast 3 m. east).
1st (A) Apollonia Beach (Limassol 3 m.).
1st (B) Alasia; Astir.
       Awaiting classification: Panorama; Continental; Metropole; Palace;
       Amathus Beach (due to open summer 1973).
3rd   Acropole; Rose; Vienna.
4th   Astoria.
This being a port and commercial centre, the majority of hotels are in the centre of the
town in order to cater for a business clientele as well as tourism.
Restaurants and Bars
Acropolis, Gladstone St.
Akroyali, 28th October St.
Britannia, Franklin Roosevelt Ave.
Diana, Makarios III Ave.
Elyse, Makarios III Ave.
Lofty's, Paphos Rd.
Metropolitan (Chinese food), off Makarios III Ave.
Mimosa, Hadjipavlou St.
Niyazi Kebab (Turkish food), Ismet Pasha St.
The needs of visiting businessmen, and the proximity of the British sovereign base
at Episkopi has favoured the proliferation of restaurants of all kinds, ranging upwards
from milk-bars, fish-and-chip parlours, pastry-shops and cafés to the more expensive
establishments which serve both international and local food. Not all can be included
here. The principal localities for good eating are Makarios Avenue, Chr. Hadjipavlou
St and Ayios Andreas St. Other restaurants are strung along the Limassol–Nicosia
road. These include the Avenida, Kifissia, Kyma and Potamos Yermasios Restaurant-
Bars.
Night clubs
Akroyali, Kyma, Cave du Roi and Disc-a-gogo (discotheques in Makarios III
Avenue); Olympia (cabaret), Zenon St, and Tropicana Night Cellar club, on the
by-pass.
Churches
Anglican St Barnabas, Leontios St (*Map* **1**).
Roman Catholic St Joseph, 28th October St (*Map* **7**).
Cinemas
Hellas; Pallas; Regal; Rialto; Yiordhamlis.
Festival
Folk-dancing festival in *Public Gardens,* early July.
Bathing
One of the most popular beaches for bathing is the sandy 'Ladies Mile', which is
reached by driving west out of town on Roosevelt Avenue (Route C on Limassol
map). The beach to the east of the town is mainly pebbles, except where the Miramare
Hotel has specially imported sand. The Nautical Club, approx. 2 m. on the Nicosia
road, accepts temporary members.

Despite the lack of deep water, which involves the transfer of
cargo and passengers by lighter, the port of Limassol is a busy one
and will increase in importance when the construction of a deep-

water harbour becomes effective, probably in 1973. The town is second to Nicosia in size. It combines sophistication with the claims of industry. Hotels and public services are excellent, the shops well stocked, and café and restaurant life are pleasant and vivid in both the Greek and Turkish quarters of the town. In the same way that some people are natural party-givers, Limassol goes all out for fun and entertainment, and takes the fullest advantage of high days and holidays. The greatest and most extrovert of these is the spring carnival, which rivals those of the French Riviera for exuberance.

The industries of Limassol make a solid foundation for these pleasures. The chief exports are wine and carobs, both of which play a major part in the island's economy, and the odd, sweet smell of carobs hangs heavy on the air during the harvesting and shipping season. Because Limassol provides the means for processing agricultural produce – it has wine, brandy, beer, fruit canning and soft drinks factories – combined with facilities for shipping fruit and vegetables from the neighbouring large plantations, the town is of great importance not only in its own immediate neighbourhood but also to farms and villages as far afield as the district of Paphos. It is significant and altogether charming that in the autumn road signs on the outskirts of Limassol should proclaim: 'DANGER: GRAPE JUICE ON THE ROAD' – as though the produce of the country has been transported in a giant and overflowing cornucopia.

HISTORY

Most of the history of the town can be told in relation to its castle. In fact, there are no other local sites of any importance, and therefore no need to search them out as a preliminary to reconstructing the events of the past. In the Middle Ages Limassol rose to great importance, taking the place of its close neighbour Amathus, where Richard Cœur de Lion landed in 1191. Subsequently, however, decline set in, as a result of destruction inflicted by the Genoese in 1373 and by Saracens in 1426, and periodic damage caused by earthquake and sometimes by flood. In view of these disasters it is not surprising that for many centuries Famagusta ranked superior. In fact, Limassol did not begin the long climb back to high status until the eighteenth century – the beginning of an era of commercial growth.

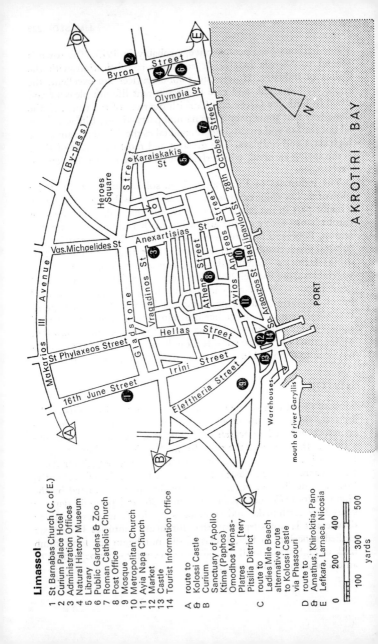

Limassol

1 St Barnabas Church (C. of E.)
2 Curium Palace Hotel
3 Administration Offices
4 Natural History Museum
5 Library
6 Public Gardens & Zoo
7 Roman Catholic Church
8 Post Office
9 Mosque
10 Metropolitan Church
11 Ayia Napa Church
12 Market
13 Castle
14 Tourist Information Office

A route to
  Kolossi Castle
B Curium
  Sanctuary of Apollo
  Ktima (Paphos)
  Omodhos Monas-
  Platres   [tery
  Pitsilia District
C route to
  Ladies Mile Beach
  alternative route
  to Kolossi Castle
  via Phassouri
D route to
& Amathus, Khirokitia, Pano
E Lefkara, Larnaca, Nicosia

0   100   300   500
     200   400
        yards

CASTLE*

Though Byzantine fortifications of *c.* 1226 at one time occupied the site of the present castle, little remains of these except part of the east wall, which is the west wall of the present castle, and certain traces within the east chapel and among the foundations.

In 1191 the fleet carrying Richard Cœur de Lion to the Crusades encountered storms so fierce that his ships were scattered between Crete and Rhodes. The story which followed is best told in the words of the Chronicle ascribed to Benedict, abbot of Peterborough, 1177–93:

> ... three large vessels were driven by the aforesaid tempest to the island of Cyprus, and, being wrecked and broken up, sank in sight of the port of Limezun ... Isaac the Emperor of Cyprus seized the chattels of those who were drowned, and robbed of their money all who escaped from the shipwreck. Moreover, in the fury of his savagery, worse than any beast of prey, he refused permission to enter the port to a galliot which had been driven thither by the wind, and which carried the Queen of Sicily [Joanna, the Queen Dowager], and the daughter of the king of Navarre [Berengaria, who was betrothed to King Richard]. When news of this was brought to the king he hastened to their rescue, with many galleys and a great following of ships, and found the ladies outside the port of Limezun, exposed to the winds and the sea. Then in great wrath he sent messengers to the Emperor of Cyprus, once, twice and yet a third time, making his request with mild entreaty, that his fellow pilgrims, whom the Emperor was keeping in durance, should be restored to him together with their belongings. To whom the Emperor made answer with proud words, refusing to surrender either the prisoners or their belongings, and saying that he had no fear of the king of England or of his threats.
>
> Then spake the king to all his army, saying 'To arms, and follow me! Let me take vengeance for the insults which this traitor hath put upon God and ourselves, in that he oppresses innocent men whom he refuses to surrender to us.'†

* At the date of going to press the Castle is still occupied by Turkish/Cypriot military forces. However, since this is the one important historical monument in Limassol, visitors wishing to see over it are advised to make advance application to the officer in charge, in the hope that restrictions may be lifted in their favour.

† *Excerpta Cypria*, p. 6.

Richard thereupon landed at Amathus and proceeded to slaughter the forces of the emperor, though he wisely forbore from following the survivors into the mountains. When plans for wresting the possession of the island from the emperor were well in hand, Richard and his betrothed made rendezvous in Limassol, where their marriage was solemnized on May 12th, the feast of St Nereus, Achilleus and Pancratius. Berengaria was crowned Queen of England on the day of her marriage. It is of interest in this connection that the altar at present in the east chapel of the castle displays evidence of having been at one time converted to the Latin rite – that is, from a square to a rectangle. Some authorities suggest that the altar stone was originally pagan, before being adapted for use in the Byzantine era, and that it was enlarged at the time of the royal marriage by the addition of a portable altar from one of the ships of the English fleet.

In the early thirteenth century, at a time when earthquake damage to the town was being made good, the castle was enlarged to contain the church erected by the Knights Templar during the Crusading period. The castle was leased by the Lusignans to the Templars after the fall of Acre in 1291, and it became their headquarters. The Knights Hospitaller, who had similarly removed to Limassol, later transferred their headquarters to Rhodes. Under the Knights Templar the Gothic windows were covered, and the structure thickened to such an extent that there was provision for secret passages inside the fabric of the walls. The masonry of the east chapel bears marks which may be the signatures of individual masons, but could conceivably be clues to treasure hidden during that period of building. When the Knights Templar were banned by the Pope in 1308 the Lusignans regained possession.

The Genoese set fire to the town and took the castle in 1373. The skeleton of a soldier, 6 ft 4 ins. in height, has recently been discovered in the castle. He was laid out Viking fashion, with his right hand to his heart, and his left at the place where the hilt of his sword would have been. His skull had been split by a single blow. His height and conformation suggest that he was a Scottish soldier who died in the defence of the castle against the Genoese. His bones have been allowed to remain in the place where they were found, and in the position of burial.

Another cache of bones is attributed to the year 1426, when the Egyptian Mamelukes under Sultan Aschraf Barsabei gained admittance to the castle through the aid of a prisoner. One of the skeletons unearthed here had every bone of his body broken, and it may be supposed that this might have been the traitor who assisted the barbarians.

When the Mamelukes agreed to leave the island in exchange for an annual tribute the Lusignans again assumed control of Limassol Castle and assigned it to the Knights of St John of Jerusalem. During the period which followed, the Knights transformed the great western hall into a church in Gothic style, and converted the chapel into prison cells.

In 1538, nearly fifty years after the annexation of the island by Venice, and prior to the large-scale Turkish attack, a small party of Turks, ostensibly guests (though they refrained from accepting wine), took the castle. The occurrence was prevented from becoming an international incident by the Turks being declared pirates. Soon after these usurpers were ousted, the Venetians began to implement a policy of fortification against the expected Turkish invasion. As in other cities of Cyprus, they made use of materials taken from existing buildings, razing them to the ground for the sake of their stone, and levelling everything else that remained in order to assure a clear field of fire. In this way many churches were destroyed and other antiquities lost – among them a large portion of the Byzantine castle. The Great Hall, which the Knights of St John had converted into a church, became the subject of dissension between ecclesiastical and military interests. Finally, a compromise was reached, whereby a clear demarcation line was made: the church would be situated below, the fortifications above.

The alterations to Limassol Castle continued until 1567, when the locality was severely shaken by earthquake. A portion of the roof of the Great Hall and its vaulting fell in when the central supporting pillar collapsed. The town had to be partially abandoned as uninhabitable, and work on the castle came to a halt.

With the advent of the Turks in 1570, Limassol was thoroughly and brutally pillaged. The usurpers took over the rebuilding of the castle in a form suited to their needs: by restoring the upper west wall of the Great Hall, and building a protective tower at the entrance. The damaged vaulting in the West Hall was rearranged, and wooden beams were substituted for the original pillars. Until 1878 this great room, the structure of which reveals the whole history of the castle, was used by the Turks as a prison, and continued to function as such until 1940 under the British regime. In 1950 the vaults were strengthened by the replacement of the central arch.

Churches

Though Gunnis, in *Historic Cyprus*, states that the Orthodox churches of Limassol are without interest, his reason being that they are of no great age, we suggest that visitors should look in at the nineteenth-century Metropolitan Church (*Map* 10) and Ayia Napa (*Map* 11).

OTHER SIGHTS

Besides the *Public Gardens*, there are *Zoological Gardens*, containing specimens of moufflon for visitors unable to see this rare wild sheep in natural surroundings, and with a *Natural History Museum* attached (both open on weekdays 10 a.m. to 12 noon, 2 p.m. to 5 p.m.). The creation of a *District Museum* to replace that which was housed in the castle is under consideration. It will probably occupy a site not far from the Curium Palace Hotel. There is also a small *Folk Museum* in Heroes Square, which may be seen on application to the *Library* in Ayios Andreas St. This is an excellent library, mainly of books in Greek. The wine factories and the distillery welcome visitors.

EXCURSIONS FROM LIMASSOL
Kolossi Castle, Curium and Sanctuary of Apollo

Route Take either the main Limassol–Paphos road (Routes A or B on Limassol map), turning left for Kolossi Castle (7 m.), which stands a short distance south of the road, or the longer route to the south (Route C on Limassol map) through the Phassouri plantations (+3 m.). A fast road known as the M.1 south of Kolossi cuts down mileage to Paphos. These routes join near Episkopi village, to which a detour (+1 m.) should be made to the Museum. Continue to Curium (10 m.), the Stadium, and the Sanctuary of Apollo (11 m.).

For Ktima (Paphos) continue via Petra tou Romiou, Kouklia, the Temple of Aphrodite at Palea Paphos and Yeroskipos (pp. 265–9) (+33 m.).

Ancient Monuments and Museum
Kolossi Castle
Opening hours
Mid-May to mid-Sept. Daily 9 a.m. to 12 noon
3 p.m. to 6.30 p.m.
Mid-Sept. to mid-May Daily 9 a.m. to 1 p.m.
2 p.m. to 4.30 p.m.

Episkopi Museum
Opening hours
Mid-May to mid-Sept. Weekdays 8 a.m. to 1 p.m.
4 p.m. to 6 p.m.
Sundays 10 a.m. to 1 p.m.
Mid-Sept. to mid-May Weekdays 8.30 a.m. to 1 p.m.
2.30 p.m. to 4.30 p.m.
Sundays 10 a.m. to 1 p.m.

Curium (main site)
Custodian's office 400 yds inside entrance.
Opening hours
Mid-May to mid-Sept. Daily 7 a.m. to 7 p.m.
Mid-Sept. to mid-May 7.30 a.m. to dusk.
The restaurant provides refreshment and a splendid view of the sea.

Sanctuary of Apollo
Custodian in attendance.
Opening hours
Mid-May to mid-Sept. 9 a.m. to 12 noon.
3 p.m. to 6.30 p.m.
Mid-Sept. to mid-May 9 a.m. to 1 p.m.
2 p.m. to 4.30 p.m.
There is no custodian at the Stadium.

[+3 m.] Though Kolossi is 7 m. from Limassol by the direct road, a more pleasant approach is by a southern route through the *Phassouri Plantations*, which adds 3 m. to the distance. The Cyprus Palestine Plantation was formed in 1933, and since then experts from Israel have built up a thriving concern, growing and exporting citrus, dried fruit and pecan nuts. Their example was followed a few years later by a Limassol businessman, who has developed a very large farm at Zakaki for the cultivation of fruit of every variety suitable to the soil and climate. Honey is a profitable sideline. As well as presenting an impressive example of the development of the country's natural resources, visits to these farms are very pleasant. Arrangements should be made through the Limassol Tourist Office (or by telephoning the company at Limassol 2131), but even if the vast plantations are seen only from the road on the way to Kolossi, the shade and shelter of the cypress and bamboo wind-breaks and the tall eucalyptus trees draining the swamps all contribute to a pleasant drive through avenues of fruit trees.

A turning left at Phassouri village leads in about 3 m. to **Akrotiri** on the shores of a *Salt Lake*. Access to *Akrotiri Monastery (St Nicolaos)* two miles farther on is gained through the gate into the Akrotiri British base, for which a pass is required (consult Limassol Tourist Information Bureau).

[7 m.] The village and castle of Kolossi (opening hours p. 235) are just to the left off the main direct road from Limassol.

HISTORY OF KOLOSSI CASTLE

This dates from before the building of the present great keep, which was erected *c.* 1454 by the Knights of the Order of St John of Jerusalem, otherwise known as the Knights Hospitaller. In 1191 Isaac Comnenus and his forces camped here when they unsuccessfully opposed the invasion of Richard Cœur de Lion. It is likely that a castle was first built on the site in 1210, when the property was granted to the Hospitallers. Nothing survives of this earlier building. About ten years after the fall of Acre in 1291, and after the removal of the headquarters of the Order to Limassol, Kolossi became the centre of the conventual life of the Hospitallers, and except for a brief occupation by the Knights Templar fulfilled this role until the removal of their headquarters to Rhodes in 1310. Kolossi was then retained as a Commandery – incidentally the richest overseas possession of the Order, deriving a substantial income from the sale of Commandaria wine, and from vineyards and sugar plantations. The status of the Commandery, and its ownership of several villages, was confirmed by the Chapter in 1380.

It is likely that the Genoese campaigns of 1373 and raids by the Mamelukes early in the following century resulted in so much damage (though the castle was never taken) that it had to be entirely rebuilt. By this time, and despite the hazards and unrest of the period, the Knights Hospitaller had developed their great estates in the form of villages and vineyards geared to the production of wine famous throughout Christendom. In addition a factory used for processing raw sugar is situated to the east of the keep, and though repaired under Turkish occupation in the late sixteenth century – probably necessitated by earthquake damage – part of its structure is believed to antedate any of the remains of the castle itself, with the possible exception of the well-head to the south of the main entrance.

When the island was annexed by Venice in 1489, Giorgio Cornaro, brother of Queen Catherine, was rewarded for his complicity in the transaction by a grant of the villages of the Commandery and the revenues arising from them. This property remained in the ownership of the Cornaro family until the Turkish invasion of 1570.

DESCRIPTION OF CASTLE

The great square keep is imposing in its solidity, and beautiful for the colour of its stone. It consists of three storeys with walls 9 ft thick, with a machicoulis under the ramparts immediately above the drawbridge and entrance on the south side. This overhanging defensive device was provided with openings from which stones could be dropped on the castle's besiegers. The west wall has a marble panel bearing the royal arms of Cyprus, flanked by those of two Grand Masters of Rhodes. Below them is the coat of arms of Louis de Magnac, Grand Commander of Cyprus 1450–68, who is believed to have been responsible for the present form of the castle.

The building was never intended to be entered through the ground floor, which has three large vaulted rooms that were used for stores, with cisterns beneath, the sole communication with the upper floors originally being through a trap-door. The main entrance, which was defended by the drawbridge and machicoulis, leads into the main hall at the second-floor level, where there was a second room containing a large fireplace, which was probably the kitchen. Both these rooms have pointed vaults. On the right of the entrance there is a large mural painting of the Crucifixion, below which the arms of Louis de Magnac appear again. A spiral staircase of good proportions in the south-east corner leads to the third storey, which again consists of two large vaulted rooms, set at right-angles to the two below, which were the apartments of the Grand Commanders. Each room has four windows with seats in the thickness of the wall, as well as a magnificent fireplace reminiscent of contemporary French design and decoration, and again incorporating the de Magnac arms. There is also a privy. The battlements are reached by a continuation of the spiral staircase. This portion of the castle, as well as the entrance, was largely rebuilt in the course of restoration in 1933. It has been suggested that the height of each of the four main rooms was divided by wooden flooring carried on beams, thus providing the extra accommodation which is notably lacking in the present interior.

Remains of outbuildings below the drawbridge were probably stables and stores. These were accessible through a postern gate. It will be seen that the medieval *Aqueduct* north of the sugar factory is still used for irrigation. Both the mill and the factory were finally put out of business as a result of competition from the West Indian sugar plantations.

[8 m.] Continue northwards, then turn left to join the direct Limassol–Paphos road, which crosses the Kouris river beyond Erimi. On the farther side of the bridge a road (right) leads to Platres (see route from Omodhos and the Pitsilia district, p. 244). Turn here, but after 30 yds fork left at the signpost for Courion (alias Episkopi) Museum. The village of Episkopi, which is divided between Greek and Turkish communities, should not be confused with the British sovereign base with its suburban housing 4 m. to the west. A series of direction signs lead circuitously to the new Museum, which houses a very interesting collection of local discoveries, easily the most exciting being statuary from the newly excavated Roman villa at Curium. This includes the figures of Hermes in his role as Pastor or Protector of Shepherds and of Asclepios, the God of Medicine, as well as a beautiful head of Aphrodite crowned with a diadem.

[10 m.] Continue through the Turkish sector of the village to regain the main road, which now ascends the artificial escarpment upon which Curium was built, probably with the object of protecting the Paphos Gate of the city.

The main site of *Curium* is on the left or seaward side of the road.

HISTORY OF CURIUM

Though Curium was in existence in the fourth millennium B.C., and is mentioned by Herodotus as the home of Argives from the Peloponnesus in 1200 B.C., the first important reference to it in history relates to the Graeco-Persian wars. A swing of allegiance at the time of the Battle of Salamis (Greece) in 480 B.C. dramatically brought Curium to prominence. The city-state later supported Alexander the Great in the Siege of Tyre, and this time contributed to the overthrow of the Persians. It is evident from the various excavations on the site that there was no decline of greatness under Ptolemaic or Roman rule. When the time came, Christianity was embraced as fervently as the previous cult of Apollo Hylates. Philoneides, an early bishop, was martyred in the reign of Diocletian (284–305), and one of his successors was largely responsible for presenting the Church's claims to autonomy to the Council of Ephesus in A.D. 431. The earthquakes of 332 and 342, which destroyed Salamis and Paphos, did a great deal of damage, but Curium was not finally abandoned until the Arab raids of the seventh century. At that period the bishopric was transferred to Episkopi, giving the village its name.

DESCRIPTION OF SITE

Curium is not nearly as extensive or scattered a site as Salamis, and every feature of interest is close to the car park at its centre. Archaeologists from Pennsylvania who excavated the site in 1952 identified a *Civic Reception Centre* for distinguished visitors immediately adjacent to the main entrance to the site. This juxtaposition of the functions of the twentieth with those of the fourth century A.D. is entertaining. The floor of what was a colonnaded building gives a fascinating welcome. The mosaic depicts one of the livelier scenes of Greek legend. Achilles is shown in the disguise of a maiden at the court of the king of Skyros at the moment when Odysseus is in the act of unmasking the impersonation and sounding an alarm. Achilles has been 'snapped' in the act of throwing off his maidenly sandals and seizing a spear which he has kept ready to hand. Other rooms on either side of this courtyard contain traces of mosaic work, but none as complete or as exciting as the Achilles.

There are remains near by of a *Roman Aqueduct*. At this point it would have been 18 ft high.

The next area of importance to be reached is also on the left of the approach road. It is here that the Department of Antiquities, in continuing the work of the American expedition begun some forty years previously, discovered a complex of late Roman buildings with mosaic pavements depicting gladiatorial combats. The site has been identified as that of a *Roman Villa*. A wealth of statuary was found, and is now to be seen in the Episkopi Museum. (At the time of going to press this site was not open to the public, because work was not complete.)

The road now leads towards the car park, restaurant and custodian's office, beyond which you come to the early *Christian Basilica* on the right. This is believed to have been the cathedral church of the bishops of Curium in the fifth century. The main part measured approximately 180 by 120 ft, and the nave was separated from the aisles by a double row of substantial pillars in granite with marble bases and capitals. The foundations of four more pillars demonstrate that these supported the baldachin over the altar. There are fragments of mosaic all over the place, but the entire site has been consistently robbed right down to the foundations, so thoroughly that the remainder of the church buildings to the east of the forecourt at the west end have never been identified. There are also small annexes to the east, which leave room for a small open court immediately opposite the apse, and extend as far as the pavement of the street. The site of the baptistry is to the north.

Theatre

The theatre, which was excavated in 1949–50 and has recently been restored, has a superb site above the sea. Its original form (second century B.C.) may have been circular. This was later reduced to a semicircle, before being enlarged in the second century A.D. so that it could provide seating accommodation for about 3,500 people. The seats were reached by gangways and a vaulted corridor behind the auditorium. The stage and scene-building were re-modelled at least three times before being adapted for spectacles involving wild animals (probably early third century A.D.). After this the theatre shows signs of having returned to conventional use before being abandoned in the fourth century. The modern recon-struction work (1961) had as its primary aim the performance of classical Greek tragedies and comedies, with Shakespeare and con-certs contributing to the programmes. Performances summer week-ends.

Baths and Annexe of Eustolios

These remains are higher up the hill to the east, and are later in date than the abandonment of the theatre. The entrance vesti-bule, which is approached from the theatre (from the west), has servants' quarters on the left and unidentified rooms on the right. There is a welcoming inscription set into the floor of the vestibule: 'ENTER . . . AND GOOD LUCK TO THE HOUSE.' A rect-angular courtyard with porticoes around three sides is beyond, near a fountain and a pool. Fragments of mosaics have survived, the most important of which is an inscription to one Eustolios, the builder of 'this cool refuge sheltered from the winds'. The in-scription goes on to refer to Phoebus Apollo as the original deity of the site, then to Christ. It is thought that these buildings were originally part of a luxurious villa, but that at the time when the mosaics and the baths were installed they were adapted for public recreation, perhaps on the lines of an exclusive club. The baths were situated higher up the slope, and were approached from below by a flight of steps. A central room has mosaics in four panels set into the floor. One shows a partridge, and another a symbolic representation of *Ktisis*, or Creation, in the form of a female figure holding what appears to be a standard linear foot measure. The smaller rooms consist of the usual Roman frigidarium, tepidarium and caldarium, with foot-baths, firing appliances, plumbing works and ducts to carry hot air from the hypocausts. All the arrange-ments reveal good and economic planning, with due allowance for aesthetics. The water supply came from a large cistern on the northern slope, and this was presumably fed by the aqueduct already observed at the entrance to the site.

The remaining two excavated sites of Curium are reached by returning to the main entrance and turning left on to the road to Paphos.

[10½ m.] The **Stadium,** which dates from the second century A.D. to *c*. 404, is to the north of the road, less than ½ m. west of the main entrance to Curium. It was excavated by the Pennsylvania University Museum in 1939 and 1947, and although the remains then discovered revealed little more than the foundations, neither the U-shaped plan nor the positions of the three entrance gates are in doubt. The starting-point for the races has also been identified. The seven rows of seating would have accommodated about 6,000 spectators. A small section has been reconstructed to show the arrangement of the seating.

[11 m.] SANCTUARY OF APOLLO

A sign-posted track about half a mile farther west along the main Paphos road leads to the Sanctuary of Apollo, in his role of Hylates, the God of the Woodlands. Though the sanctuary was rebuilt many times as the result of earthquake damage, the god seems to have been consistently worshipped here from the eighth century B.C. to the fourth A.D. While the official pamphlet is of great value for reference, one of the most satisfactory ways of seeing the site is by first skirting the *South Building* by turning right on leaving the custodian's office. After rounding a corner you will then enter the site by the *Paphos Gate*, which was originally flanked by two columns, coming to a paved area before turning left for the flight of steps leading to the *North-West Building*. These rooms were believed to have provided accommodation for visitors, or possibly storage space for their offerings. Returning across the pavement brings you to the long portico with its Doric columns which gives access to the five rooms of the *South Building*, which may have been used for the same purposes as those of the North-West Building. Two of them are known to have been erected by Trajan in A.D. 101. On the way to a *narrow street* opposite you pass a semicircular depression which during the course of excavation by the Pennsylvania University Museum 1934–54 was identified as a *pit* used for the disposal of redundant votive objects, since it contained terra-cotta figurines and pottery dating from the fifth century B.C. until the Roman period. The straight paved street now leads to the site of the *Temple of Apollo*, which was approached by a flight of steps and a portico of five columns. The small dimensions of the temple are explained by the fact that it was the custom in Cyprus for rituals to take place out of doors. Return a short distance before turning left into the *Archaic Precinct*. Excavations in this area have brought to light an altar and a large quantity of votive objects similar to those from the votive pit, but predating them (eighth–fifth century B.C.). This precinct has a small forecourt to the south, beyond which there is a small room which may have been occupied by the priest. The barred windows of the room opposite indicate that it might have been the *Treasury*. A passage between further sets of small rooms leads to a flight of steps at the eastern end of the paved area, and to what was the *Curium Gate*, a monumental entrance which bore an inscription in honour of Trajan A smaller flight of steps to the right leads to the *Palaestra*, where athletes exercised and played games. Note the stone jar – probably put there to contain oil or water for their use – standing in the north-west corner of the court. This set of buildings was outside the sanctuary proper, which has well-defined walls. The same applies to the *Baths*, which are north of the Palaestra, and consist of rooms providing a range of temperatures according to the Roman custom.

The car park and the custodian's office are regained through the south-west corner of the Palaestra.

Omodhos Monastery, Platres and Pitsilia District

Route Follow the Paphos road out of Limassol (Routes A or B on Limassol map) forking right after Erimi (7 m.) for Omodhos Monastery (26 m.), Pano Platres (37 m.) and Trooditissa Monastery (36 m.).

A day's excursion on minor roads may be made to the Pitsilia District by taking the road from Pano Platres past Mesopotamos Monastery (7 m.), joining the main road at Kato Amiandos (13 m.). Turn right at Karvouna crossroads (15½ m.) for Kyperounda and Khandria (22 m.). Keep right for Agros (28 m.) and continue east to Palekhori (38 m.) before turning left. Make a detour at Alona (47 m.) for Platanistasa (+2 m.) and, 2 m. after Polystipos (49 m.), for Lagoudhera (+4 m.), returning by way of Khandria (51 m.) to Pano Platres (+73 m.).

N.B. This calls for negotiation of some bad sections of mountain road. If thought fit, the excursion can be shortened by cutting out Agros, Platanistasa, etc., and going and returning to Laghoudhera via Khandria.

One way back to Limassol from Pano Platres is by returning to Mandria and then branching left to join the main road east of Perapedhi, an interesting village with a flourishing co-operative society run by local apple-growers. After 2 m. turn right on to the main north–south road, and follow the Kouris valley to Ypsonas, 5 m. from Limassol on the Paphos road (+29 m.).

For Nicosia turn left at the main north–south road for route via Karvouna Cross-roads. Evrykhou and Peristerona (pp. 135–9) (+55 m.). Alternatively, continue north-east from Palekhori, via Apliki (40 m.) and Klirou (49 m.) (+57 m.). A connection could alternatively be made at Troödos or Prodhromos with the mountain route described on pp. 139–42, covering the other hill resorts and villages.

Paphos is reached from Pano Platres by returning to Omodhos and later forking right for Mallia and again for Ayios Nikolaos before descending through the Dhiovrizos valley to join the main Limassol–Paphos road 1½ m. west of Kouklia (p. 266) (+37 m.).

Tourist Information Bureau Municipal Pavilion, Pano Platres.
Hotels

At Platres:	1st (A)	Forest Park; Splendid.
	1st (C)	Grand; Minerva; Pendeli.
	2nd (A)	New Helvetia.
	2nd (B)	Spring.
	3rd	Pafsilypon; Palace; Petit Palais; Vienna.
	4th	Kallithea; Semiramis.
At Perapedhi:	3rd	Paradise.
	4th	Perapedhi.
At Agros:	4th	Vlachos.

Restaurants and Bars
In addition to the restaurants and cocktail bars of the hotels, the following outdoor restaurant and café-bar should not be overlooked: Psilodhendron, near Pano Platres.

Cinema
There is a summer season at the open-air cinema at Platres. In addition to up-to-date films there are occasional theatrical productions.

Exhibitions
Perapedhi Agricultural Show mid-August. Dancing exhibitions.

[7 m.] Fork right off the Paphos road after crossing the bridge at **Erimi.**

[22 m.] Turn to the right soon after the small side-turning to Kissousa and follow signposts to Platres. This part of the drive through the foothills is very pretty. The country consists of small valleys debouching into larger watercourses, and it is intensively cultivated, mainly with olives and vineyards. The villages have brick kilns where, in summer and autumn, bricks are stacked out of doors for drying.

[26 m.] MONASTERY OF OMODHOS

This is no longer used as such, but it well repays a visit to its church, and to see the interesting woodwork in the *Synod Hall* and in the ceiling of the first-floor cloister to the north of the enclosure. This country craftsmanship, which is elaborate enough to have been classified as 'rococo', is attributed to Christanthos, the bishop of Paphos who was massacred by the Turks in company with other Orthodox prelates. The small *Museum* also contains relics of the guerrillas who took refuge in the mountains during the years of EOKA activity. The clothing of several of these fighters, including some garments said to have belonged to Colonel Grivas, is preserved with as much reverence as ecclesiastical relics. Another room houses a small Folk Museum.

The *Church of the Holy Cross* is fairly modern, though not modernistic, and has regrettably replaced a venerable Byzantine church, no trace of which has been left. However, the new dimensions are impressive, about 100 by 35 ft internally, which combined with proportionate height imparts a sense of dignity. The famous relics of the church include the skull of St Philip, which has been authenticated as having been a gift from a Byzantine emperor, and a portion of the True Cross and the bonds which bound the hands of Christ. The latter are believed to have been brought to Cyprus by St Helena, and like the fragments of the Cross have been incorporated into large crosses of silver-gilt repoussé work. Another feature of interest, especially to English visitors, is the gravestone set into the north wall of the church. This commemorates an ex-officer of the Hundredth Regiment of Foot who distinguished himself at the Siege of Ancona when he was in the imperial service of Tsar Paul, and who died in Omodhos Monastery in 1811.

The square in the village of Omodhos can be a lively place, with a great deal of local activity, particularly that connected with viti-culture and the merchandising of fruit. Lace of traditional designs suitable for the edging of linen continues to be made by village women. The fair held on September 14th every year is one of the most stimulating and fascinating in the whole island, partly due to the opportunity it gives for the gathering of people from the remoter mountain villages.

[29 m.] Mandria

[32 m.] About 1½ m. beyond **Kato Platres** there is a T-junction, the right turning of which goes direct to Pano Platres, while the left turn leads in 4 m. to *Trooditissa Monastery* (passing a right turning to Troödos after about 2 m.).

This is not one of the most interesting of the monasteries from an architectural point of view, the church having been rebuilt in 1731 with three aisles. The charm of the monastery has until recently been lessened by galvanized roofing, but this has now been replaced by tiles of local manufacture. Owing to a splendid location among pine woods at a height of 4,566 ft above sea-level, under Mount Olympus which is 2,000 ft higher, this monastery possesses the atmosphere of a serene mountain retreat and is in fact the summer residence of the bishop of Paphos. The first church on the site is thought to have been built *c.* 1250 as a shrine for an icon of the Virgin brought at great hazard from Asia Minor. This sacred relic is preserved in the present church under the usual protective covering of silver-gilt repoussé work. Also of interest is the holy belt which hangs near the principal icon of the Virgin. This is believed to confer fertility on any woman who wears it, and in return she is expected to dedicate the resulting boy-child to the service of the monastery. In certain circumstances she may bestow a wax image or some other gift as an alternative thank-offering. Quite a substantial sum of money was spent on repairs to the monastery in 1967–8.

[32 m.] The right branch of the T-junction leads in 1 m. to **Pano Platres.**

This is the largest of the hill resorts and there is a good choice of hotels in all price ranges (p. 244), and facilities for sport and organized entertainment (including an open-air cinema). The Summer Festival, towards the end of the season, attracts many interesting exhibitions demonstrating the life, folk-lore and activities of the mountain people. The altitude of Platres (3,700 ft) is not exacting, and it is a very popular health resort, in the past having been frequented by such personalities as King Farouk of Egypt, as well as by Service personnel from the coastal regions of the island. One of the chief attractions is a lovely perennial stream, the *Khrysos Potamos*, which is an unusual feature in mountains which tend to be waterless except after rainfall. This constant water supply is used to advantage at an attractive eating place at Psilodhendron, where the spit on which kebabs are grilled is turned by a miniature water-wheel. The neighbourhood is delightful for woodland walks or horseback excursions through country which bears a close resemblance to some of the glens of Scotland. One of the more impressive beauty spots is known as the Caledonian Falls, reached by a ¾ hr. walk from Psilodhendron.

Platres would also make a good centre for visiting the resorts and villages on the northern slopes of the Troödos range described on pp. 140–2.

PITSILIA DISTRICT

Visitors to Platres who have a day to spare are recommended to explore the Pitsilia region to the east of the southern range. With the exception of Papoutsa (5,098 ft), the mountains here are for the most part less high. The roads lead through charming hilly country, frequented in the summer by local people from the cities, and less well known to foreigners. The soil and southern aspect of the region is favourable for the cultivation of grapes. In fact, the famous Commandaria wine of the Knights Hospitaller came from its villages or *commandarias*. The village co-operatives of Zoopiyi, Kalokhorio and Ayios Konstantinos are still the chief producers of this dessert wine made from half-dried grapes. These villages, however, lie south of the recommended route from Platres, and east of the main road from Limassol.

All the distances in the circular route described below are from Pano Platres. First take the upper road out of the resort, passing *Mesopotamos*, the site of a monastery no longer used as such, near which there is a fine waterfall in the forest.

[13 m.] At **Kato Amiandos** turn left on to the Nicosia–Limassol mountain road.

[15½ m.] At Karvouna Crossroads take the right turn sign-posted to the Sanatorium, then follow the twisting road which leads east past **Kyperounda** – a village named from the Greek word for cypresses.

[22 m.] Turn right again at **Khandria**.

[28 m.] **Agros** is a charming village where there is simple hotel accommodation (p. 244). This is a district where it is possible to rent small houses or rooms for holiday periods.

[38 m.] The road leading eastwards out of Agros reaches **Palekhori** on the north side of the watershed. This village has great attraction, being built steeply on either side of the headwaters of the Peristerona river, the banks of which are outlined by tall poplars. Records of the name already being established in the thirteenth century prove that even at that early date the village was an old one, since *paleo* has that significance in the Greek language. Unfortunately its churches have suffered from over-zealous restoration, and that of St Luke, once renowned for its frescoes, has been demolished. However, this is less of a loss from the point of view of a day's sightseeing, because by making two slight diversions from the hilly road which bends back in a north-westerly direction from Palekhori to Khandria, two most interesting and attractive Byzantine churches are within easy reach.

[47 m.] A turning to the right at **Alona** leads to the *Church of Stavros tou Ayasmati* (or Holy Cross) at Platanistasa. This is an excellent example of the later Byzantine style, and is notable for its wall-paintings. Because the church has no dome, the pictures cannot be arranged in the usual order of precedence, and are in two tiers, the upper one depicting the life of Christ and the Virgin Mary, and the lower levels containing representations of the saints, among whom St Mamas riding his lion and St Demetrios on the west end of the south wall are particularly attractive. An inscription of 1466 over the south door asserts modestly that 'the gift is God's, the hand that of Philip the painter'.

[51 m.] Having returned to Alona, continue westwards and turn right after **Polystipos** for **Lagoudhera** two miles farther on. The *Church of Panayia tou Arakou* here is rated second only to Asinou, and is most certainly worth a diversion. It stands above the village on the road to Sarandi. A shed-like roof and verandas have been added to enclose the original domed twelfth-century building. The interior is in such great contrast that it comes as a revelation. The wonderful wall-paintings display in brilliant colour the whole sequence of Christian belief, beginning with Christ Pantokrator, Ruler of the World, supreme in the dome. He is surrounded by angels and prophets, then biblical scenes, descending in fact and in importance to the figures of saints and martyrs in the lower walls, arches and vaults. These church paintings were completed in 1193. Much needed restoration has been undertaken by Dumbarton Oaks (Harvard University).

The full circle is completed by returning to Khandria.

Amathus, Khirokitia and Pano Lefkara

Route Follow the coast road running eastwards from Limassol (Routes D or E on Limassol map) for Amathus (5½ m.), Khirokitia (23 m.) and Pano Lefkara (33½ m.).
  For Nicosia continue north on minor road, forking right after 3 m. for Kornos (p. 227) and main north–south road (+28 m.) *or* return to Limassol road, turning left at Skarinou station, and forking left at Kophinou (+32 m.).
  For Larnaca return to Limassol road as above, but fork right in Kophinou (+22 m.).
Ancient Monument
Khirokitia
Opening hours
Summer 9 a.m. to noon
           3 p.m. to 6.30 p.m.
Winter. At any reasonable hour. Contact the custodian at the roadside *khan* or station.

[2 m.] East of Limassol the road runs parallel to a continuous pebble beach, where there are cafés and restaurants shaded by mimosa and eucalyptus. The new Miramare hotel, reached by a side-turning, has terraces and sand.

[5½ m.] *Amathus,* which was the capital of one of the former nine city-kingdoms but is now ruined and partially engulfed by the sea, nevertheless presents a romantic sight with its one salient fragment of wall jutting out over the water. Though there is scope for underwater exploration, there is little here for the casual sightseer by land, unless continuing excavations produce discoveries which have escaped the treasure-seekers of the past. Evidence that these treasure-seekers included in their number not only the pillagers of tombs in search of articles which might be sold for their face value but also some of the greatest French and American archaeologists of the nineteenth century is contained in the Louvre in Paris and in the Metropolitan Museum in New York.

A temple of Heracles (known to the Phoenicians as Melkarth) was situated here, also one dedicated jointly to Aphrodite and Adonis. Both these shrines were renowned in the ancient world. Amathus became one of the most important centres in Cyprus for the copper industry, and flourished well into the Byzantine period, though when Richard Cœur de Lion landed in 1191 the city was already in decline, if not yet deserted. One of the most famous men to be born in Amathus was John the Almoner, the original patron of the Order of St John of Jerusalem.

Immediately opposite a *kentron* to the west of the jutting piece of wall there are the remains of three circular stone chambers and, twenty yards farther inland, a 'royal' tomb cut into the rock. The key may be obtained from the Antiquities Office in the Administration Offices in Anexartisias St, Limassol. Another tomb, this time on the seaward side of the road, is indicated by a signpost a few hundred yards in the Limassol direction.

[9½ m.] To the right will be seen a large cement factory and Moni Power Station, by means of which it is expected that every village in Cyprus will be provided with electricity.

[13 m.] A turning to the right leads to the *Monastery of Ayios Yeoryios* for women.

[23 m.] The entrance to *Khirokitia* is on the right of the minor road behind the road station (opening hours p. 249).

KHIROKITIA

The remains of very early civilizations are sometimes of limited interest to the average sightseer because too much is demanded in the way of background specialist knowledge and there is not always a great deal for the untrained eye to see. In the case of Khirokitia all this is true, but nevertheless a visit to the site is to be recommended, not only because the settlement is the earliest so far discovered in Cyprus (*c.* 5800–5250 B.C.), and is easy of access, but also because the life of its people can be sufficiently reconstructed by comparing the visible remains with the detailed leaflet published by the Cyprus Antiquities Department. Further information can also be obtained from an advance inspection of the exhibits in the Larnaca Archaeological Museum. But even without this useful preliminary a short tour of the excavations cannot fail to be interesting.

HISTORY

Finds of animal bones, some of them fashioned into crude household articles, prove that the people of Khirokitia domesticated animals. Blades of sickles demonstrate that they cultivated grain. As regards the utensils they used, this was a period of transition when the people were moving from gouging river stones into practical shapes to the manufacture of pottery distinguishable by a pattern made with a comb-like implement when the surface was still wet. The technical standard of their tools is evidence that they were good wood-workers and carpenters. And it is certain that the people of Khirokitia had commercial relations of some sort with both the Asian and European mainlands. This is suggested by the fact that blades of obsidian – which is a natural glass of volcanic origin not endemic in Cyprus – have been found among their household effects.

DESCRIPTION OF SITE

The site is on a steep sugar-loaf hill on the farther side of the Maroni river. It will be seen that the river curves around Khirokitia and that there are springs in the river-bed even when the flow in summer has ceased, this being the reason for the choice of the site for settlement.

One of the major items of archaeological interest here is the *wall* which runs the length of the site. This could not have been a fortification, because there are buildings on either side of it. Experts have come to the conclusion that it was in fact the main street of the settlement, along which the inhabitants hauled water and stones from the river. Excavations on either side of this road have brought to light foundations of *tholoi*, the beehive dwellings of that era, separated one from another by narrow passage-ways.

When excavation work was undertaken by the Department of Antiquities in 1936 (it had to be discontinued during the war and was not resumed until 1946) it became apparent that there were several building levels, and it could be presumed that the round huts were successively allowed to fall into disrepair preparatory to their remains being flattened and new structures superimposed. The circular foundations were constructed of stones brought from the river, and the walls were made of mud or of bricks formed from sun-baked mud. What is particularly interesting about this succession of building periods is that, because it was customary to bury the dead in the floor of the dwellings, many skeletons have been found in the layers of a single house.

The method of interment was to dig shallow graves, and to lay out the dead with their knees contracted to their chins. Superstitious fear of death is evidenced by the fact that a weight was often placed on the dead person's body – to discourage haunting. Many of the domestic utensils and ornaments found on the site were buried with their owners, or presented to them on burial, and in some instances there appears to have been a ceremonial breaking of stone vessels. It is remarkable that the graves of women contain more offerings than those of men.

Visitors will be advised by the custodian to follow the recognized route, which has been plotted so as to follow the southeastern edge of the excavations, skirting four areas of building, and progressing to the north side of what is known as Area III, from where there is a good prospect of the entire site and its relation to the surrounding country. The Department of Antiquities leaflet goes into greater detail than is possible here, giving descriptions of the individual houses at different levels, and itemizing the archaeological finds at various spots.

[25½ m.] About 3 m. farther along the main road from the Khirokitia turning, at Skarinou station (not to be confused with the village of the same name which lies to the north), take a left turning which leads up into the hills. This passes through comparatively open country, in the main unterraced but 'spotty' with carob trees, as described by that indefatigable Victorian traveller, Mrs Lewis, in *A Lady's Impressions of Cyprus*.

[33½ m.] **PANO LEFKARA**

This is a hill village reminiscent of many such in Italy, astride a shoulder of the mountains. Below it, off the road, there is a separate, lower village, Kato Lefkara, which engages in similar industries but is not so much visited.

The charm of Pano Lefkara is immediately apparent. It has houses with colour-washed walls and tiled roofs, and looks cosmopolitan, as though in keeping with the habits of its male inhabitants, who for centuries have travelled Europe as packmen, selling the Lefkaritika lace for which their native town is famous. It is believed that Leonardo da Vinci bought lace here in 1481, and took it back to Milan as a gift to the cathedral.

The women traditionally remain at home making lace. In fine weather they sit outside their houses and in alleys off the narrow main street, forming a picturesque and nostalgic sight in these days of mechanization. The work is excellent. As well as lace, the needlewomen of Lefkara do drawn-thread work on linen or cotton in splendid traditional geometric designs which are well suited to modern table-linen.

Another local industry, and one of equal fascination, is the manufacture of *lokoum*, or Turkish Delight. Nothing farther from the modern idea of a factory could be conceived. The sugar is piled in great copper cauldrons over enclosed wood fires, and when it reaches the correct temperature it is spun till the consistency is milky and opaque. At this stage the flavouring is added, also the nuts, which have been lightly roasted in a flat pan and stirred by hand to ensure even browning. The hot glutinous mass is then tipped into trays lined with icing sugar, and left until it is cool enough to cut. It is then well packaged, ready to be dispatched all over the world.

This is a place of great charm, comparable with Safed in Israel for paintable quality. Although there is not a great deal to see in the way of churches or archaeological remains, it is a delight to walk through the streets and the clusters of houses and gardens. The people are hospitable and especially conversational.

PAPHOS (KTIMA)

Population 11,000.
Information
Library and Tourist office; 28th October Square.
Hotels (in Ktima)
1st (A) New Olympus.
2nd (A) Paphos Palace.
4th   Kinyras.
Until recent times there has been little demand for hotel accommodation in this comparatively backward part of the island. But new roads, projected development schemes and the multiplicity of archaeological discoveries look like changing this situation.
Restaurants and Bars
Acropolis, Mousallas Heights.
Christophorou, Harbour.
Hondros, Kato Paphos St.
Myrra, Kato Paphos St.
Theodorou, Harbour.
Trianon (local food), Athens Avenue.
Tcholias, Coral Bay.
The two principal hotels have bars and restaurants. The harbour restaurants specialize in fresh fish, and have facilities for eating on the waterfront.
Cinemas Attikon; Titania; Zena.
Bathing
The municipal bathing place east of the harbour is convenient for changing, and makes a good place for skin-diving. A local boatman should be employed for more ambitious underwater exploration of the ancient breakwater and the Moulia Rocks. Coral Bay (8 m. northwards) is in process of development into a resort with all amenities.

The visitor to Cyprus is apt to become confused when Paphos is mentioned, because the modern capital of the district is named Ktima, the port nearly 2 m. to the south is Nea (New) or Kato (Lower) Paphos, and Kouklia (9½ m. to the east) was formerly known as Palea (or Old) Paphos. And the site of a yet older port is identifiable east of the present harbour. However, it is more usual to speak of going to Paphos than to Ktima, even though the latter is a modern town, and the former an area of depopulated ruins.

Ktima is a town which has not attracted much industrialism, though road improvements to the east will inevitably bring it closer to the rest of the island. There is something very leisured about the town, and an atmosphere that shows that it does not aspire to any further greatness than satisfying the needs of the large agricultural and forest district of Paphos and welcoming visitors to the most secluded corner of the island.

Until the discovery of the Roman villa and its mosaics in 1962, the strange Tombs of the Kings were the chief attraction, coupled with the charms of the harbour and its Turkish fort.

HISTORY

Though Ktima is known to have been inhabited in the Neolithic period, its documented history began in the seventh to tenth centuries A.D., at the time when the inhabitants of Nea Paphos were forced by raiding Arabs to retire inland to the safer rocky plateau from which approaching enemies could readily be seen. Earthquake damage and malarial infestation subsequently brought about the complete evacuation of the old city and port, which under the Ptolemies and the Romans had been superior to Salamis.

PRINCIPAL REMAINS

Mosaics (House of Dionysos)
Map 23.

Opening hours
Mid-May to mid-Sept. Daily 7.30 a.m. to 7 p.m.
Mid-Sept. to mid-May   7 a.m. to dusk
Custodian in attendance.

A few hundred yards inland from the port of Nea Paphos a flat-roofed metal structure safeguards from sun and weather what is undoubtedly one of the greatest treasures of the Mediterranean countries. In 1962, exposed by ploughing rather than by trial archaeological diggings, there came to light a portion of mosaic similar to that of a much damaged fragment of similar work on an adjacent site. But the difference in this case was that as investigations proceeded a very large Roman villa was uncovered and identified, and found to be comprised of twenty-two rooms grouped around an open court and colonnade. In contrast to the walls, which had been shattered by earthquake to a few feet from the ground, the floors were substantially intact, and fourteen of the rooms were found to contain distinctive mosaic designs in a miraculous state of preservation. The subjects are mainly mythological: Pyramus and Thisbe; Dionysos and Icarios; Poseidon and Amphitriti; Meleager and Atalanta; Ganymede being carried off by an eagle; Apollo and Daphne and, among others, a fascinating Triumph of Dionysos. Each is captioned, using the Latin spelling of proper names. There are also realistic hunting scenes, including a variety of wild animals, as well as beautiful patterns made up of ancient symbols. Because of the numerous representations of the God of Wine, these remains are now popularly known as the House of Dionysos.

These may be viewed at close range from cat-walks built over the interior walls of the villa, so that the elaborate design and colouring of the floors may be viewed from a height on all four sides. Some restoration has been necessary to counteract the effect of partial subsidence, but in other respects the floors are as perfect as when they first were laid.

The villa was originally two storeys high, and possibly belonged to an influential governor or rich merchant of the third century A.D. It was destroyed by the earthquakes of the fourth century. A street ran alongside the villa to the south.

In the course of excavation a large amphora was found containing coins in mint condition dating from the reigns of Ptolemy V to Ptolemy XI; also a skeleton presumed to be that of a slave crushed by a collapsed wall while attempting to escape from the earthquake with a hoard of looted coins. The coins, some more of which were found in 1964 during the excavation of the villa's water supply, are of great importance in dating the villa.

The mosaics are one of the most beautiful sights, as well as the most easily read, in the whole of the island and, even if there were nothing else to view in the locality, warrant a special visit to Paphos. Further excavations to the north-west of the House of Dionysos have brought to light a second important building of the Roman period, which experts have identified provisionally as a palace. This contains a circular room with a mosaic floor representing the Cretan labyrinth and the classical protagonists, the Minotaur, Thesaus and Ariadne. Situated also to the north-west there is another room believed to be a workshop of the Hellenistic period used for the minting of coins. This is a discovery of particular interest to numismatists. At the time of going to press these and adjacent discoveries are not yet ready for inspection by the general public.

Basilica of Panayia Limeniotissa
Map 27.
On the left of the road leading from the harbour to the House of Dionysos the remains of a large three-aisled basilica of the fifth century A.D. has been excavated by the Department of Antiquities. Its destruction probably dates from A.D. 653, when an Arab invasion overwhelmed the city. Evidence in the form of Arabic inscriptions prove that the site was occupied by the invaders in the

latter half of the seventh century. A second but smaller three-aisled basilica was built on the same site early in the following century, probably after the withdrawal of the Arabs, materials from the original church being used in its construction. This second church is probably identical with the one mentioned by St Neophytos as having been destroyed by earthquake in the last half of the twelfth century. Still another church, built in the nave of its predecessor, is known to have existed until comparatively recent times. At the time of going to press these remains are not open to the public, though they can be seen from the road.

Nea Paphos Fort*
Map 29.

The site of the Roman villa was presumably selected so that it might command a good prospect of the port of Nea Paphos which, however, presents a different aspect today – not only because it has recently been improved for the use of fishing boats, but because it is dominated by the small Turkish fort. Though this incorporates fragments of a Venetian castle, it is purely Turkish in design, and completely symmetrical. It was built in 1592 by Hafouz Ahmed Pasha, the Governor of Cyprus who 'left a good religious work in this very strong castle'. This fort, and the Venetian fortifications which preceded it, replaced Byzantine defences which had been modified by the Lusignans. Until recent years it was employed as a salt store, a use which is damaging to stonework.

Roman Theatre
Map 18.

Excavations have revealed that the late Roman theatre to the south-east of the lighthouse contains fourteen rows of seating which unfortunately have been stripped of their stone facing. The orchestra and the stage buildings have also been uncovered. One interesting feature is a subterranean tunnel below the central axis of the auditorium. A rough road leads around the lighthouse and the House of Dionysos to the harbour.

Byzantine Fortress
Map 24.

For many years attention has been drawn to a slightly elevated site overlooking the harbour, to which the popular name of Saranta

I

* Access prohibited at time of going to press.

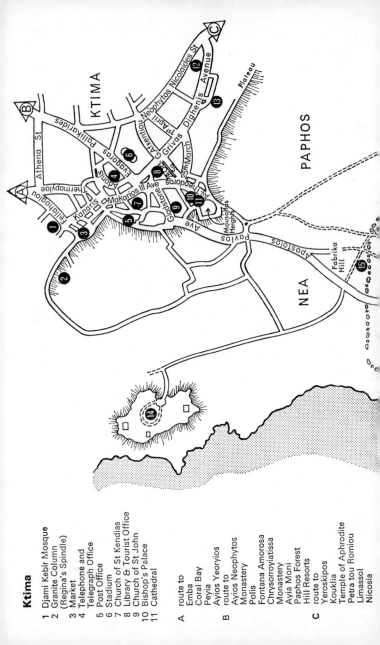

Ktima

1 Djami Kebir Mosque
2 Granite Column
   (Regina's Spindle)
3 Market
4 Telephone and
   Telegraph Office
5 Post Office
6 Stadium
7 Church of St Kendias
8 Library & Tourist Office
9 Church of St John
10 Bishop's Palace
11 Cathedral

A route to
   Emba
   Coral Bay
   Peyia
   Ayios Yeoryios
B route to
   Ayios Neophytos
   Monastery
   Polis
   Fontana Amorosa
   Chrysorroyiatissa
   Monastery
   Ayia Moni
   Paphos Forest
   Hill Resorts
C route to
   Yeroskipos
   Kouklia
   Temple of Aphrodite
   Petra tou Romiou
   Limassol
   Nicosia

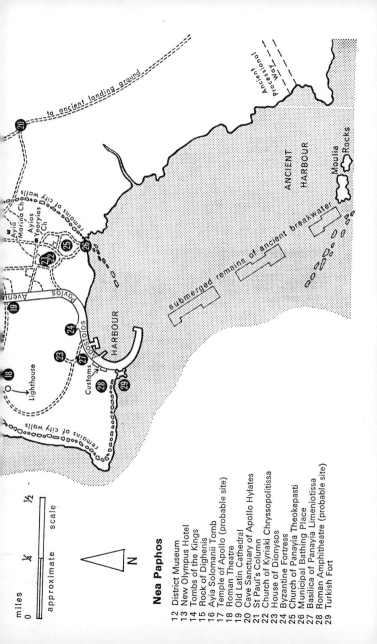

Nea Paphos

12 District Museum
13 New Olympus Hotel
14 Tombs of the Kings
15 Rock of Dighenis
16 Ayia Solomanii Tomb
17 Temple of Apollo (probable site)
18 Roman Theatre
19 Old Latin Cathedral
20 Cave Sanctuary of Apollo Hylates
21 St Paul's Column
22 Church of Kyriaki Chryssopolitissa
23 House of Dionysos
24 Byzantine Fortress
25 Church of Panayia Theokepasti
26 Municipal Bathing Place
27 Basilica of Panayia Limeniotissa
28 Roman Amphitheatre (probable site)
29 Turkish Fort

miles
0   ¼   ½

approximate scale

N

Kolones or Forty Columns was given on account of the mass of fallen masonry it contained. Yet little could be made of it by an uninstructed eye, and the numbers of its columns fell far short of the fabled forty. However, recent excavation under the auspices of the British School of Archaeology in Athens has now uncovered a Byzantine fortress of some magnitude, whose construction entailed the use of many more than forty columns. Some have been re-used horizontally in a period of subsequent rebuilding. The original castle is thought to have been constructed after the early Arab raids on Paphos. Later it fell into disrepair, was strengthened in the tenth century and then was occupied by the Crusaders. An earthquake shattered it in 1222. At the time of going to press the work of excavation and reconstruction still proceeds, and when this is completed it is hoped that detailed plans will be available to visitors to the site.

Old Latin Cathedral
Map **19**.
On the return journey in the direction of Ktima, and immediately before the left turning to the modern lighthouse, there will be seen the survival of what was once the great Latin Cathedral of Paphos.

Nothing is left except the angle made by two of its fallen walls. Yet this lonely and insignificant remnant serves as a pointer to the legend that the ground on which the cathedral was built has miraculous propensities: it is believed that when earth taken from the site is mixed with water and consumed it promotes a good flow of milk for nursing mothers.

Even less remains of a *Temple of Apollo* (*Map* **17**) which is thought to have existed on the north side of the road to the lighthouse.

Tombs of the Kings
Map **14**.
Until the discovery of the Roman villa and its mosaics, the chief archaeological fame of Paphos lay in the necropolis known romantically but probably inaccurately as the Tombs of the Kings, in the area reached by a road north of that to the lighthouse. Other names for the locality are *Palaeokastra* (old castles) and *Taphi ton Vassileon* (burial-place of the kings). The tombs, which go back to the Late Bronze Age (*c.* 1600–1050 B.C.) and continue into the

Hellenistic period, are unlikely to be those of kings, because royalty did not exist at the earlier dates.

Though the road to the tombs, which branches off the main road opposite the salient Rock of Dighenis, is impossible to miss, the tombs themselves, because of their number and complexity and the fact that they have few surface indications of their locations, are difficult to find. They should ideally be viewed under expert guidance after inquiry at the District Museum or in the hotels and cafés of Ktima. There is no appointed guide on the spot, as at other sites under the jurisdiction of the Department of Antiquities.

The account given by Mrs Lewis after her visit to Paphos in 1893 is in many respects still valid:

> We occupied all the next afternoon in riding our ponies round and about the whole circuit of the ruins of Nea-Paphos (now called by the Turks Baffo), our courteous entertainers walking beside us as cicerones and doing their utmost to introduce order into our minds, bewildered by the formless and infinite chaos of the ruins of different epochs. Columns, capitals, pedestas, and hewn stones of every size and form, all quarried in far-off lands, lie broadcast, amid the modern village of sun-dried bricks.

This will explain the need for a 'courteous entertainer', since the main discrepancy between Mrs Lewis's description and what is to be seen in modern times is that the population of 'modern' Nea Paphos has declined to under five hundred, none of whom live in proximity to the Tombs of the Kings.

In this area of confusion there are more than a hundred tombs hewn out of the rock. Some of the burial chambers are plain, unadorned cavities, others have been provided with Doric pillars and porticoes carved in the rock-face. As far as can be ascertained, all have been pillaged, many of them at times as far distant as the Roman period. Carved crosses testify that many of the tombs were at one time converted for Christian worship.

Other Tombs

As the tombs are scattered, and comprehensive exploration would involve a great amount of time, it is convenient to be able to locate two representative Hellenistic caves distinct from the

Tombs of the Kings and close to the road leading from Ktima to the harbour. These two are close together, and may be found without difficulty.

The tomb known as *Ayia Solomanii* (St Hannah) (*Map* 16) is one of the most ancient in Cyprus. It is underground, and reached by steps in the shade of a vast fig tree. Incidentally, this tree is regarded as being sacred, and is frequently decorated with rags displayed as votive offerings in gratitude to the saint, thus echoing the pagan tree-worship practised in Cyprus in early times. The tomb served its original purpose in the Hellenistic period, but came to be used as a hermitage in the fourth century A.D. The dedication is to St Solomanii, whose seven sons were martyred for their Jewish faith in 168 B.C. It is thought to have been the synagogue for the Jews of Paphos. The traces of ninth-century frescoes are the earliest in the island, and are accompanied by a tenth-century representation of the Dismembering of Christ's Body (otherwise the Distribution of the Holy Eucharist), which is an unusual subject for wall-paintings. The well on the site, now sometimes dry, had a reputation for curing eye diseases.

Cave Sanctuary of Apollo Hylates

Map 20.

Though this must be rated among the principal features of archaeological interest in the locality, it is very much off the beaten track and, since the interest is largely academic rather than apparent, it merits investigation only by the specialist visitor. The period is Greek (600–295 B.C.), and the construction bears a resemblance to what is known of the layout of the famous shrine of the Oracle at Delphi, in that there is provision in both for an underground chamber from which the mystic utterances of the Oracle could be relayed to the Guardian of the Sanctuary before being interpreted for the benefit of supplicants. It should be remembered that the original landing-place at Paphos, which was used by throngs of pilgrims bound for the spring festival at the Temple of Aphrodite at Palea (Old) Paphos (p. 268) is situated just under 2 m. to the south of this shrine of Apollo Hylates, and not at the present harbour. The original point of disembarkation was protected from rough seas by the Moulia rocks and an ancient breakwater which as the result of an earthquake now lies submerged in deep water.

Much of the construction of this breakwater and other marine installations have been explored in recent times by underwater enthusiasts of the Royal Engineers stationed in Cyprus. Some of their finds from the harbour area, and also from the coast not far from the Tombs of the Kings, are housed in the Paphos District Museum.

Other Ruins

The probable site of a second *Roman Theatre* (*Map* **28**) north of the Turkish fort contains little to see.

The line of the *Roman City Walls* can be traced almost in its entirety, beginning at the harbour of Nea Paphos, following the line of the coast due west and then north, and turning inland around the modern lighthouse to swing east below the Rock of Dighenis, and reaching the coast south of the Church of Panayia Theoskepasti at a point where St Paul and St Barnabas are thought to have embarked on their further voyages.

There is also known to have been a *Temple* (*Map* **17**) on the southern slopes of Fabrika Hill, where tablets of the second century B.C. were found. These are in the Paphos District Museum.

An interesting story is attached to two other spots: the *Rock of Dighenis* (*Map* **15**) – the legendary hero-figure of Byzantine Cyprus – and a *granite column* to the north (*Map* **2**). When Dighenis was courting the elusive and wilful 'queen' of the island, who went by the all-embracing name of Regina, she promised to yield to him if he could manage to bring her water from the far Kyrenia mountain range. With great difficulty he accomplished this prodigious task, only to be rewarded by laughter and scorn. Whereupon he seized a large chunk of rock and hurled it at the queen's palace, while she retaliated by throwing her spindle at her enraged lover – and here their missiles remain in perpetuity.

CHURCHES

Church of St Kyriaki Chryssopolitissa
Map **22**.

This is pure Byzantine in form. Though it was erected as a Latin church, it was converted to the Greek rite during the Turkish occupation of Cyprus. (It is of interest that the Orthodox Greek Church was never so viciously persecuted by the Turks as was the Latin Church.) One of the more interesting icons showing Christ as a youth is displayed on the Holy doors of the iconostasis.

An unidentified site near the church contains fragments of some fine *Columns* (*Map* 21), some of which still stand upright, and which may have formed part of the residence of a Roman proconsul, or have belonged to a forum. The interest in the columns lies in the legend – which does not appear in the New Testament – that St Paul was chained to one of these when he received the 'forty stripes save one', a punishment supposed to refer to a whip with thirty-nine lashes rather than to the number of blows administered. St Paul's visit to Paphos in A.D. 45 is recorded in Acts xiii 6–12. In company with St Barnabas he furthered the cause of Christianity by his conversion of the Roman proconsul Sergius Paulus, who was won over by witnessing the local prophet, Elymas the Sorcerer, struck down by sudden blindness by these two great itinerant early Christians.

Church of Panayia Theoskepasti

Map 25.
This 'Church of the Shrouded Madonna' has been completely re-built and restored. Its chief attraction is the legend that the building was protected from the invading Arabs by a miraculous cloud which rendered it invisible to their eyes.

MUSEUMS

Paphos District Museum

Grivas Dighenis Ave.; Map 5.

Opening hours
Mid-May to mid-Sept. weekdays 8 a.m. to 1 p.m.
4 p.m. to 6 p.m.
Sundays 10 a.m. to 1 p.m.
Mid-Sept. to mid-May weekdays 8.30 a.m. to 1 p.m.
2.30 p.m. to 4.30 p.m.
Sundays 10 a.m. to 1 p.m.

Housed in a modern building on the right of the Limassol road on entering Ktima, the museum contains an interesting collection of pottery, some contemporary with Khirokitia (p. 250), as well as amphoræ, Roman glass and fragments of statuary. A large proportion of the exhibits come from Marion, the ancient city which existed near Polis on the north coast of the Paphos District (p. 272), but the chief features are a wide variety of objects from the House of Dionysos.

Private Collection of Professor Eliades

1 *Exo Vrysis St, Ktima; apply for admission at any reasonable hour.*

Professor George S. Eliades, the Hon. Curator of the Paphos District Museum, has an interesting collection of early pottery and a small folk museum at his house, which he will gladly show to visitors. When available, he will also advise on the sites of Nea Paphos which he has excavated for many years.

EXCURSIONS FROM PAPHOS (KTIMA)

Yeroskipos and Temple of Aphrodite, Palea Paphos

Route Leave Ktima by the Limassol road (Route C on Ktima/Paphos map) or Yeroskipos (2 m.), Kouklia and Palea Paphos (9½ m.) and Petra tou Romiou (15 m.).

For Limassol continue along the main road via Curium and Kolossi Castle (pp. 236–8) to Limassol (+29 m.).

Ancient Monuments

Temple of Aphrodite and La Covocle (*Lusignan Manor*)
Custodian in attendance.

Opening hours

Mid-May to mid-Sept. 9 a.m. to 12 noon.
3 p.m. to 6.30 p.m.
Mid-Sept. to mid-May 9 a.m. to 1 p.m.
2 p.m. to 4.30 p.m.

Closed on Mondays.

[2 m.] YEROSKIPOS

A key to the functions of this village is provided by its name, which is a corruption of 'Hieroskepos', the Sacred Garden. It was a halting-place for the crowds of pilgrims who had disembarked at the old harbour of Paphos and were bound for the Temple of Aphrodite at Palea Paphos, where there was a great spring festival for the worship of the deity in her aspect of goddess of springtime and flowers. The whole route was lined with trees and planted with flowers and shrubs selected for their fragrance. A minor claim to fame for this village is the manufacture of excellent Turkish Delight or *lokoum*.

Church of St Paraskevi

Nowadays the village contains very few reminders of its pagan period. What gives it greatest interest is the Church of St Paraskevi. Its patron saint was a Roman convert born in the second century and martyred in the reign of Marcus Aurelius. This church is the second five-domed Byzantine church in Cyprus, Peristerona being the other. Both are distinguished by three axial domes, with the remaining two domes at a lower level over the north and south transepts. Their prototypes, which were both erected under Justinian, are the Church of St John at Ephesus and the Coronation Church of the Holy Apostles at Constantinople. The interior of the Church of St Paraskevi has been subdivided by walls which support the domes and are pierced by circular arches. The nave has been enlarged twice, the most recent occasion being in 1931, but the church has suffered little from this or earlier restorations. A chapel at the south-west, reached from the south transept (in this church the transepts do not project from the nave) may have been a mortuary chapel similar to the one at Kiti. Another chapel to the north-west is used as a store for icons. The fifteenth-century icons in the church are very good examples of the art of that period. They include part of a scene showing the Betrayal of Christ, with the soldiers accoutred in curious medieval armour, and a fragment of the Last Supper in which the figures recline in oriental fashion. The double-sided (originally portable) icon now on the left of the iconostasis is probably also of fifteenth-century workmanship and portrays the Virgin with Child on one side, and a later painting of the Crucifixion on the reverse.

Roman Temple

The site of a small Roman temple is near the church. A few of its capitals and the remains of columns lie scattered in the vicinity.

[9½ m.] The *Temple of Aphrodite*, the remains of *Palea (Old) Paphos* and *La Covocle*, a Lusignan Manor (opening hours p. 265), are reached from the village of **Kouklia**, a short distance north of the main road. There is a necropolis of the Bronze Age and also a later settlement dating from 1200–1000 B.C. to the east of the village.

HISTORY OF PALEA PAPHOS

Old Paphos became the capital of the island in the fourth century B.C. Its foundation is attributed by Pausanias to the legendary Agapenor, who distinguished himself in the Trojan Wars. A later mythological king believed to have reigned here was Pygmalion, the sculptor who fell in love with his creation of a beautiful female statue, to which Aphrodite gave life and named Galatea. The child of the union was named Paphos. Then later still came Kinyras, the high priest of Aphrodite's shrine, who was foolhardy enough to challenge Apollo to a musical contest and paid forfeit with his life. A dynasty sprang from him which was to rule the city for almost a thousand years.

The first historical documentation of Palea Paphos occurs in an Assyrian tablet in the British Museum. This mentions a king named Ithuander or Ittudagon in 672 B.C. The priest-king successors of Kinyras, who celebrated the secret Egyptian rites of Adonis and Aphrodite, ruled until the time of their ill-fated rebellion against Ptolemy I in 295 B.C. Though forfeiting civic power, the city remained the religious centre of the island until the Romans under Cato took possession in 56 B.C. Earthquakes in the fourth century A.D. – the same which destroyed Nea Paphos to the west – were followed by a decree of the Byzantine Emperor Theodosius (379–96) whereby all pagan temples, including the renowned Temple of Aphrodite, were forced to cease functioning. Kouklia regained importance during the rule of the Lusignans, and became the site of a royal pavilion named 'La Covocle', from which the present name of the village and site is derived. Saracen raids at the turn of the fourteenth to fifteenth century finally put an end to a city of prime importance, of which the present-day small hamlet is a humble successor.

For some years a German archaeological mission headed by Professor Dr F. G. Maier of the University of Konstanz has been engaged upon a topographical survey of the whole area of Palea Paphos. Portions of the fortifications of the ancient city have been uncovered and finds have included ivory from the Mycenaean period.

TEMPLE OF APHRODITE

The ground plan of the Temple of Aphrodite shows it to have been designed with covered and uncovered courts of a Phoenician character, but constructed with the use of Greek building techniques. The exact purpose of many of the chambers exposed by excavation remains obscure. It is likely, however, that large processions entered through the east gate, from the direction of Curium, while the pilgrims coming from Paphos Harbour used the southern portico. This debouched into a wide open court, which in turn led by a flight of steps to the central hall. The large central open court had chambers on its east side and a stoa on the north. Buildings to the south of the south entrance have Cyclopean walls, which are the oldest remains on the site.

The great spring festival of Aphrodite was celebrated by the pilgrims in various ways according to their degree of initiation. There were games for the populace on the first day, purification ceremonies and sea-bathing on the second, and bloodless sacrifices to the goddess on the third, culminating in presentations of ritual cake, the *Pyramous*, by the high priest. In the second degree, the rites of Adonis comprised acts of mourning for the premature death of the golden youth. This was followed by a triumphant and orgiastic celebration of his resurrection. The third degree underwent initiation into the mysteries of both cults, with doves, an obelisk and the image of a bearded goddess as the chief symbols. The culmination was the presentation of salt symbolizing Aphrodite's birth from the sea, together with phallic symbols to denote fertility. These were acknowledged by the pilgrims by payment in coin.

In the course of excavations in 1887 under the auspices of the Hellenic Society and the British School at Athens, an attempt was made to relate the site to representations of it appearing on Roman coinage of the first century A.D. But conclusions were hampered not only by the misleading limitations inherent in coin design but also by evidence that the Romans had made substantial changes and additions not only in 15 B.C. under Augustus but later as the result of earthquake damage in the reigns of Tiberius and Vespasian. A crusading knight, Seigneur de Villamont, has commented that 'at the prayer of St Barnabas, a native of Cyprus, an idol of Venus and her temple fell shateretd to the ground'. It is considered by some archaeologists that further discoveries in the district should reveal that what is at present known as the Temple of Aphrodite is in fact no more than an annexe to a greater temple which is as yet undiscovered. Further excavations are being undertaken by the University of St Andrews.

LA COVOCLE

The château of the Lusignans, *La Covocle* (from the Latin *cubiculum*), is to the south of the temple. A royal domain was administered from here and the sugar factory attached to it secured its reputation as a place of importance in the economy of Cyprus during the Venetian occupation, following recovery from damage by Saracen raiders. A great vaulted stable contains an interesting collection of mosaics – some from the north peristyle of the temple – and pottery found in the vicinity.

[15 m.] *Petra tou Romiou* is the name given to a crop of huge rocks jutting into the sea, some miles farther to the east. This mythical birthplace of Venus is constantly awash with brilliant foam. There are no archaeological remains and it is a place for relaxation, for swimming and for contemplation of the legend which has arisen as a consequence of the bright foam carried on the waves. However convincingly marine biologists explain this phenomenon as being due to an abnormal incidence of disintegrating animal and marine organisms, the myth remains indestructible. In the words of Homer's Hymn No. 6: 'The moist breeze of Zephyr brought her there on the waves of the sea with a noise of thunder amid the soft foam, and the gold-clad Horae received her with joy. They decked her with precious jewels and set on her immortal head a beautiful crown of gold, and in her ears ear-rings of copper and gold.'

A later legend also attaches itself to this spot, to the effect that the national hero Dighenis, when insultingly reviled as 'Romiou' – or Greek – by invading Saracens, hurled vast rocks at them and destroyed their fleet. These are the rocks which give such a beautiful shape to the bays, which though near the main road, are far from human habitation.

This is a place which should be visited when there is no necessity for hurrying on elsewhere.

Ayios Neophytos Monastery, Polis and Fontana Amorosa

Route Leave Ktima by the north-east road (Route B on Ktima/Paphos map) for diversion to Ayios Neophytos Monastery (+6 m.), returning to main road for Stroumbi (12 m.), Polis (24½ m.) and Fontana Amorosa (30 m.).

For Nicosia or Kyrenia return to Polis and continue on coast road along the shores of Khrysokhou Bay, passing Vouni and Soli (pp. 128–31): by-pass Morphou for Nicosia (+75 m.) or continue north-eastwards to join the indirect Nicosia–Kyrenia road near Dhiorios for the coastal route to Kyrenia (+91 m.). (This will make rather a long day, and an overnight stop should be considered.)

Hotels

At Polis: 3rd Akamas.
At Fontana Amorosa: Tourist Pavilion.

[3 m.] A left turn off the Polis road leads through the village of **Trimithousa** and in about 3 m. reaches the *Monastery of Ayios Neophytos*, which is situated on the slope of the hills facing the sea.

HISTORY OF AYIOS NEOPHYTOS

The founder saint of the monastery was an interesting figure. He was born in 1134 at Kato Dhrys, near Kato Lefkara, and ran away from home when his parents suggested that he should marry. He enrolled as a novice in the Monastery of St Chrysostomos below Buffavento, and later became sacristan there. But he longed to exchange community life for that of a hermit, and set off with the intention of finding a suitable cave in Asia Minor. However, he was detained at Paphos and prevented from leaving the country. On his release at the age of twenty-five, Neophytos discovered the present site, found it suitable for his purpose and cut a cave in the rock with his own hands. It is ironic that his sanctity and desire for solitude attracted scores of followers, and that what was to have been a lonely refuge became the nucleus of a community, the Encleistra, and the foundation of the hospitable monastery which bears the saint's name.

HERMITAGE AND MONASTIC BUILDINGS

The monastery and the hermitage are described beautifully by D. G. Hogarth in his *Devia Cypria* (1889). The description is as true today as it was when the Victorian archaeologist visited Cyprus:

The present monastery buildings are situated in a little paradise of running water and deep groves of olive, pomegranate and lemon trees, immediately to the south of the cave in which the saint first took refuge. The latter, carved by the hands of Neophytus himself into a dwelling room and a small chapel, is still the goal of pious pilgrimage; and except for the frescoes which have been daubed over the walls and roof, remains much as its first tenant left it. In the little room, 11 ft by 8 ft at its largest, are his coffin-shaped bed, excavated in a recess of the rock (into which the faithful still climb, and turn round thrice), a little rock-cut table and seat, and over the latter a modern cupboard filled with the skulls of the hermit's followers ...

Actually there are three linked caves cut in the rock, and these form a very small chapel, a sanctuary and the saint's own dwelling place as described by Hogarth. The earliest wall-painting 'daubed' on the north side of the chapel may date from the late twelfth century. The sanctuary has a representation of St Neophytos supported by angels. The paintings in the cell are cruder, and depict the Resurrection, in which the saint is seen to be kneeling at the feet of Christ. Without doubt it is at this primitive table that St Neophytos wrote his *Ritual Ordinance* dealing with early Greek monasticism, also his commentary retailing the misfortunes of Cyprus at the time of Richard Cœur de Lion, 'the English king, the wretch', as well as many theological treatises, a large proportion of which are still in existence. By that time St Neophytos had attracted such a large number of followers that he felt impelled to form them into a community. To give himself something of the seclusion which he had sought as a young man, towards the end of his life he excavated a cave higher in the cliff for his own occupation. However, he never failed to make himself accessible to his community, and to the people of Paphos who flocked to hear his sermons.

The block of monastic buildings is situated to the east of the saint's retreat. These form a shady place of cloistral calm, and have guest rooms looking seawards. The church of the monastery, on the north of the enclosure, is approached by a flight of steps. It is built on the usual medieval plan, with three aisles and barrel-vaulted roof carried on columns which have capitals decorated with curiously thin acanthus leaves. The saint's bones were removed from the Encleistra in 1750, and are kept in a wooden sarcophagus, with the exception of the skull, which is housed in a silver reliquary.

[12 m.] Return to the main road and continue northwards to **Stroumbi**, a village famous for wine and surrounded by vineyards. It is said that its name comes from a prosperous fat man (*stroumbos*) who was the landowner in medieval times. This makes a good halting-place for tasting the wine of the country districts and comparing it with factory products. Yet Stroumbi is a sad place, having been devastated by the earthquake of 1953. Much of it has been rebuilt in severely functional earthquake-resistant cubes. One consolation is that the disaster occurred at six in the morning when the majority of the villagers were already out and about, so that many escaped death.

Soon after Stroumbi the watershed is reached, and the road northwards descends into the valley of the Stavros Psokas river, with the Troödos Mountains on the right.

[24½ m.] POLIS

The modern town is situated to the west of the site of ancient *Marion*, which was founded by Athenians in the seventh century B.C. and soon became an important copper town. Its greatness lasted until 312 B.C., when Ptolemy's forces destroyed the city and transferred its inhabitants to Paphos. It was then rebuilt to the south of the present town under Ptolemy Philadelphus (285–47 B.C.), who renamed it Arsinoe after his sister. But the name fell out of usage, and the place came to be called simply Polis, or city. When the ancient necropolis was excavated by Richter in 1886 over four hundred tombs were opened, and two-thirds of the contents were sold by public auction in Paris. British and Swedish excavations followed. Nowadays there is little to interest the sightseer, and it is doubted whether further excavation work would yield results.

A left turn out of Polis leads along the north-eastern shore of the Akamas Peninsula. (The western coast is barren and inaccessible.)

[27 m.] **Lachi** has a small harbour, and there are also remains of an ancient jetty below the level of the sea. After leaving the village, take a right-hand fork on to a secondary road that continues along the coast.

[30 m.] FONTANA AMOROSA

A farm (Potami Chiftlik) is reached, and the car may be left in a park near the tourist pavilion. The rest of the way to the Fontana Amorosa is by footpath through what appears to be an enchanted garden of fig trees, carobs, bamboos, cyclamen and other small flowers. But Ariosto, the Italian poet (1474–1533), has put it better in his great romantic epic *Orlando Furioso*: 'There is a slope seven miles long which rises from the seashore and is planted with myrtle, cedar, bitter oranges, laurel and many other aromatic trees, bushes, roses, lilies and crocuses which give off a beautiful fragrance which the sea breeze wafts from the earth and carries to the sea.' He adds that the district has women and virgins of outstanding beauty, and to old and young women the goddess gives ardent love to the end of their lives.

The fragrance of flowers and herbs, which is an important part of the cult of Aphrodite, seems to linger here whatever the season. The actual Fountain of Love is a grotto into which water from a perennial spring drips through curtains of maidenhair fern, and is overhung by a very old fig tree. When Mr Drummond, the British Consul at Aleppo, visited the spring in 1750 he had no curiosity to taste the water, 'the effect of which upon old people like me is said to be that of making the spirit willing while the flesh continues weak . . .'

This is another place which should be enjoyed at leisure, with plenty of time for sea-bathing.

Chrysorroyiatissa and Ayia Moni Monasteries

Route Leave Ktima by the north-east Polis road (Route B on Ktima/Paphos map), forking right 1 m. before Stroumbi for Chrysorroyiatissa Monastery (26 m.) and Ayia Moni Monastery (28 m.).

   The excursion can be extended to Stavros tis Psokas, Cedars Valley and Kykko Monastery by driving back through Pano Panayia and on to Asproyia and the Ezouza valley to connect with the mountain road described on p. 135. In this case it would not be advisable to return to Ktima the same day, because plenty of time is required to negotiate the winding mountain roads. A night could be spent by arrangement at the Stavros tis Psokas Forest Station, or at one of the mountain resorts.

[10½ m.] A short distance before Stroumbi take a right fork.

[12½ m.] **Polemi**

[14½ m.] **Psathi**

[16 m.] Fork right in **Ayios Dhimitrianos.**

[18½ m.] Keep to the left in **Kannaviou.**

[20 m.] Fork right for Pano Panayia.

[24½ m.] **Pano Panayia** is the birthplace of Archbishop Makarios III, and he lived there until he became a novice at Kykko Monastery before completing his education at the Pancyprian Gymnasium.

[26 m.] A sharp right turn in Pano Panayia leads to the *Chrysorroyiatissa Monastery*, which is surrounded by some of the most splendid scenery in all Cyprus.

MONASTERY OF CHRYSORROYIATISSA

According to tradition, its founder was Ignatios, a hermit who lived on Mount Kremaste. From here he had a vision of a fire burning on the sea-shore far below, and on seeking it out he discovered the miraculous, luminous icon traditionally painted by St Luke and kept at Isauria in Asia Minor, where it had been saved from destruction by a woman who had cast it into the sea during the

Iconoclastic Wars. The icon's luminosity having drawn him to it, Ignatios was directed by the Virgin to build a shrine for it on Mount Royia. This mountain has derived its name from the word for pomegranate or, according to another authority, from 'the golden breasts' of the Virgin. As happened in similar circumstances elsewhere, the presence of the miraculous icon attracted monks, deacons and students to its mountain site. The monastery flourished until the period of Turkish rule, but after 1572 it was deprived of much of its property and there was a danger that it would have to be abandoned. By this time it had come to be known to the Turks as the Monastery of the Bell, because one of the abbots had managed to gain exemption from the ban on bells imposed by the Turkish authorities until the year 1856. A famous bishop of Paphos, Panaretos (1767–90), was able to initiate effective restoration work, and from the eighteenth century onwards the old monastery developed into what it is today: a hospitable and holy place set 3,768 ft above sea-level among idyllic scenery, with forest to the north, bare hills and fertile valleys to the south, wooded country stretching away towards the Akamas Peninsula and the sea on the west, and great mountains on its eastern flank. Though substantial damage by fire was done to the monastic buildings in recent years, they have now been restored.

The miraculous icon of the Blessed Virgin Mary is held in especial veneration by criminals and the condemned. A silver-gilt protective case was made for it in 1762 and an elaborate frame fitted a little later. However, the hidden icon is well illustrated in a copper-plate engraving of 1801 preserved in the church. This is the work of John Cornaros, the famous Cretan icon painter. It is surrounded by illustrations of the history of the icon and its discovery.

[28 m.] It is well worth while proceeding another 2 m. to the disused *Monastery of Ayia Moni*, the property of Kykko Monastery. Though the church is essentially medieval in design, besides having been reconstructed in 1638, it is a very early Christian foundation, as is suggested by the decorative band of acanthus leaves below the apsidial semi-dome. Moreover, the church is believed to have been built on the site of a pagan temple to Hera, the Juno of the Romans. The cruciform marble font is of particular interest.

Emba, Coral Bay, Ayios Yeoryios Church and Peyia Basilica

Route Take the road north (Route A on Ktima/Paphos map) and after ½ mile fork right for Emba (+2 m.), returning to continue northwards, by-passing Khlorakas and keeping left for Maa (Coral Bay) (7 m.).

Return a short distance on previous road, then turn left at signpost for Peyia, but before entering that village turn sharp left again for Peyia Basilica and Ayios Yeoryios (15 m.).
Ancient Monument
Peyia Basilica
Custodian in attendance.
Opening hours
Mid-May to mid-Sept. 9 a.m. to 12 noon.
3 p.m. to 6.30 p.m.
Mid-Sept. to mid-May 9 a.m. to 1 p.m.
2 p.m. to 4.30 p.m.

[2 m.] A right fork after ½ m. leads to **Emba**, which makes a very pleasant short excursion, especially in spring, when the neighbourhood is carpeted with flowers. The *Church of the Blessed Virgin Mary* is large and of Byzantine design, with three aisles crowned by two domes each of which was finished by a small marble pillar of the Roman period – a rather touching architectural conceit. The narthex was added in 1744. An external staircase leads from the north of this narthex to the roof. Though the church's frescoes suffered considerably from crude repainting by a local artist in 1886, these are now decaying, and do not offer too severe a contrast to the original representation of Christ Pantakrator in the dome. The greatest of the treasures preserved here are an early sixteenth-century two-panelled icon, now under glass, showing the Twelve Apostles, six to a panel, above Venetian coats of arms; and a Gospel printed in Venice in 1539, bound in leather with an embossed medallion of Christ on the cover.

[7 m.] *Coral Bay*, Maa on the map, is reached by returning towards Ktima and forking back to the right, by-passing **Khlorakas,** and has a reputation as a beautiful bathing place, where the sand is coloured pink by tiny fragments of coral. It has a small restaurant overlooking the sea. A large-scale development scheme under way at the time of going to press indicates that though the bay's seclusion must be dissipated, it will acquire modern entertainment and amenities for new residents as well as casual visitors. A 300-bed hotel is to be followed by some 50 villas.

[10 m.] Return a short distance and ascend a bluff where a left turn is signposted **Peyia**. This is an attractive hill village facing the coastal area which has given its name to an ancient Christian town to the west, of which the original name has been lost. Before entering the village proper, just after passing the Police Station, turn left at the signpost for Ayios Yeorios.

[15 m.] The road comes to an end at the site of **Peyia Basilica** (left) and the *Chapel of Ayios Yeoryios* (right). There is also a small restaurant on the cliff, with steps down to a rocky bay.

The remains of Peyia Basilica (actually three superimposed churches) were discovered in 1951, to be excavated at the same time as adjacent baths. Corinthian capitals and sections of flooring assist in the identification of basic features. There are also amusing mosaics of wild beasts: a boar, a lion, a bull and a bear, while others have been left covered with sand in order to preserve them.

Opposite is the charming *Chapel of Ayios Yeoryios*, which, however, contains little of antiquarian interest except an altar formed by two Byzantine capitals placed one above the other. As this is beyond the iconostasis, it is not readily viewed. The whole area of Cape Drepanum was occupied by the important Roman city of *Drepanum*. The ruins extend over approximately a quarter of a square mile, but they have never been properly excavated. Because of its remoteness on a rocky coast facing an offshore island, this is a place well worth visiting on a leisure day.

The tract of land to the north which forms the Akamas Peninsula is much as it was described by Hogarth in 1889: 'It is a sterile corner of Cyprus, thickly covered with scrub, abounding in deep gullies and bold rock formations, the central spine being broken into bold peaks or miniature table mountains; here and there in a tiny valley is a cultivated patch, but nine-tenths of the district produces nothing but game.'*

* *Devia Cypria.*

LINK ROUTES

Alternative routes between main towns indicate ways of taking in intermediate places of interest, and may be of use to visitors who do not wish to do their sightseeing in round trips from the various centres. Distances do not include possible detours.

NICOSIA TO KYRENIA

Route (1)* (16 m.) Via Kyrenia Pass, with detours left to St Hilarion Castle (pp. 165–70) and right to Bellapais Abbey (pp. 161–4).

Route (2) (38 m.) Via western spur of Kyrenia mountains and north coast (pp. 170–3).

Route (3) (21 m.) Via Buffavento (p. 133), Klepini and Ayios Epiktitos.

N.B. A shorter road over the mountains below Buffavento is to be constructed.

NICOSIA TO FAMAGUSTA

Route (1) (39 m.) Via new road by-passing all towns and villages.

Route (2) (50 m.) Via Kythrea (p. 145), Lefkoniko, Trikomo (p. 205) and Salamis (pp. 187–99).

NICOSIA TO LARNACA

Route (1) (26 m.) Via Pyroi.

Route (2) (40 m.) Via Kophinou, with detours to Kornos, Pyrga and Stavrovouni Monastery (pp. 224–6).

NICOSIA TO LIMASSOL

Route (1) (53 m.) Via Nisou, with detours to Dhali, Kornos, Pyrga and Stavrovouni Monastery (pp. 224–6), Kophinou, Khirokitia and Amathus (pp. 249–53).

Route (2) (87 m.) Via Troödos (pp. 139–42), Platres, Kouris valley and Ypsonas (p. 244).

Route (3) (75 m.) Via Pano Dheftera (detour to Tamassos) (pp.

---

* In current conditions used by Greek Cypriots under convoy system operated by the United Nations peace-keeping force. Foreign visitors in self-drive cars can pass at all times of day and night.

150–52), Apliki, Pitsilia district (short detours to Platanistasa and Lagoudhera), Kyperounda, Karvouna Crossroads (pp. 247–9), Kouris valley and Ypsonas (p. 244).

NICOSIA TO PAPHOS (KTIMA)

Route (1) (98 m.) See Nicosia–Limassol (Route 1) and Limassol–Ktima routes.
Route (2) (97 m.) via Troödos (pp. 139–42), Pano Platres, Omodhos Monastery (pp. 244–7), Ayios Nicolaos and joining Limassol–Paphos road near Kouklia (p. 266).
Route (3) (94 m.) Via Kato Koutraphas, Vouni and Polis (p. 272).

FAMAGUSTA TO KYRENIA

Route (1) (55 m.) Via Nicosia and Kyrenia Pass.
Route (2) (55 m.) Via Trikomo and Lefkoniko Mersiniki Pass and north coast road (p. 205).

FAMAGUSTA TO LARNACA

(25 m.) By-passing Athna.

LARNACA TO LIMASSOL

(52 m.) Via Kophinou (detour to Pano Lefkara), Khirokitia and Amathus (pp. 249–54).

LIMASSOL TO PAPHOS (KTIMA)

(45 m.) Via Kolossi Castle, Curium, Sanctuary of Apollo, with short detour to Kouklia and Palea Paphos (pp. 235–43 and 266–9).

KYRENIA TO PAPHOS (KTIMA)

(102 m.) Via Morphou, Vouni Palace (pp. 129–31) and Polis (p. 272).

SELECTED BIBLIOGRAPHY

I am indebted to the authors of the following books, all of which would make good background reading for visitors to Cyprus. Some of the more recent will be obtainable from booksellers, but the ones which are out of print might be bought second-hand, or could certainly be found in libraries.

Alastos, Doros: *Cyprus Guerilla* (Heinemann, 1960)

Balfour, Patrick (Lord Kinross): *The Orphaned Realm* (P. Marshall, 1951)

Cobham, C. D.: *Excerpta Cypria* (Cambridge University Press, 1908)

Dikaios, P.: *A Guide to the Cyprus Museum*, 3rd ed. (Nicosia, 1961); *Khirokitia* (Oxford University Press, 1953)

Durrell, Lawrence: *Bitter Lemons* (Faber & Faber, 1957)

Foley, Charles: *Island in Revolt* (Longmans Green, 1962)

Gunnis, Rupert: *Historic Cyprus*, 2nd ed. (Methuen, 1947)

Hogarth, D. G.: *Devia Cypria* (Frowde, 1889)

Home, Gordon: *Cyprus Then and Now* (Dent, 1960)

Jeffery, George: *Historic Monuments of Cyprus* (Nicosia, 1918)

Karageorghis, Vassos: *Salamis in Cyprus: Homeric, Hellenistic and Roman* (Thames and Hudson, 1970)

Lewis, Mrs: *A Lady's Impressions of Cyprus* (Remington & Co., 1894)

Luke, Sir Harry: *Cyprus under the Turks* (Milford, 1921); *Cyprus, A Portrait and an Appreciation* (Harrap, 1965)

de Mas Latrie: *Histoire de Chypre* (Paris, 1852–61)

Newman, Philip: *A Short History of Cyprus* (Longmans Green, 1940)

Orr, C. W. J.: *Cyprus under British Rule* (Scott, 1918)

Schaeffer, C. F. A.: *Enkomi-Alasia* (Paris, 1952)

Stylianou, Andreas and Judith A.: *Byzantine Cyprus* (Nicosia, 1948)

PHRASE BOOK

Travellers' Greek (Jonathan Cape, 1963)

(For Maps see p. 36.)

INDEX